I0810070

IMAGES
of America

TULARE

ON THE COVER: Benjamin Harrison made a campaign stop in Tulare on April 25, 1888. The speech was given on a section of a fallen giant sequoia that Capt. Thomas H. Thompson, president of the committee for the entertainment, brought to town. The stump had a diameter of 29 feet. (Annie R. Mitchell History Room, Tulare County Library.)

IMAGES
of America

TULARE

Sésar A. Carreño

ARCADIA
PUBLISHING

ISBN 978-1-4671-3086-8

Published by Arcadia Publishing
Charleston, South Carolina

Printed in the United States of America

Library of Congress Control Number: 2013939937

For all general information, please contact Arcadia Publishing:
Telephone 843-853-2070
Fax 843-853-0044
E-mail sales@arcadiapublishing.com
For customer service and orders:
Toll-Free 1-888-313-2665

Visit us on the Internet at www.arcadiapublishing.com

To Marilyn Hanson and Richard Hough, who inspired preservation of Tulare's history and tirelessly believed in my little project, and to my lovely Gina!

Contents

Acknowledgments

First and foremost, I want to thank the staff of the Tulare County Library (Visalia). Without their assistance, this book would never have been possible. I want to thank Rodney Soares, with Tulare County Library, who spent countless hours scanning these images, and Michael Drake, Tulare County Library manager, who believed in this project from the beginning. Another importance resource and thank-you goes to Kathleen Correia, supervising librarian, California History Room of the California State Library.

I also want to thank Richard Torrez and the Tulare Boxing Club for their support in this project. Also, thanks go to Jess Flores for allowing the use of his family photographs. A warm thank-you goes to Rev. Msgr. Richard Urizalqui of St. Aloysius Church, who, without hesitation, granted me permission to use the church archives and photographs, and to principal Joel Nunes for his assistance at St. Aloysius School.

I also wish to thank my acquisitions editor at Arcadia Publishing, Jared Nelson, for his patience (as I asked a million questions) and expert guidance.

There are several people who have paved the way for this book through their research, writing, and enthusiasm for local history. Specifically, they include Marilyn Hanson, who indulged me with access to Sequoia Genealogical Society's research library, archives, and photograph collections—a treasure trove of fascinating stories and information about the community's history. I wish to thank the late Derryl Dumermuth for his vast knowledge of Tulare; and Douglas A. Souza, who supported and believed in my little project. Thanks go to my good friend Richard Hough, who supported this book from day one, and to my fourth-grade teacher Maggie Robson, who fostered my desire to learn and to dream beyond what others thought possible. To my *hermano* Jay Berman, who has helped me in my writing like a true friend: thank you, Jay, for your guidance and encouragement that fostered my interest in local history and ultimately led to this book. Finally, to my wife, Gina, thank you for your love and encouragement, not just on this project but in everything.

INTRODUCTION

Since Tulare was founded in 1872 by the Southern Pacific Railroad, it has grown into the agricultural and dairy capital of the Central Valley. Tulare has had many unique citizens, eras, and growth spurts throughout its 140-plus years. It was founded as the end of a northbound rail line. Southern Pacific quickly built a public hall and a freight depot.

By the late 1800s, as Tulare grew into a prosperous town, the railroad added passenger service. Since most of the townsite was located in what is now considered the west side, many railroad workers built their homes near the tracks. Andrew Neff, an engineer for the railroad, constructed a beautiful home on H Street. Seymour Johnson, a master mechanic for the railroad, also built a home, as did many others.

Founded along the rail lines in a pre-automobile era, the town depended on the railroad as its lifeline. Many early Tulareans hoped that the railroad would spur the city into becoming the county seat, which was then in Visalia. But all hope of this faded when the railroad company removed the shops and the roundhouse and moved operations south to Bakersfield. Tulare felt a big economic impact when this happened, but managed to survive by shifting to other industries that relied on the railroad for shipping products out of town. Along the business corridor, which was appropriately named Front Street (later J Street) because it was in front of the rail lines, many businesses began to prosper, including hotels, shops, city offices, and restaurants.

In the early days, Tulare consisted of only a few blocks, with a population of fewer than 5,000. A series of fires soon hit the town, which consisted primarily of wood-frame buildings. The first fire occurred on July 6, 1875, destroying 43 frame buildings. The second fire broke out on July 30, 1883, around 11:00 p.m. in Isaac Levinger's store on J Street, causing about $120,000 damage to 25 buildings. Some of the loss was covered by insurance. Store owner J. Goldman & Company sustained $35,000 in damage but was only insured for $5,000. Levinger suffered a loss of $5,000 but only had insurance for $4,200. The final fire, which happened on August 16, 1886, prompted the local business community to move to K Street and to rebuild with more fire-resistant materials. That blaze caused $500,000 in damage to 77 buildings, making it the most devastating of the three fires. In the ensuing effort to save the downtown buildings, David Madden's water tower collapsed, depriving firefighters the water they needed to battle the conflagration. Six months later, the "little town that could" had rebuilt the burned out section. The first building was George Doherty's Grand Hotel. In all, more than 4.3 million bricks were used to rebuild Tulare's burned-out section.

Tulare even boasted a small Chinese American community. Ling Joe arrived in 1886 and quickly became a successful businessman, owning the Good Cheer Restaurant on J Street. Unlike most Chinese restaurant owners, he did not serve traditional Chinese food but such American dishes as pork chops. Ling placed a gong across the street and rang it at mealtime to alert his loyal customers.

Tulare's Chinatown was decimated by the Chinese Exclusion Act. The initial version, passed in 1882, prohibited the immigration of Chinese laborers. Its 1892 renewal had a significant impact on Chinese immigration. In one night, Tulare got rid of its Chinese population by rounding up people of Chinese descent and shipping them out of town on the railroad that had built the city. The only Chinese family allowed to stay was the Ling family. The exclusion law was not taken off the books until 1943.

Another sad chapter occurred in 1942, shortly after the bombing of Pearl Harbor, when the Tulare fairground was leased by the US Army. More than 4,000 Japanese Americans were temporarily held there until they were shipped out to the Gila River area in Arizona.

From the start, Tulare has been prominent in dairy production. The first dairy operations date to 1850. By 2004, the area had more than 400,000 dairy cows and almost as many as people. Since the early days, Tulare has developed one of the most advanced and productive milk industries in the United States. In 1889, Daniel Zumwalt built a cheese factory and creamery near the present-day Lincoln School. It failed in the 1893 depression.

In 1898, Wooster Cartmill reopened the Zumwalt place as a milk-skimming plant. Finally, in 1901, the Tulare Board of Trade helped organize the first co-op, Tulare Cooperative Creamery, with Cartmill as manager. But by 1909, it also failed. Later in the same year, Joseph LaMarche, president of the National Bank of Tulare, financed a better farmer-owned cooperative. Under the plan, 100 dairymen agreed to pay $100 each for a share of stock. On November 6, 1909, the Dairyman's Cooperative Creamery Association (DCCA) was formed. By 1940, the association was reporting local sales of $2 million in milk revenues. It was later acquired by Minnesota-based Land O'Lakes.

In the early 1900s, Tulare's downtown business section was centered on K Street to the east, J Street to the west, Tulare Avenue to the north, and Inyo Avenue to the south. As the city grew, and buildings started to show their age, unsavory businesses moved into the area, and J Street became an area to avoid. So as the buildings burned down or were damaged, owners made no efforts to rebuild. Starting in the 1950s through the early 1980s, many of Tulare's historic landmarks were razed in the name of progress.

After the devastating Santa Barbara earthquake of 1925 and the Long Beach earthquake of 1933, many older, historic buildings became victims of the wrecking ball because of safety and fiscal concerns. In most cases, it would have been too expensive to retrofit them to make them sufficiently earthquake-proof.

One of the first areas to be destroyed was Front Street. It had fallen on hard times and by the 1950s had a horrible reputation as a haven for illegal drinking, prostitution, and gambling. So it was decided that all the buildings from Kern Street to Tulare Avenue would be razed and the site converted into a parking lot. Some of the landmarks here were the old hotels and former bank buildings. On the corner of Tulare Avenue and J Street, a new building was constructed for J.C. Penney. The next section cleared away was from North Tulare to East San Joaquin Avenues. Some of the landmarks were Nelson's Furniture, Gainsborough Studio, a Tulare fire station, and Legg's Department Store.

In the early 1970s, two other landmarks were destroyed: The old Carnegie library was razed after serving as a childcare center, and in 1973, the Santa Fe Depot was demolished after serving as a home for a model railroad club for many years. In 1980, the Tulare Theatre was razed to make way for a Wells Fargo Bank, and the Southern Pacific Depot was burned down by arsonists. In 1983, another tragedy stuck Tulare when the venerable Tulare Hotel was burned to the ground, also by arsonists.

Today, Tulare is much more aware of its historic past and clings to its remaining homes and buildings. K Street and portions of the west side show some of the effort to retain and preserve Tulare's historic legacy.

One

Downtown Streets

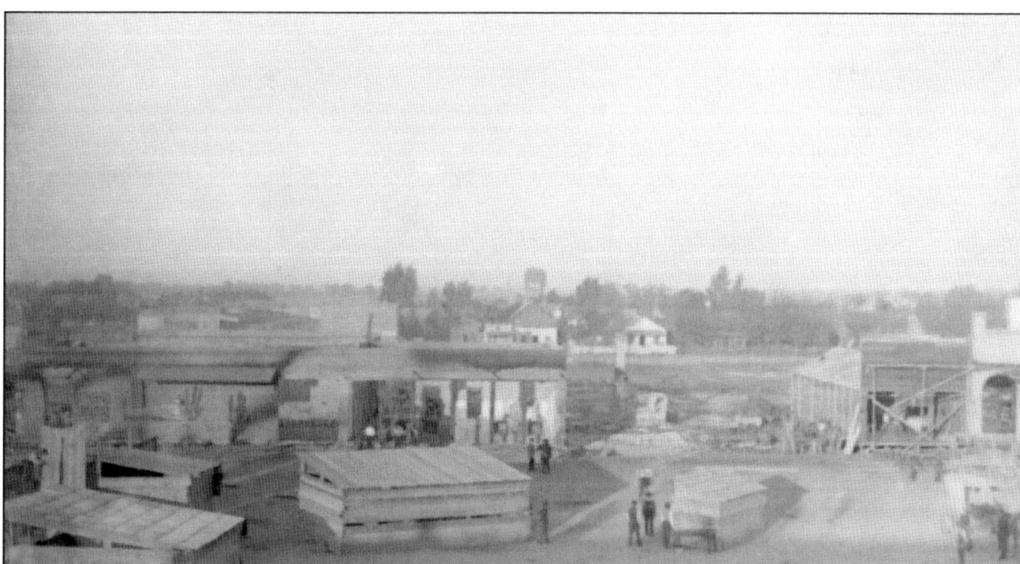

This photograph, taken from the roof of the Southern Pacific depot and freight station, shows the devastation of the Tulare fire of 1886, looking east down the 100 block of Front Street, which later became J Street. At the far right is a glimpse of the old French Hotel. Behind the burned-out buildings on Front Street is a row of homes that were not damaged by the fire. (Tulare County Library.)

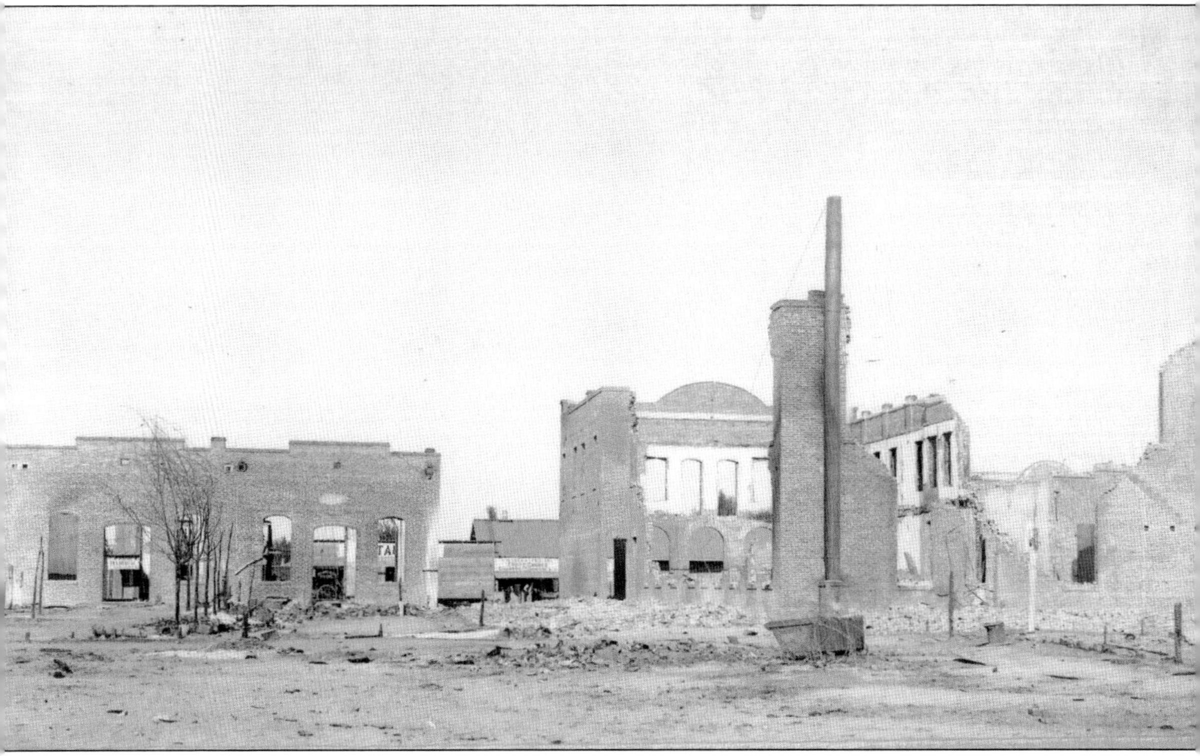

Businesses on the eastern side of Front Street (later J Street) were damaged by the Tulare fire of 1886, but many on the western side were not affected. A cigar store and restaurant adjacent to the burned-out French Hotel were among those that continued to thrive. (Tulare County Library.)

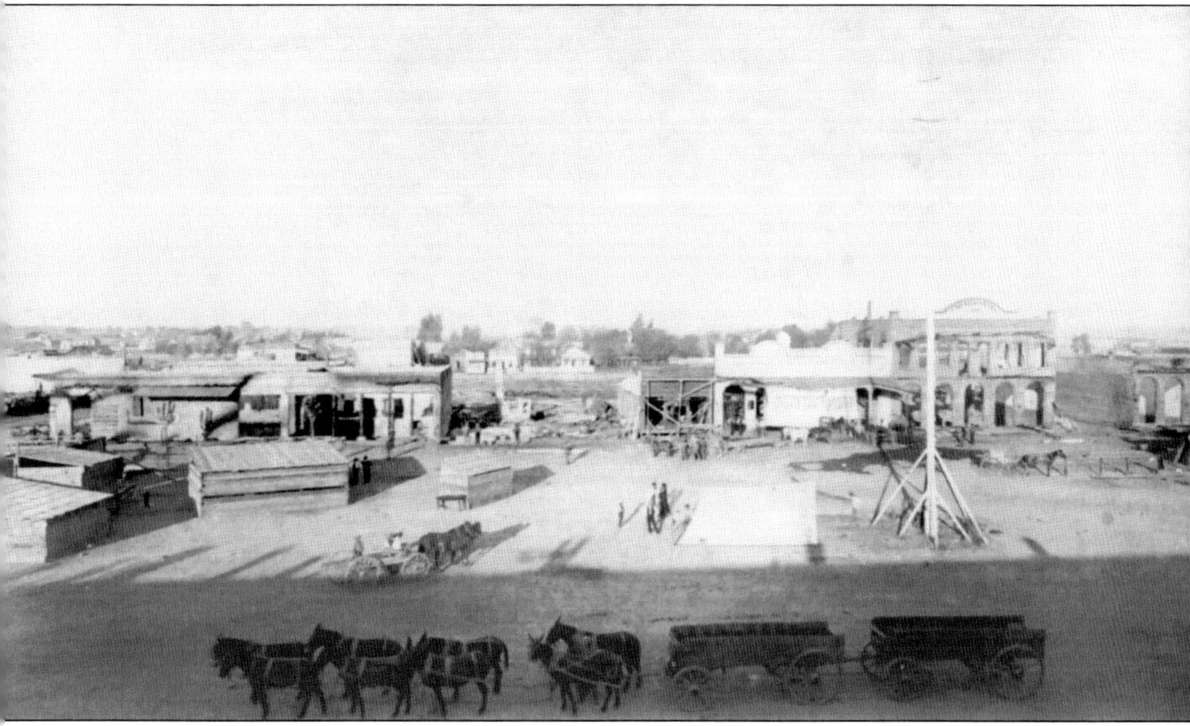

The Tulare fire of 1886 extensively crippled the young town, but industrious townspeople soon set up business using tents and temporary buildings. Examples are included in this view of Tulare and the 100 block of Front Street. Today, the former J.C. Penney building sits where the structures on the left appear. In the bottom left are two temporary buildings and the Southern Pacific right-of-way, today the site of a Walgreens parking lot. (Tulare County Library.)

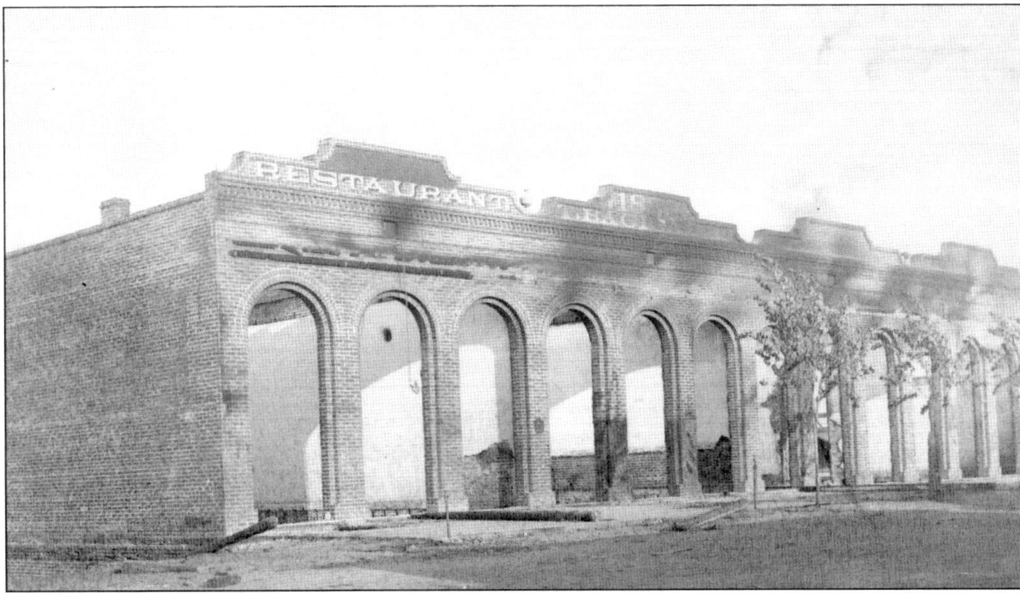

The 1886 fire began about 9:00 p.m. in the Mazeppa stable when a lantern either exploded or was knocked over by one of the animals (a horse and a cow) in a barn. The fire quickly knocked out the town's water supply, jumped a main street, and engulfed the entire business district. Structures that were reparable were rebuilt, some for the third time. (Tulare County Library.)

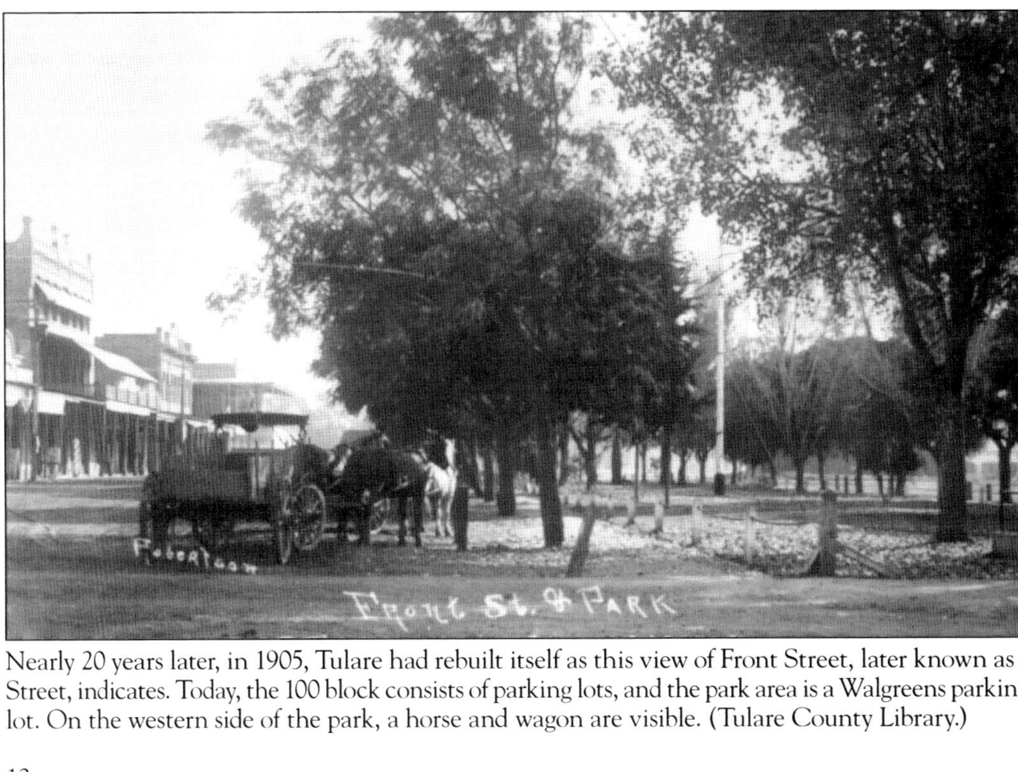

Nearly 20 years later, in 1905, Tulare had rebuilt itself as this view of Front Street, later known as J Street, indicates. Today, the 100 block consists of parking lots, and the park area is a Walgreens parking lot. On the western side of the park, a horse and wagon are visible. (Tulare County Library.)

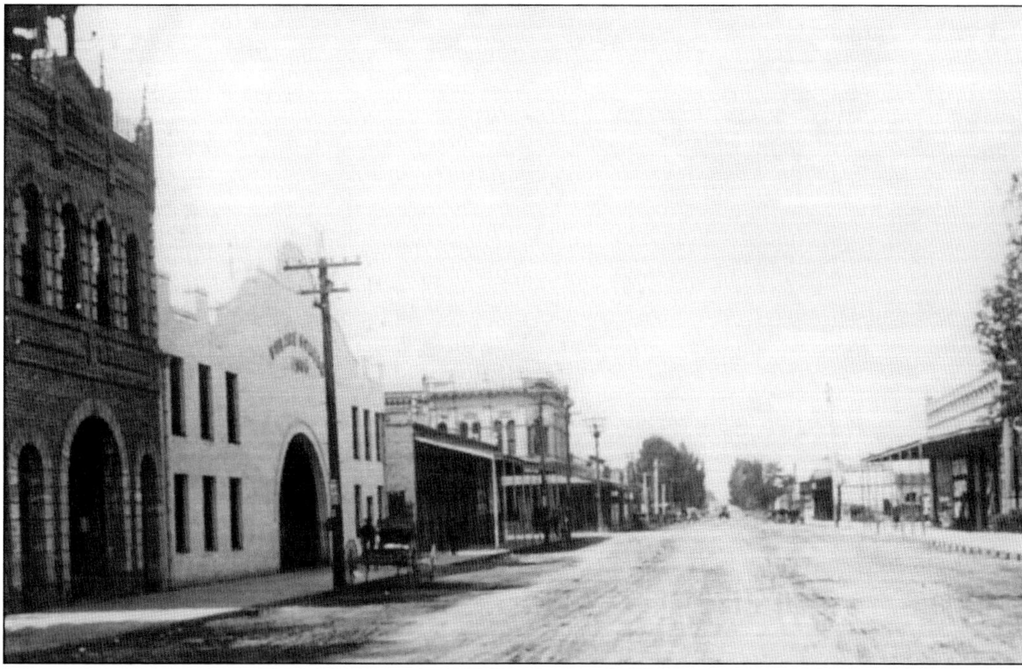

The upstairs portion of the building on the left was city hall until the current city hall was built in the late 1930s. Next to the city hall are the Tulare Stables, which still exist. The old city hall was torn down in the 1950s to make way for a breezeway and easy access to the alley and parking lots on J Street. Note the bell tower on top of the city hall and that K Street remained unpaved at the time. (Author's collection.)

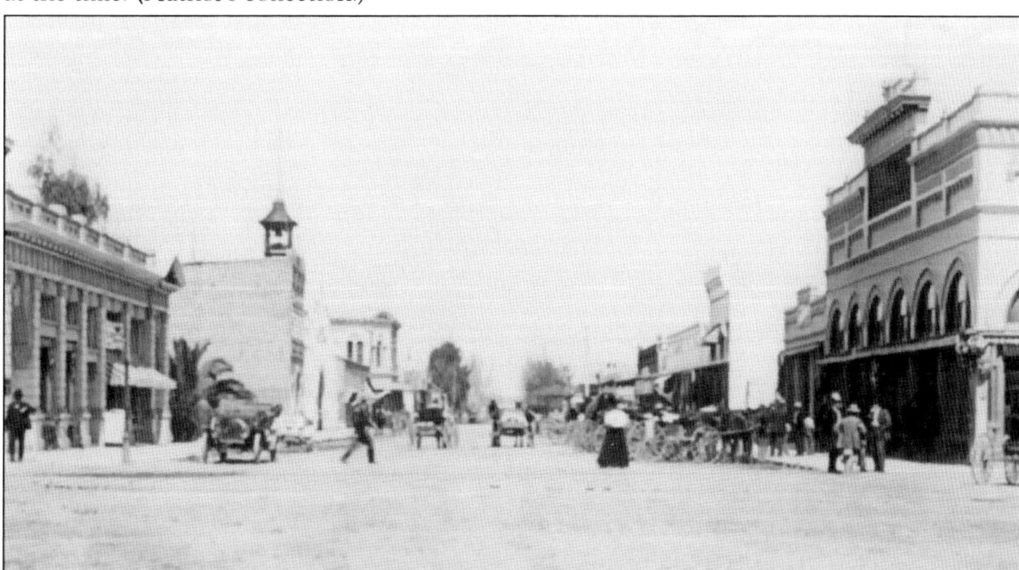

After the city's third fire in 1886, merchants rebuilt Front Street, which later became J Street, but also moved the town's business district one block east to K Street, which became its heart. On the left are the First National Bank of Tulare, the city hall, and the Tulare Stables. On the right is the Linder Hardware building. The city hall was the only building that did not survive into the 21st century. (California History Room, California State Library.)

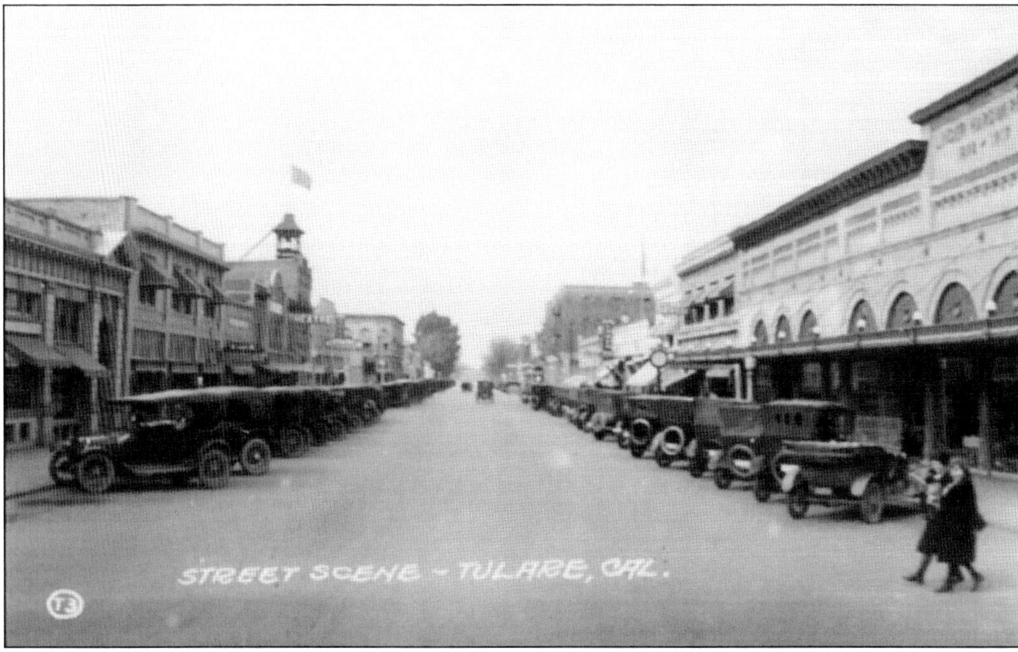

By the 1920s, K Street was lined by automobiles rather than horses and had become the central business district. Such landmarks as the Linder Hardware building and First National Bank of Tulare are still present. The city hall and Tulare Stables are on the left in this photograph. (California History Room, California State Library.)

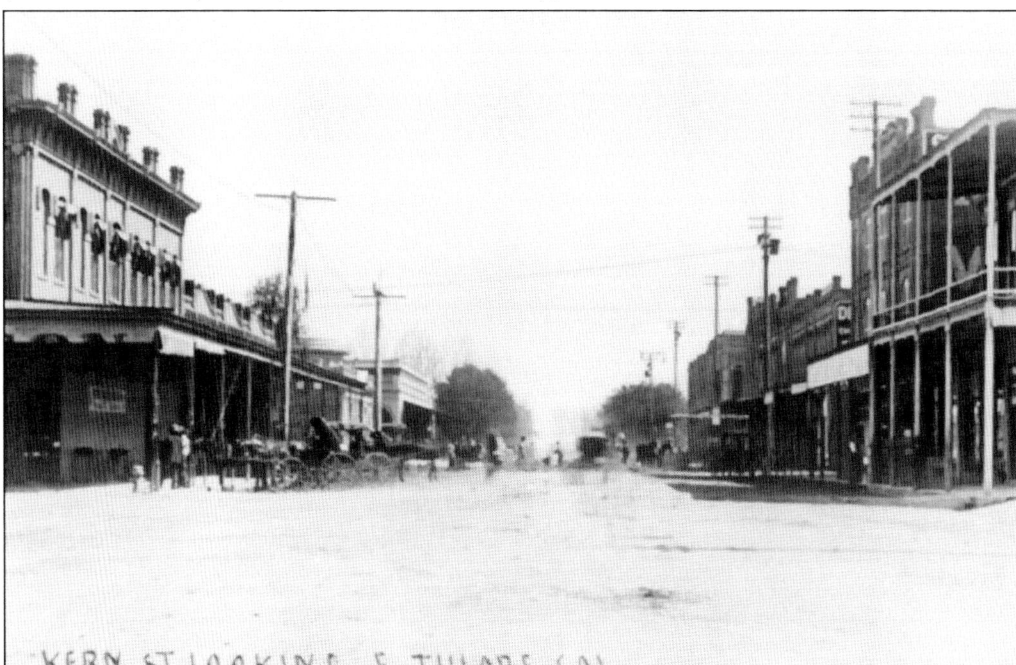

The view in this photograph, most likely taken in the early 1900s, shows Kern Street at Front Street, looking eastward. By that time, residents had many more places to shop and conduct business. Today, only the bank building and Linder Hardware still exist. (Author's collection.)

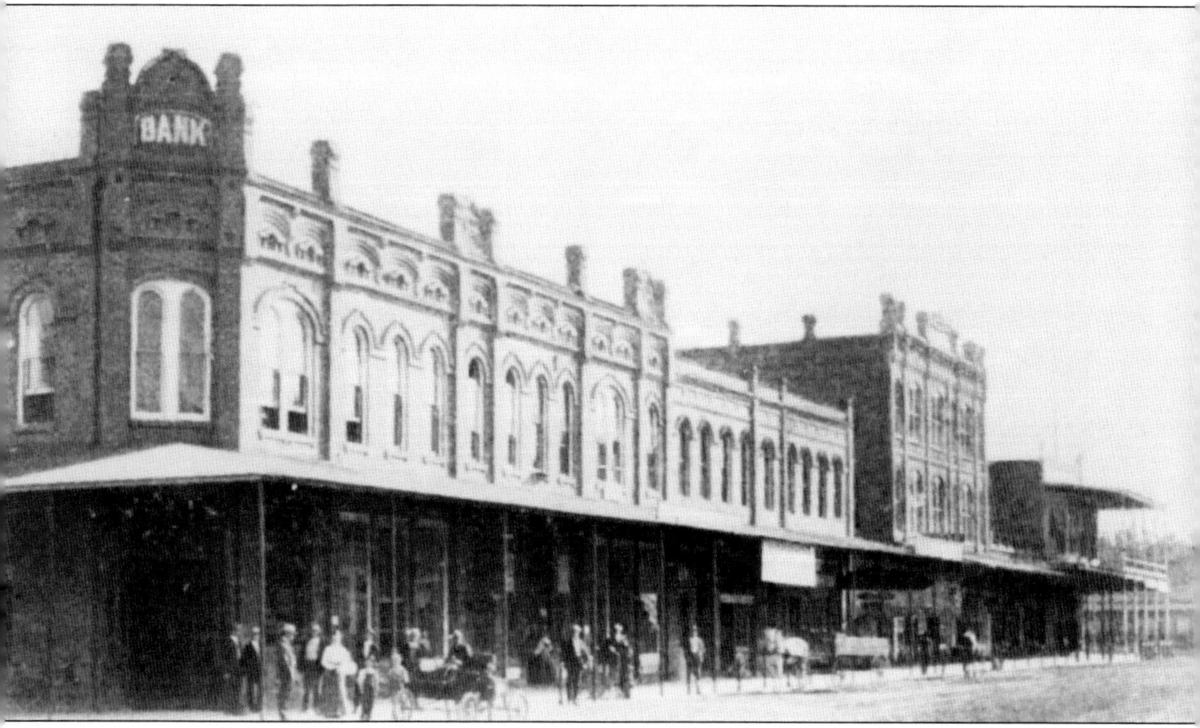

The Farmers and Merchants Bank was at the corner of Kern and Front Streets. Here, a crowd gathers to examine Tulare's first automobile, owned by a man named Goble. Much of the Front Street area was destroyed in the 1950s. Today, a newer building stands at the site. (Library of Congress.)

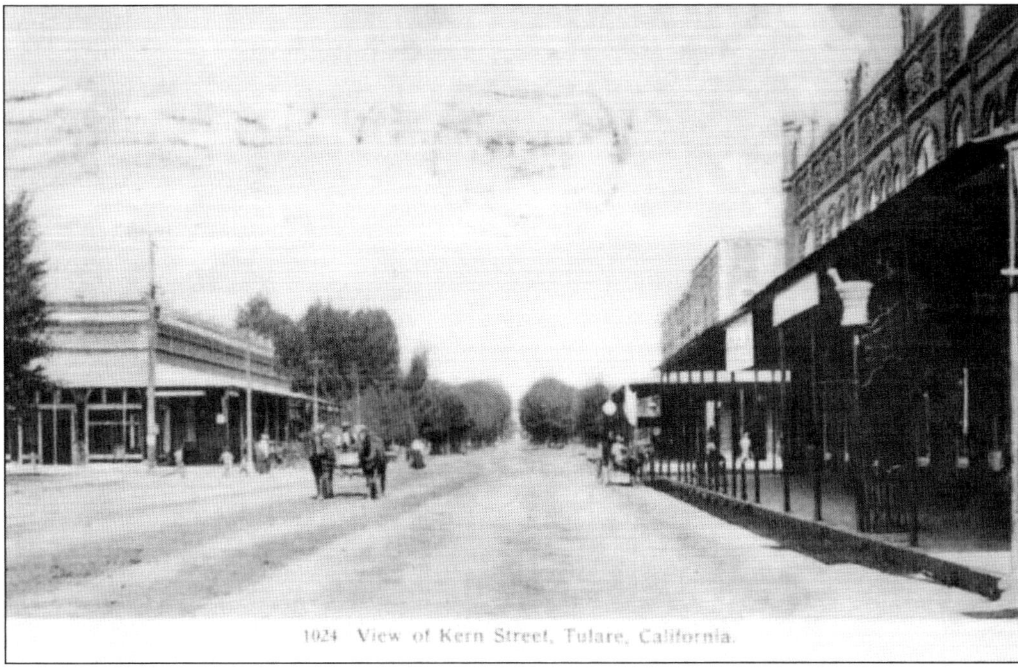

A horse-drawn wagon makes its way down Kern Avenue toward Front Street in the early 1900s. On the left is Linder's Hardware. The building across from Linder's and to the right is now the site of an open food court. The trees in the background also no longer exist. (Author's collection.)

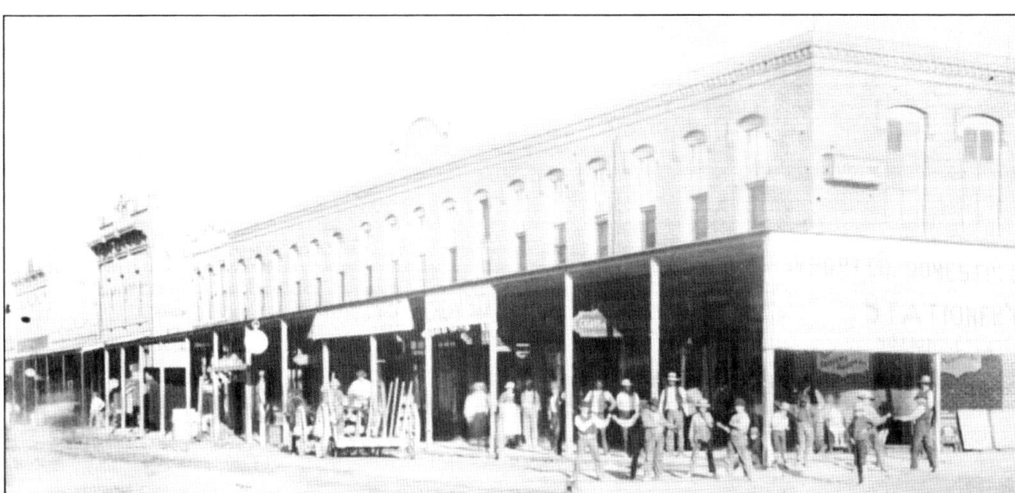

The Grand Hotel, known for distinctive ironwork around the perimeter of its roof, stood on Front Street in the late 1800s. The hotel became a haven for illegal activities as it aged and was razed along with the entire block in 1959. Today, the site is a municipal parking lot. (Tulare County Library.)

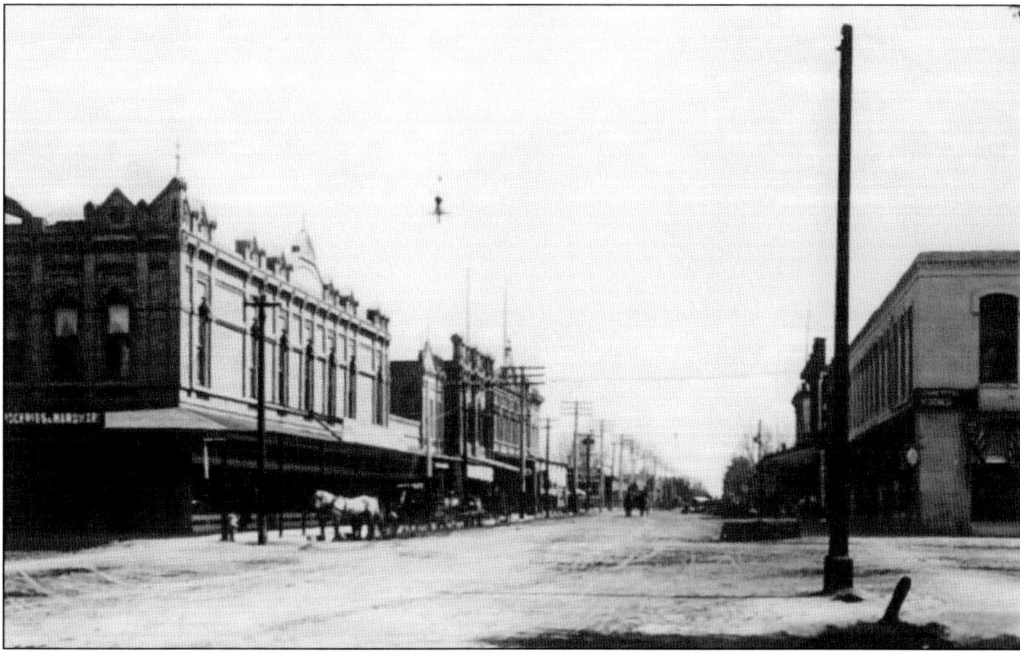

Tulare Avenue has always been one of the city's main thoroughfares. All the buildings in the photograph were razed between 1959 and 1975. The structure on the right was replaced by a building that later housed J.C. Penney and is now home to Chavez Insurance. The Rochdale Building, also long gone, was replaced by a Carl's Jr. (California History Room, California State Library.)

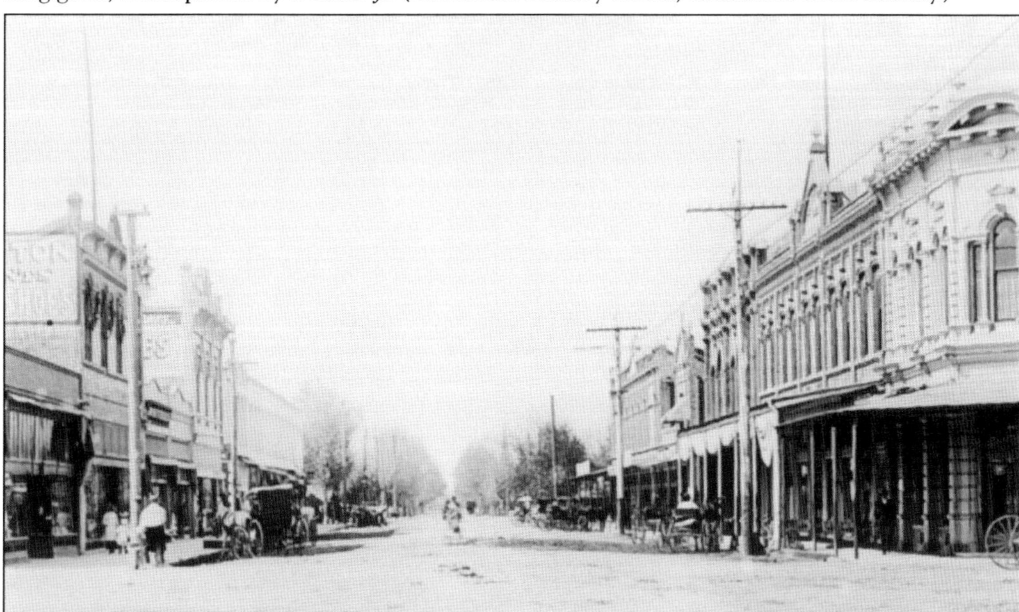

This view looking westward toward the railroad tracks shows Tulare Avenue at K Street. The buildings on the left are still in existence; one is Tulare Donuts. All the buildings on the right were razed in 1959 to make way for Tower Square, which today has shown massive decline. The building on the corner of Tulare Avenue and K Street, once Tulare Bank, today is a Westamerica Bank. (California History Room, California State Library.)

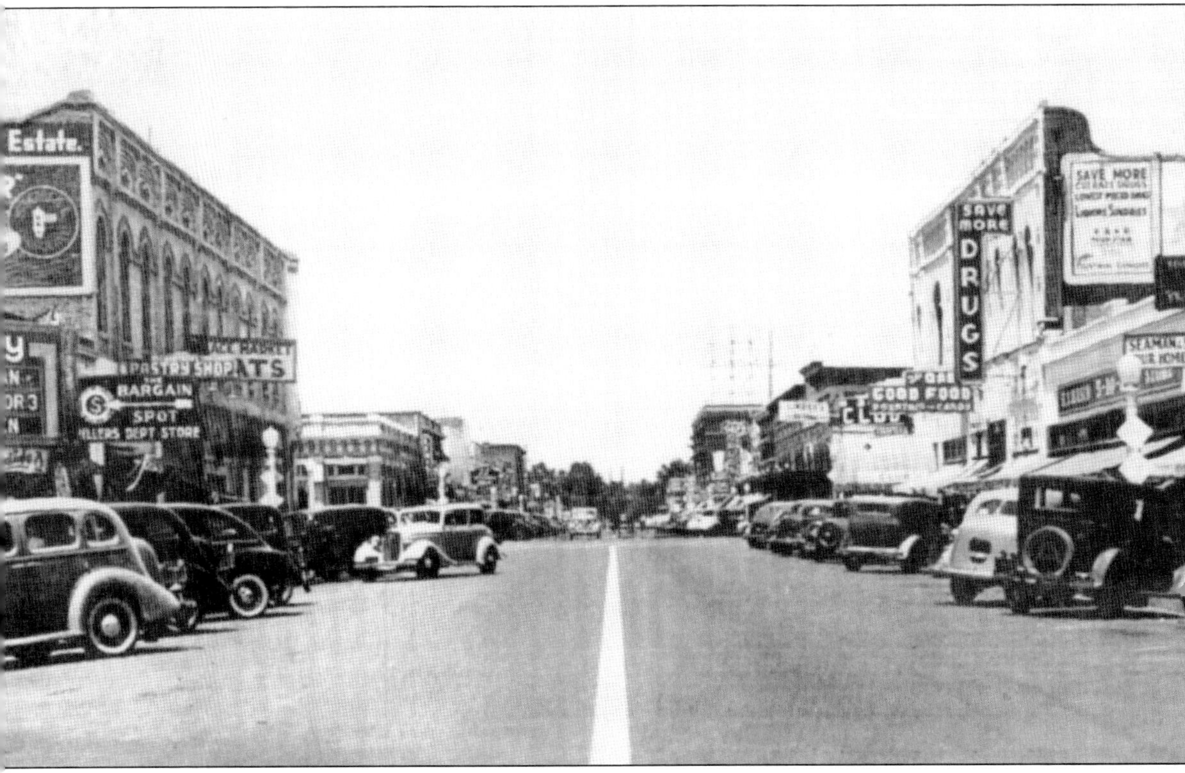

A different view of K Street, this one from Inyo Avenue, shows the bank building on the right. On the left is Linder's Hardware. The drugstore on the right has been replaced by a NAPA auto parts shop. Farther down K Street is the Tulare Hotel as it appeared in the 1930s. (Author's collection.)

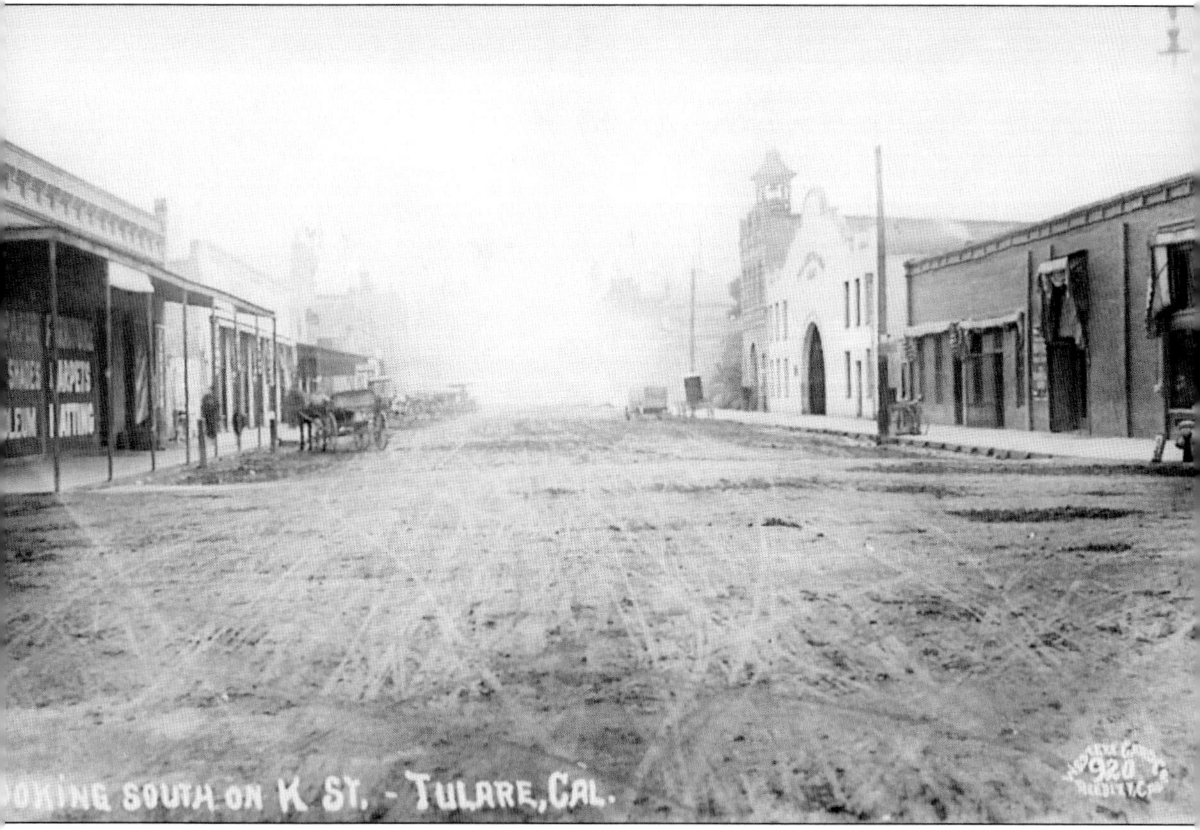

K Street was still unpaved in 1910. The building with the curved facade was the Tulare stables but today has been divided into three businesses. The city hall and fire department were located in the building with the bell tower, which was demolished in the 1950s. Although this photograph is dated 1910, some believe it may have been taken even earlier because of the lack of automobiles. (California History Room, California State Library.)

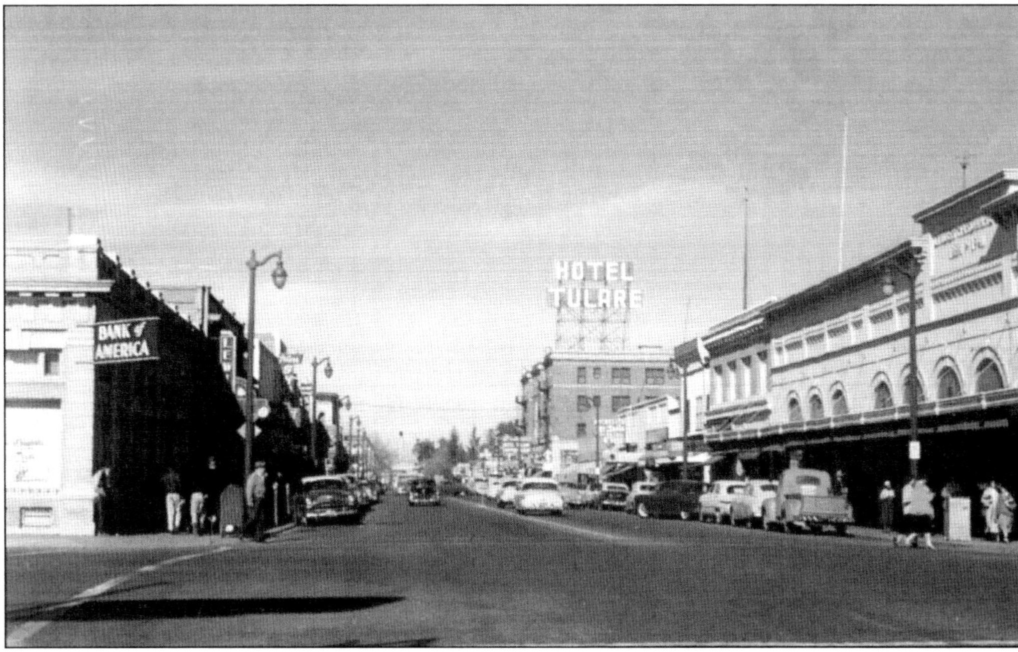

Until the end of the 1950s, K Street remained the center of Tulare's business district. In this photograph from that time, the cupola has been removed from the bank building, now a Bank of America branch. The anchors of K Street were always Linder's Hardware and the Tulare Hotel, on the right. (Author's collection.)

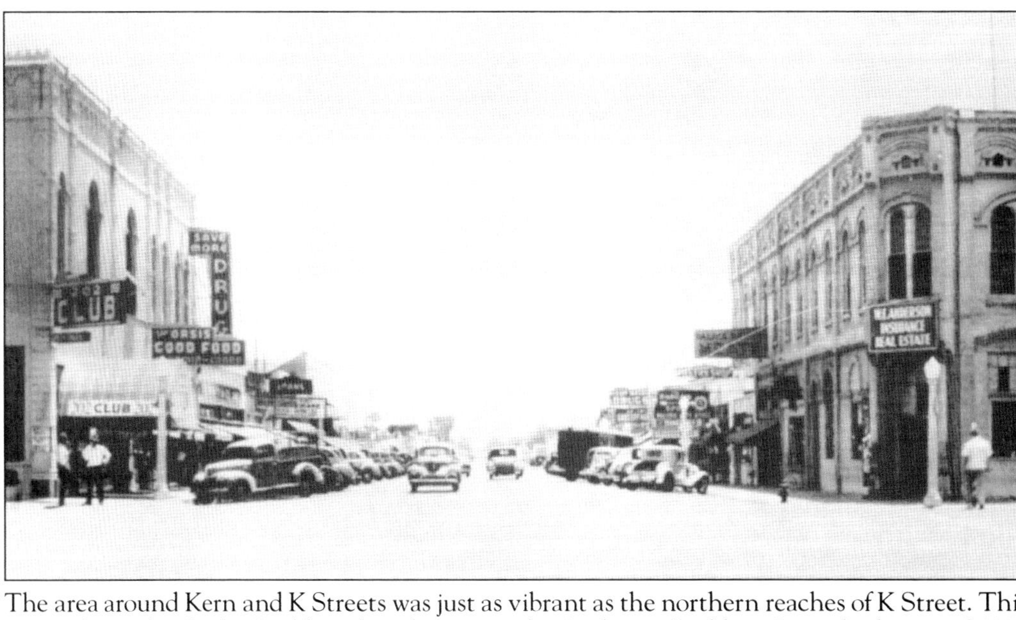

The area around Kern and K Streets was just as vibrant as the northern reaches of K Street. This image shows the Quilty Building, later known as the Anderson Building. It was built around 1890 by Israel Ham near the city's Chinatown. In the late 1890s, it housed the Farmers and Merchants Bank. Later, Capt. Thomas H. Thompson, a Civil War officer, occupied the ground floor. In 1915, Linder's used it as a temporary location after fire destroyed its building. (Author's collection.)

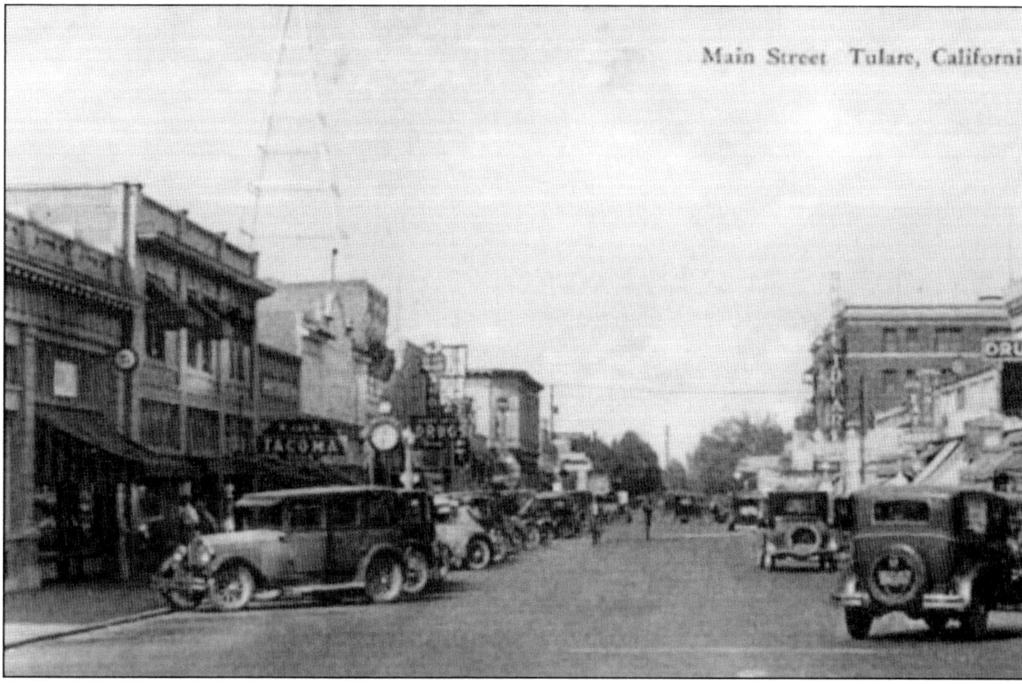

By the 1920s, K Street had been paved. Among the familiar landmarks that remained are the bank building on the left, the Tulare Stables, and the Tulare Hotel on the right. (Author's collection.)

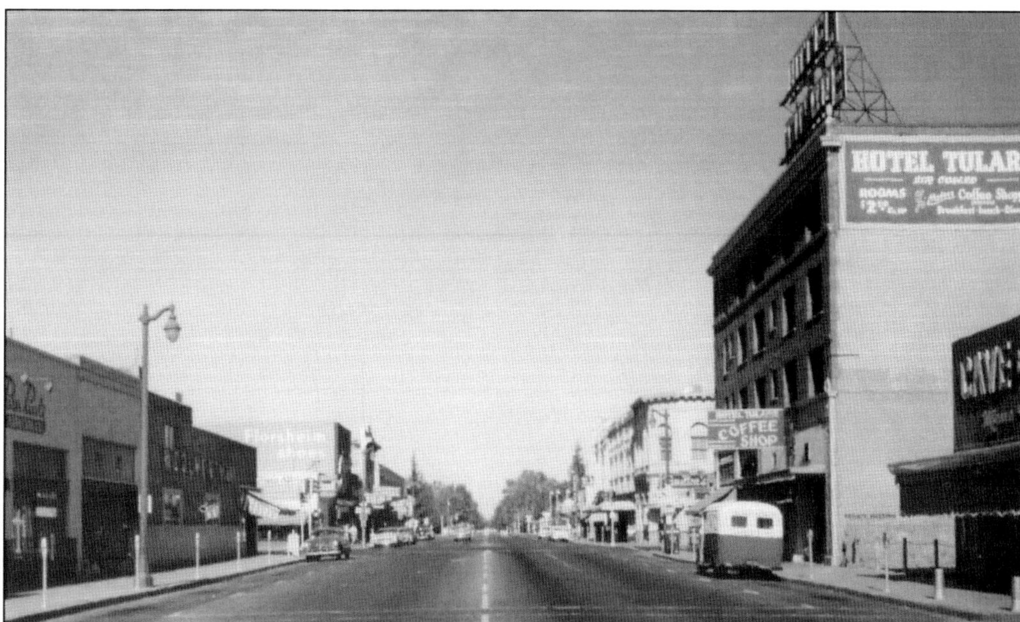

Tulare Avenue, one of the busiest streets in the city, has had many landmarks, such as the Tulare Hotel, on the right. Today, a parking lot and two arches with a plaque to commemorate the history of the hotel occupy the area. In the 1920s, Florsheim Shoes was located on the left. Farther down the street are several shade trees. Most have since been cut down. The Bank of Tulare is on the right at the corner of K Street and Tulare Avenue. (Author's collection.)

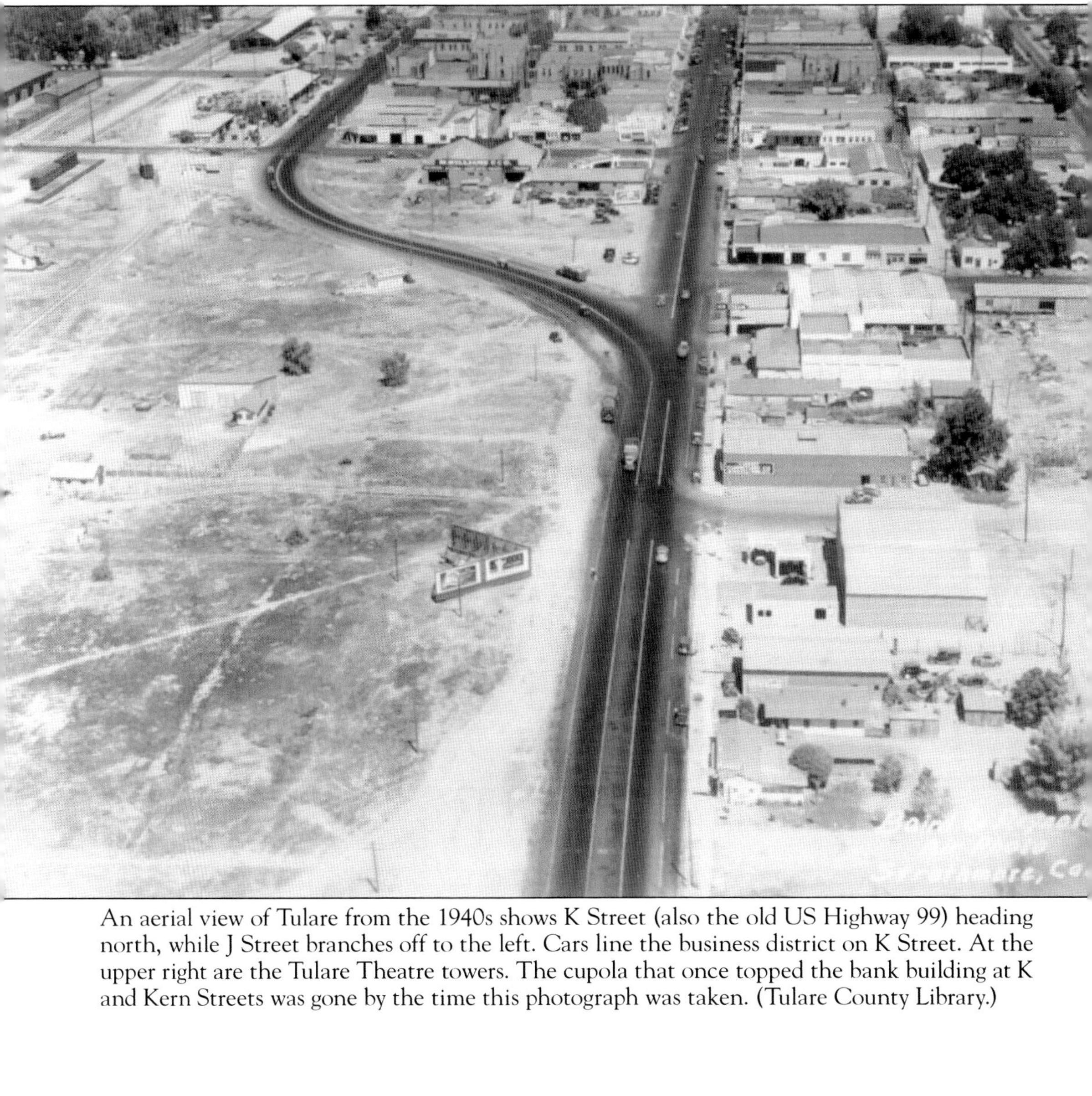

An aerial view of Tulare from the 1940s shows K Street (also the old US Highway 99) heading north, while J Street branches off to the left. Cars line the business district on K Street. At the upper right are the Tulare Theatre towers. The cupola that once topped the bank building at K and Kern Streets was gone by the time this photograph was taken. (Tulare County Library.)

Two

BUILDINGS

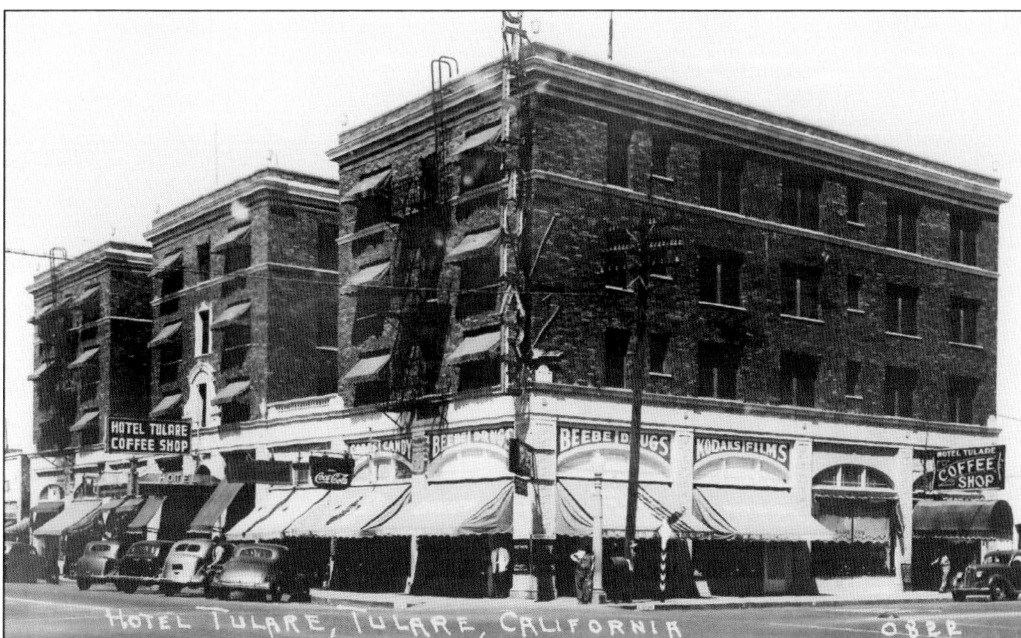

The four-story Tulare Hotel, built in the early 1920s and in use until the 1960s, was destroyed by arson on May 23, 1983. The entire block was gutted by the fire, one of the largest in the city since the 1886 blaze that destroyed much of the business district. The hotel had a huge lobby, and the ground floor had a drug store, coffee shop and other businesses. It cost $225,000 to build. When the hotel opened in June 11, 1922, Charles Kennedy of the Tulare Board of Trade was its first guest. Pres. Herbert Hoover is said to have stayed there. (Author's collection.)

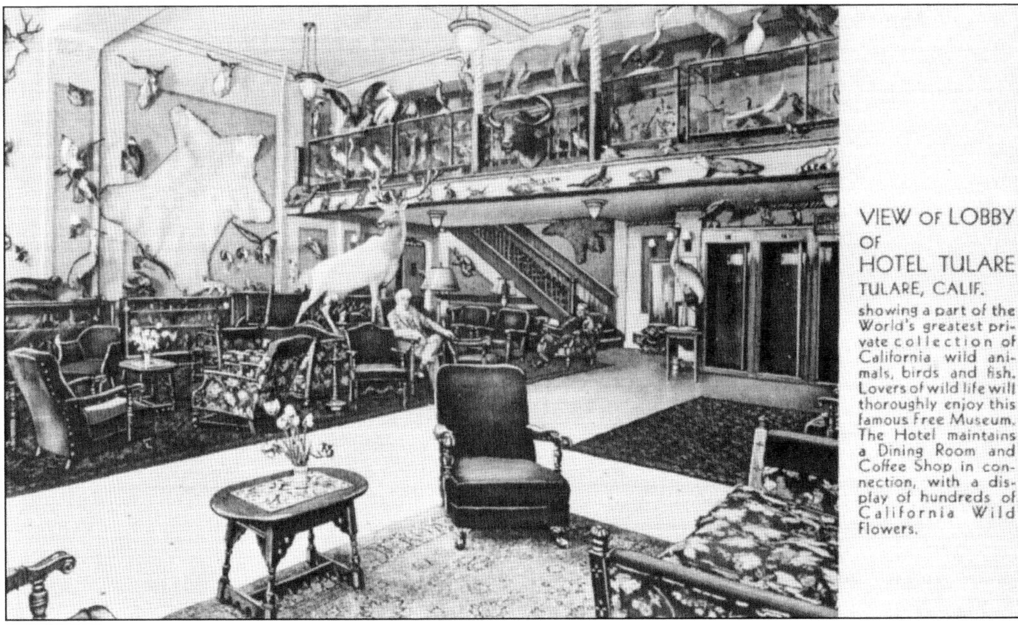

The Tulare Hotel had an extensive collection of stuffed and mounted animals and birds. Emery Whilton, who owned and operated the hotel, was an avid collector of the state's fauna. He offered guests a free museum in the lobby and claimed in a promotional brochure that the collection had 700 specimens showcasing the "World's Greatest Collection of California Wild Animals, Birds, Fish and Flowers." (Author's collection.)

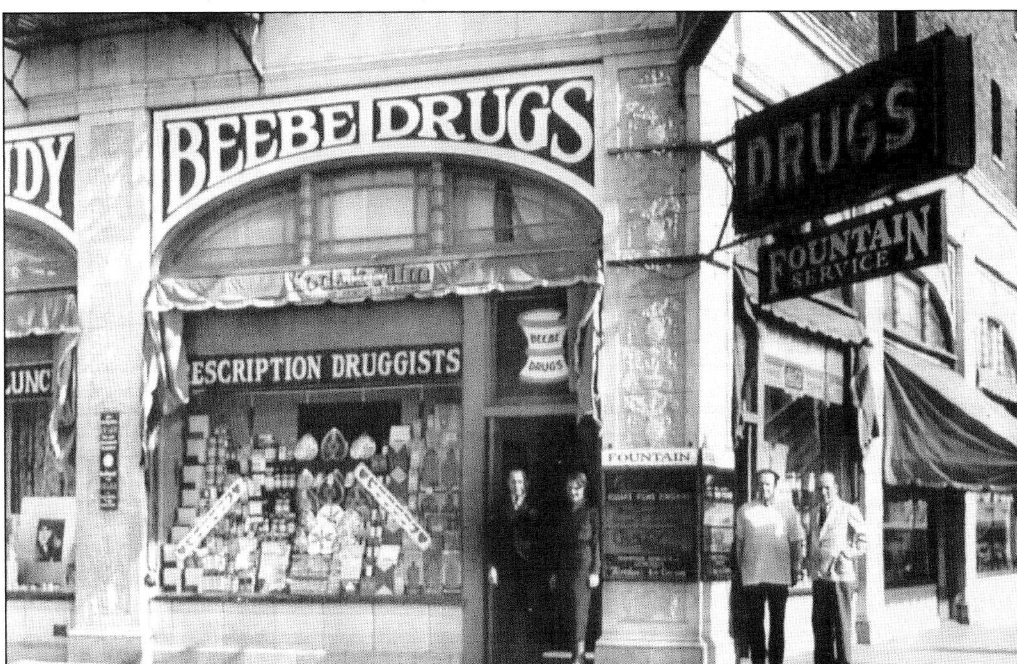

During the 1930s, the Tulare Hotel, at the corner of North K Street and Tulare Avenue, housed several businesses on the ground floor. One of them was Beebe's Drugs. Today, two arches remain from the once mighty hotel that had dominated the skyline since 1922. (Tulare County Library.)

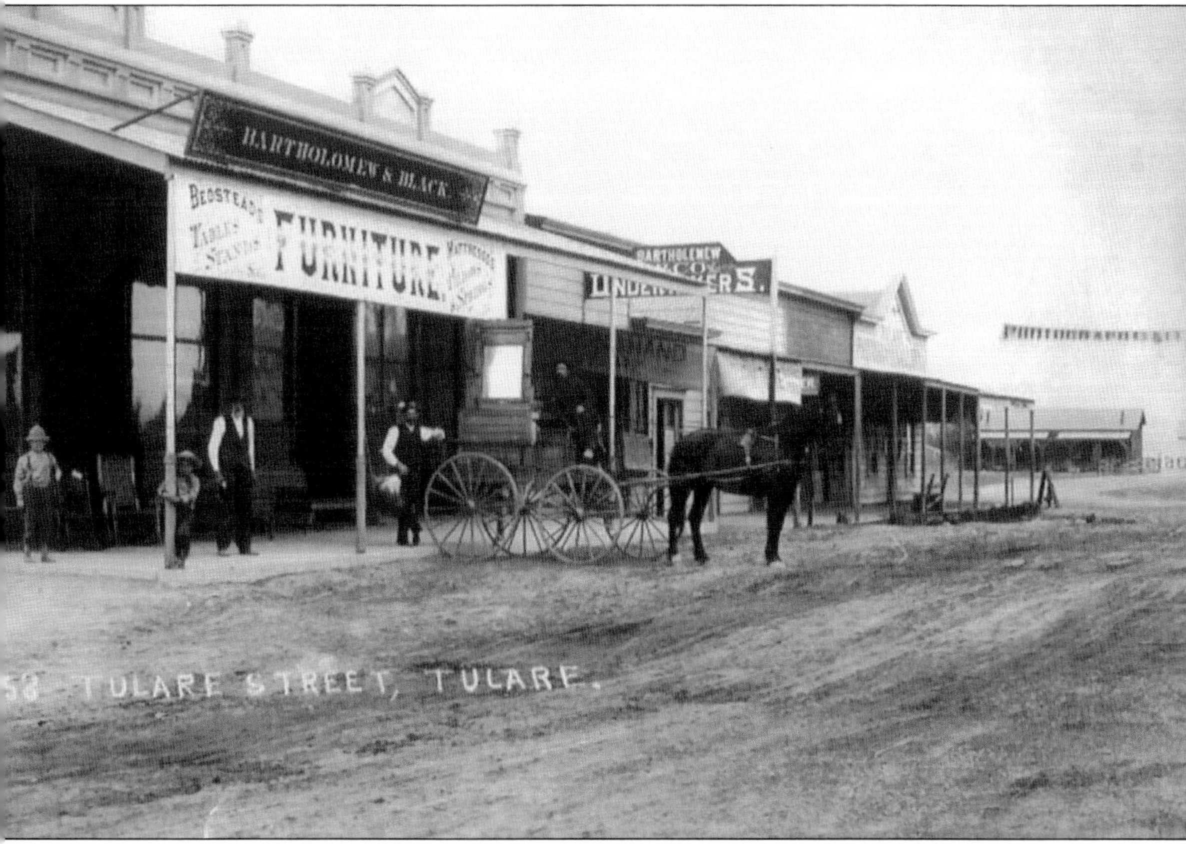

Like every city, Tulare has had its share of undertakers. In the late 1880s, Bartholomew & Company Undertakers was located on the north side of the 200 block of East Tulare Avenue. Next door to the undertaker was Bartholomew & Black, a furniture store owned by the same firm. This late-1880s image shows men loading a dresser into a horse-drawn wagon. (Tulare County Library.)

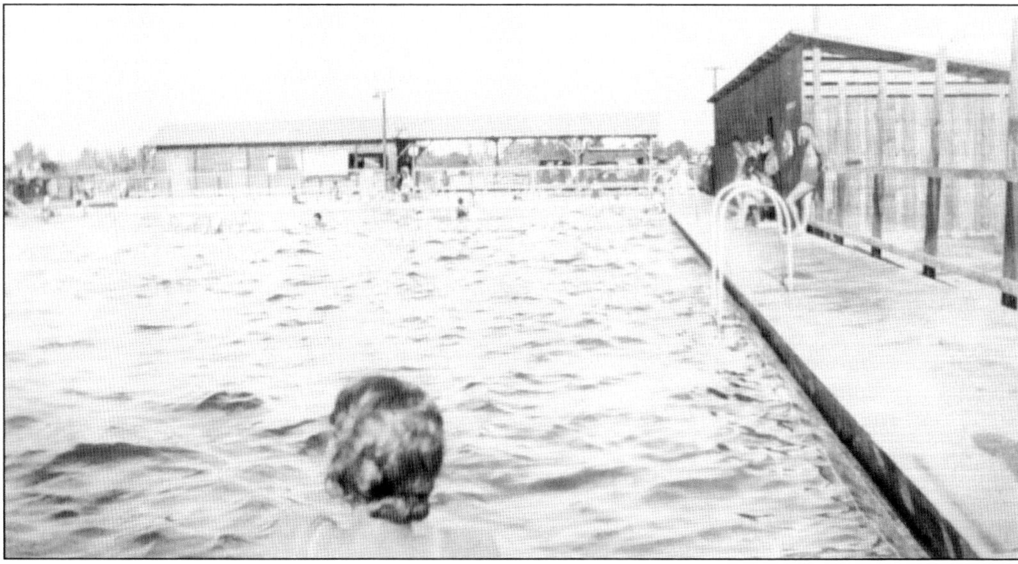

One of the earliest public pools in the city was the Blue Moon Swimming Pool, which was located on South Sacramento Street. It was completed in 1931, and was one of the largest in Tulare County. In 1937, Wilbur Bostard Sr. bought the pool along with an adjacent dance hall, which was converted into a skating rink. In 1955, the pool was replaced by the Blue Moon Market. The site has been an empty lot since 2004. (Tulare County Library.)

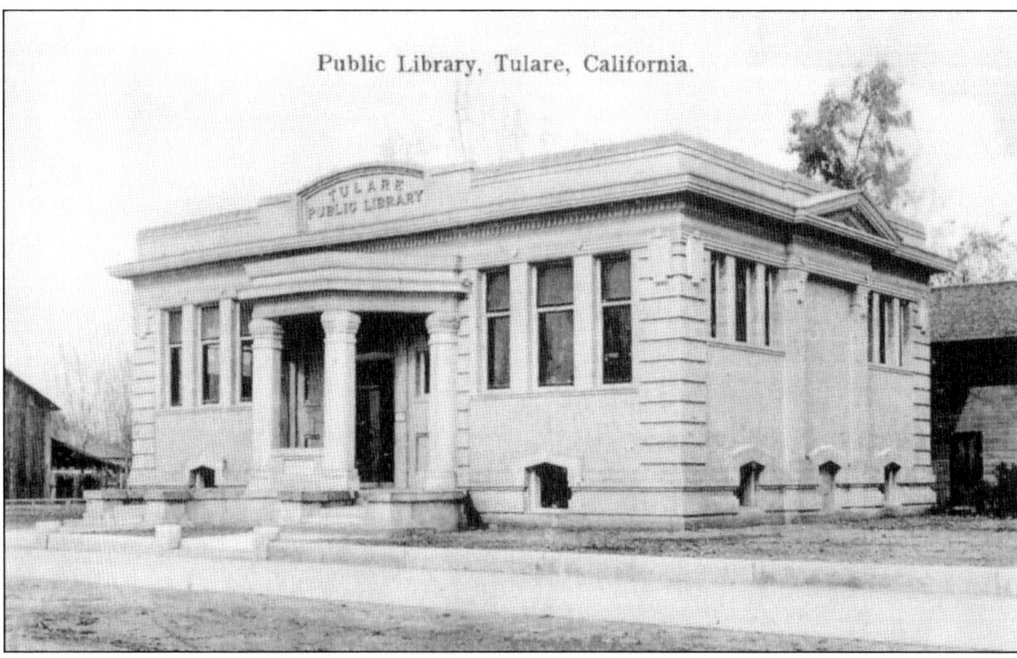

The first structure built specifically as a library for Tulare, seen in this view looking from east to west, was not very wide, possibly one reason why a much larger building, at F Street and Tulare Avenue, was used for a new library in 1963. Citizens of Tulare had collected $500 to go along with a donation from philanthropist Andrew Carnegie to start the first library. (Author's collection.)

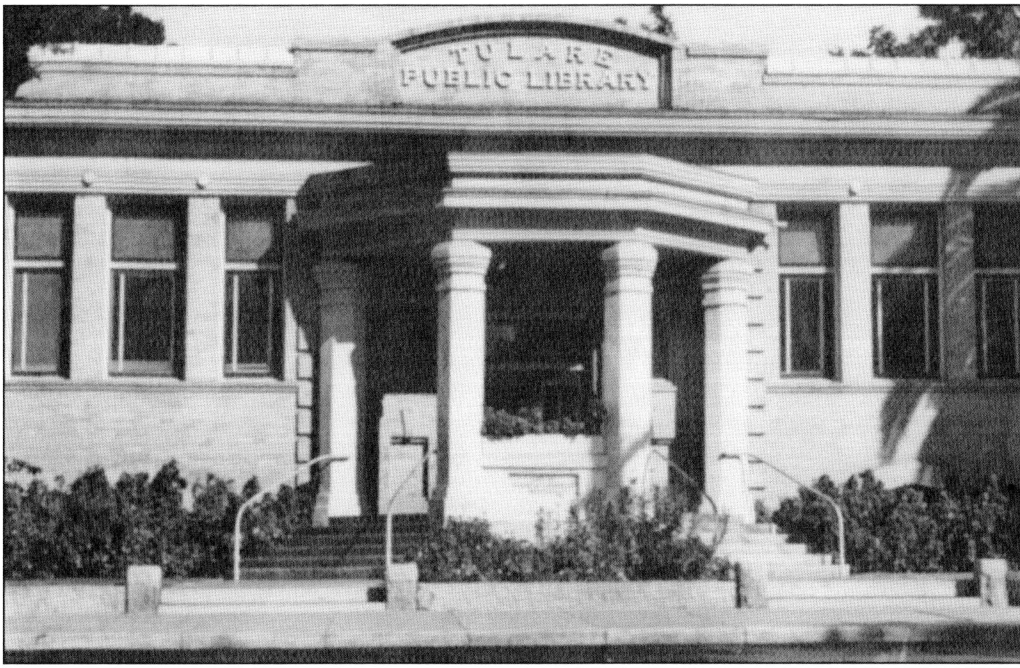

The second Tulare Library was built with funds from Carnegie in 1905. It was at the northwest corner of Kern Avenue and I Street. The building was razed in 1970 when the library moved to a location on F Street where the Central Grammar School was once located. (Author's collection.)

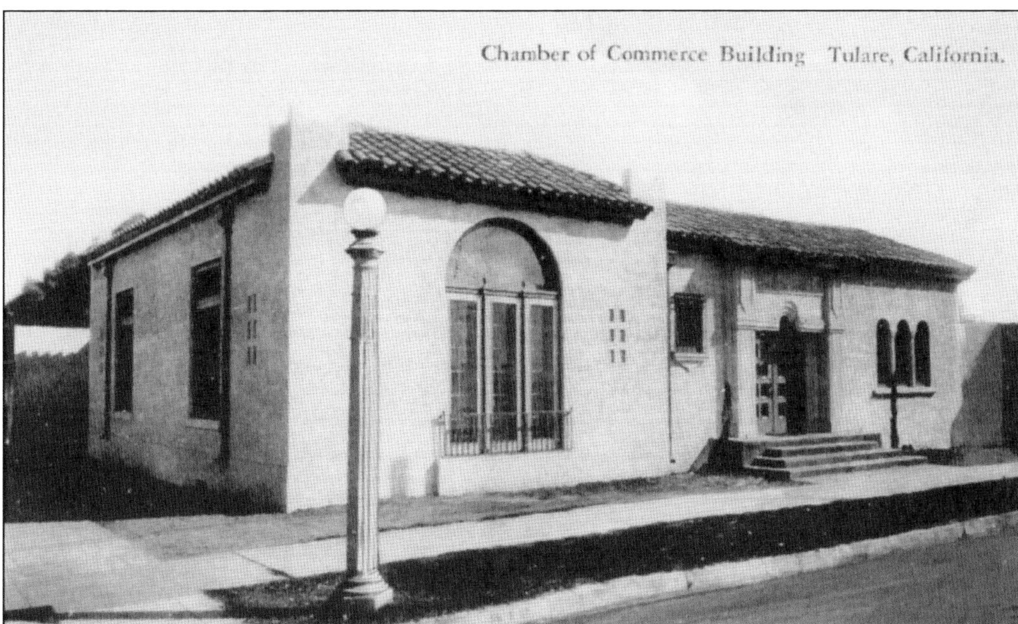

The first Tulare Chamber of Commerce building at what is now Martin Luther King Jr. Avenue and K Street is obscured by a giant mural that has been painted on it. The small building retains its original beauty nonetheless. In the rear, an annex serves as the Tulare County Fairgrounds office. (Author's collection.)

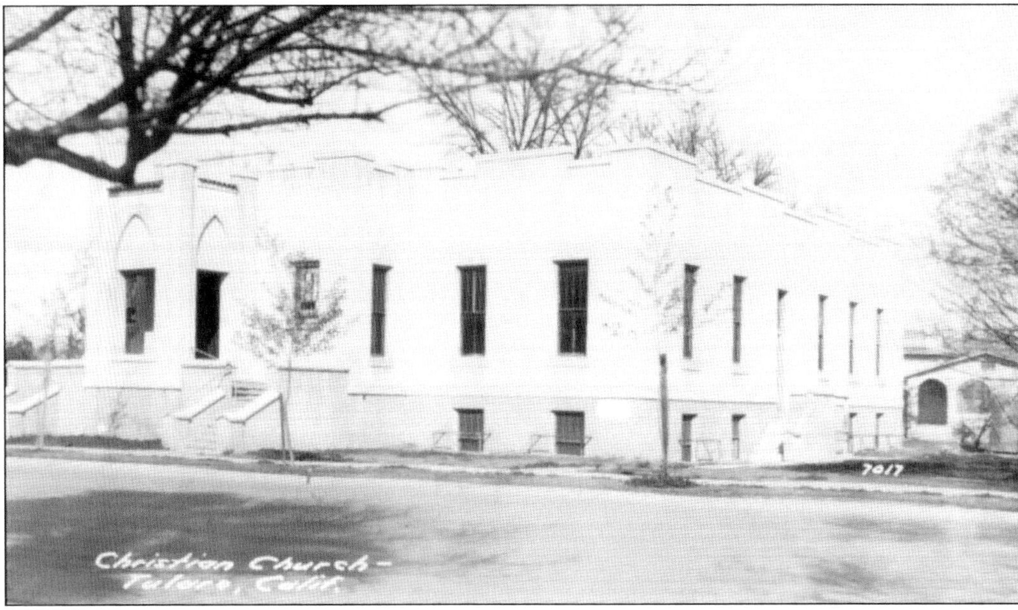

The Christian church has undergone many changes and names but still remains at G Street and Tulare Avenue. The building, one of the oldest in the city, has always been used as a church. In this early-1900s photograph, the Tulare Hospital is visible on the right near the number "7017." (Author's collection.)

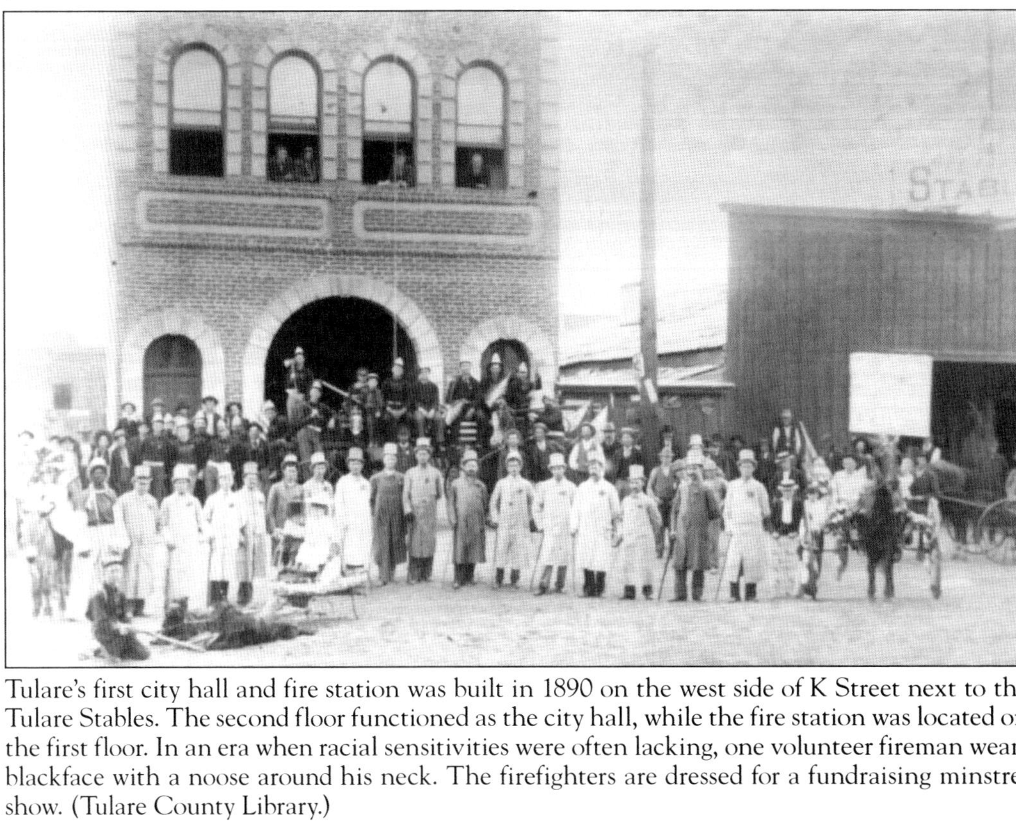

Tulare's first city hall and fire station was built in 1890 on the west side of K Street next to the Tulare Stables. The second floor functioned as the city hall, while the fire station was located on the first floor. In an era when racial sensitivities were often lacking, one volunteer fireman wears blackface with a noose around his neck. The firefighters are dressed for a fundraising minstrel show. (Tulare County Library.)

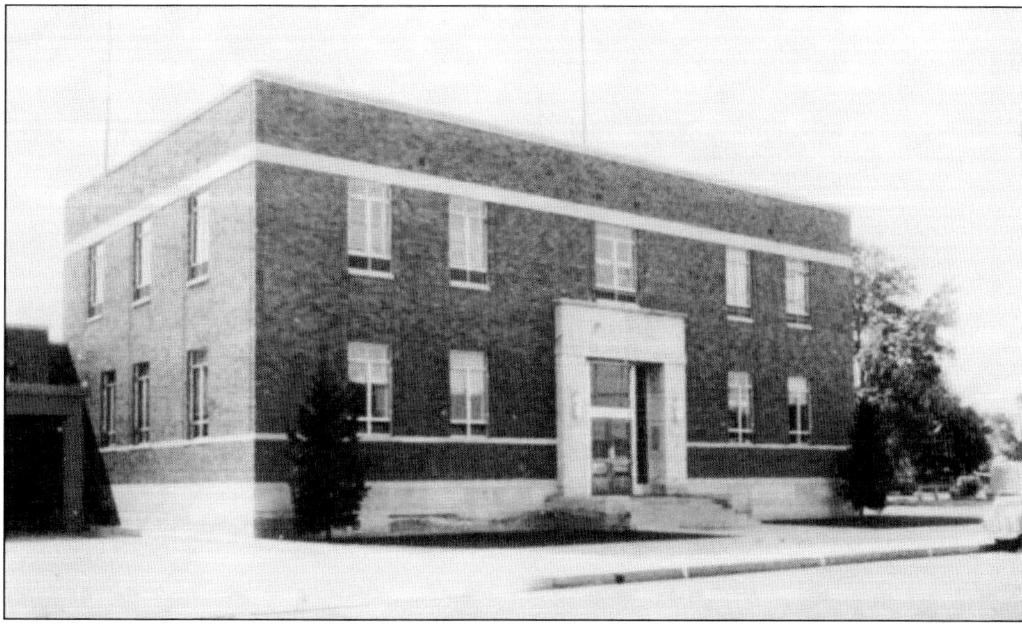

The current Tulare City Hall was built in 1937 at a cost of $76,000 plus another $35,000 in federal funds. The building, located at Kern and M Streets, also has an adjacent jail. In the late 1990s, the city hall was remodeled. (Tulare County Library.)

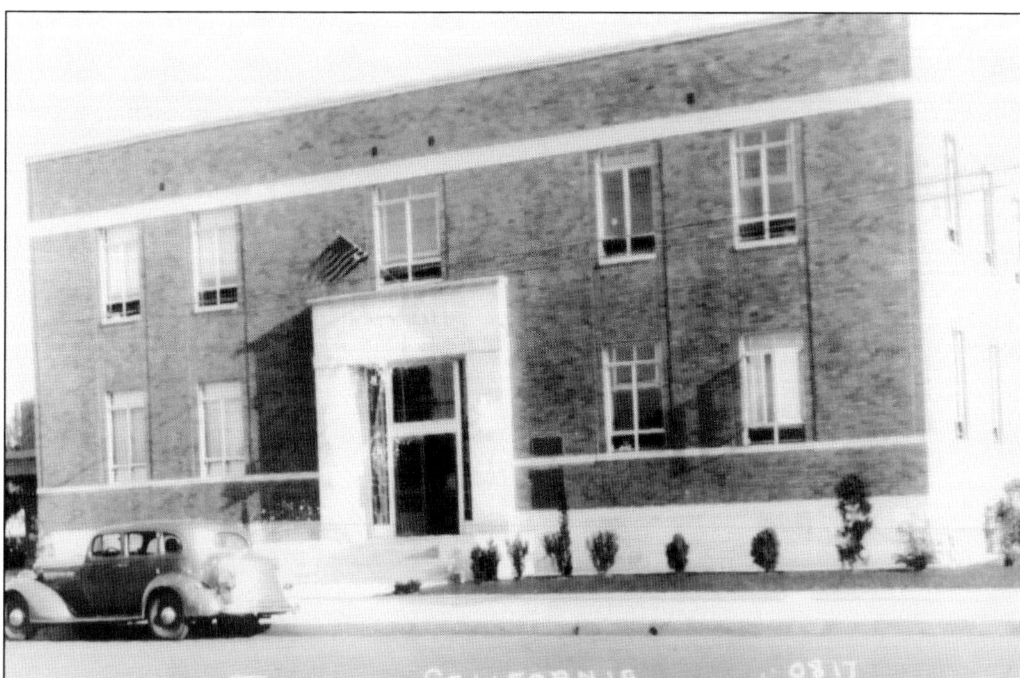

In the 1930s, when the original city hall on K Street was deemed too small, the city opted to build a larger and more modern structure. Originally, it had 8,000 square feet of space. A new wing, built in 1999, added another 4,000 square feet. (Tulare County Library.)

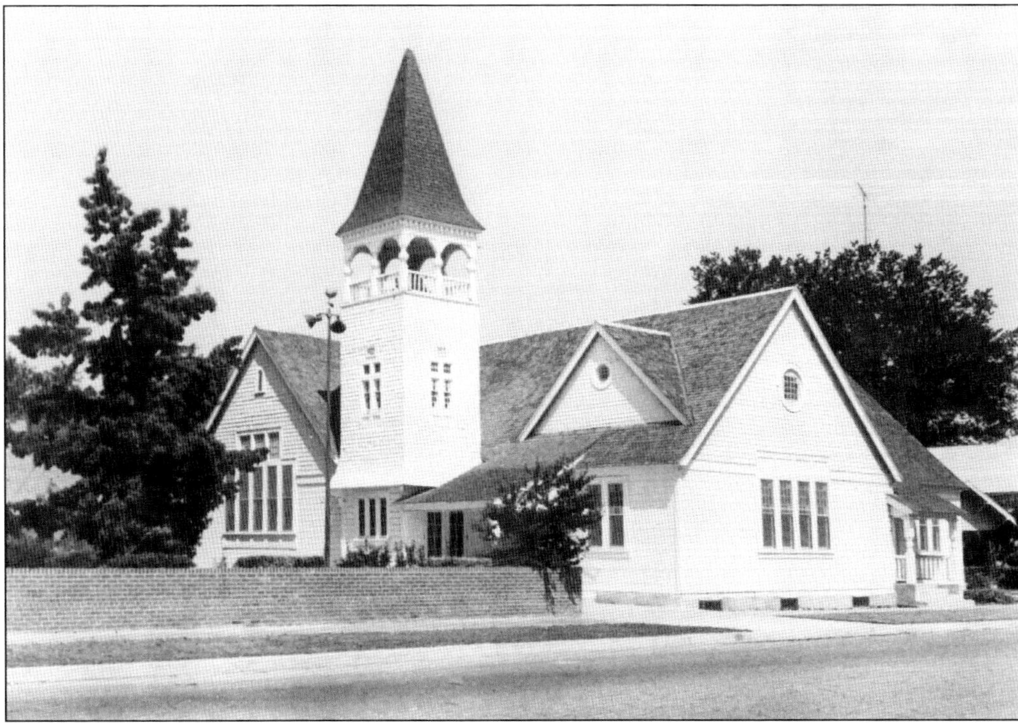

The first church in Tulare was the Congregational Church, founded in 1873 by the Rev. A.L. Rankin. The church, at King and I Streets, was destroyed by fire in 1898 but rebuilt two years later at Tulare Avenue and H Street. (Tulare County Library.)

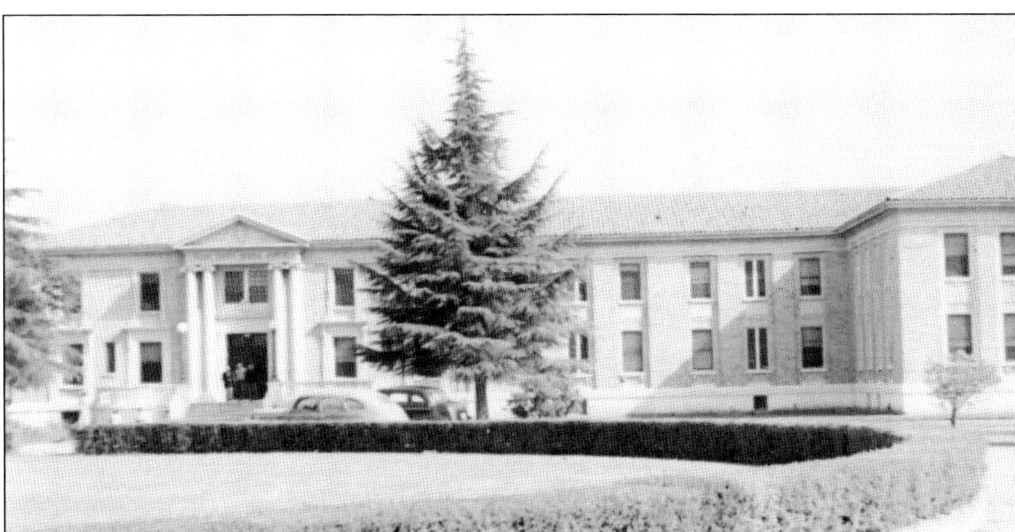

Tulare County General Hospital was opened in 1928 at Bardsley Avenue and South K Street, across the street from the county fairgrounds. The construction took place after the Tulare County Board of Supervisors decided to build the hospital in Tulare, rather than Visalia. A U-shaped driveway allowed patients to be brought to the front doors. (Tulare County Library.)

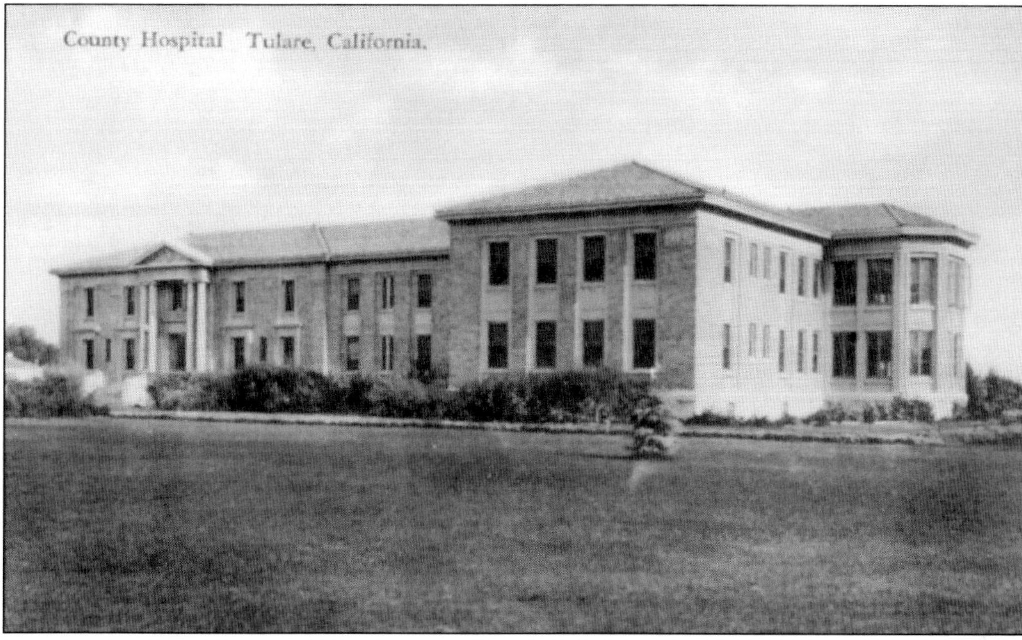

Tulare County General Hospital continued to operate until 1980, when it was replaced by the Hillman Healthcare Center at 1062 South K Street. Tulare had also built Tulare District Hospital at Cherry and Merritt Avenues. (Tulare County Library.)

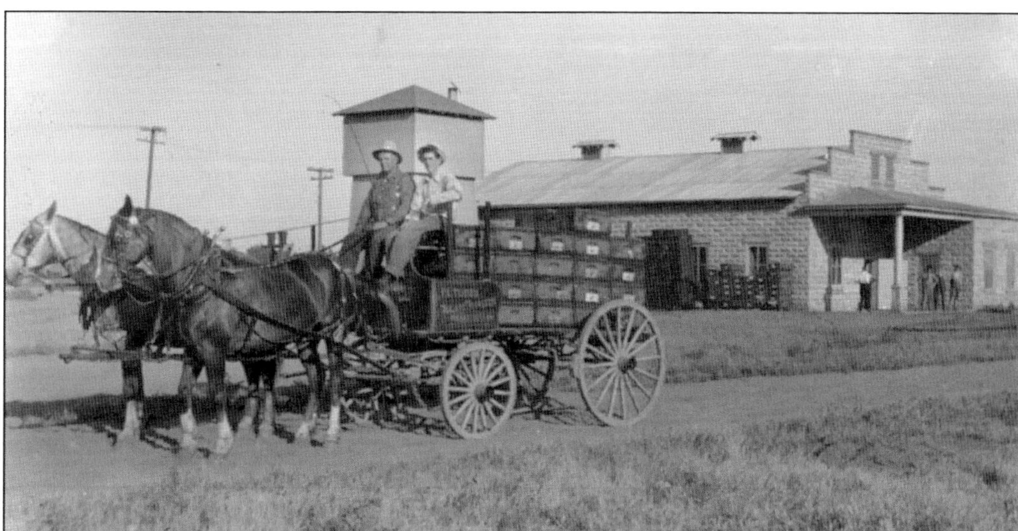

One of the most successful businesses in the Central Valley has been the Dairyman's Cooperative Creamery Association. Since 1901, when it was founded on South M Street and what is now Martin Luther King Jr. Avenue, the farmer-owned cooperative has provided members a market for their milk and helped them negotiate prices and manufacture, process, and market their products to wholesalers. The cooperative operated its own creamery to manufacture butter, but left the marketing to a Los Angeles firm. (California History Room, California State Library.)

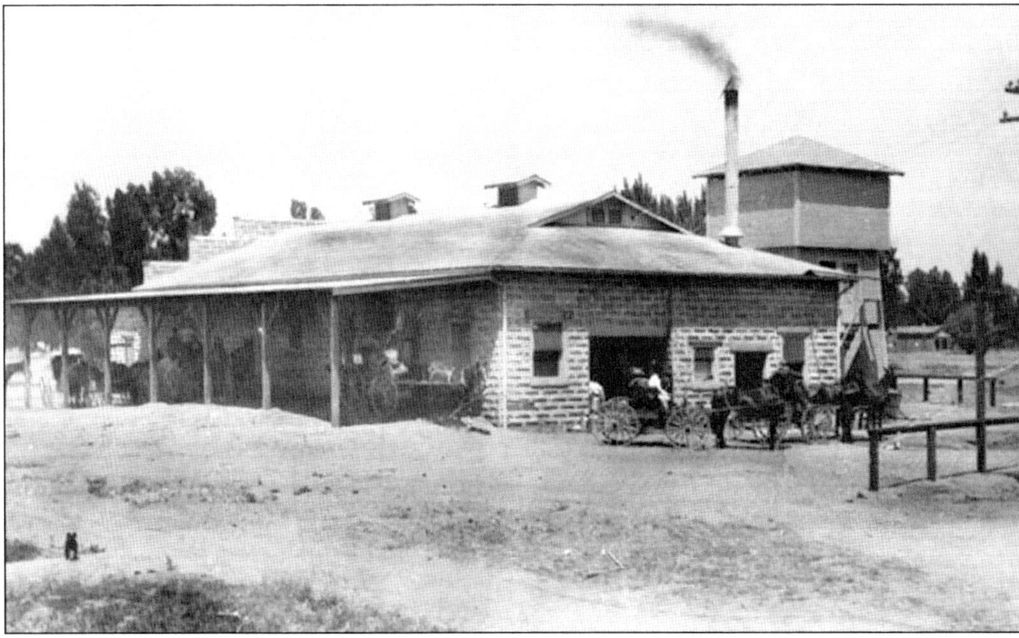

This close-up of the Dairyman's Cooperative Creamery Association dates back to shortly after its construction a century ago. It has been replaced by a multimillion-dollar facility. (California History Room, California State Library.)

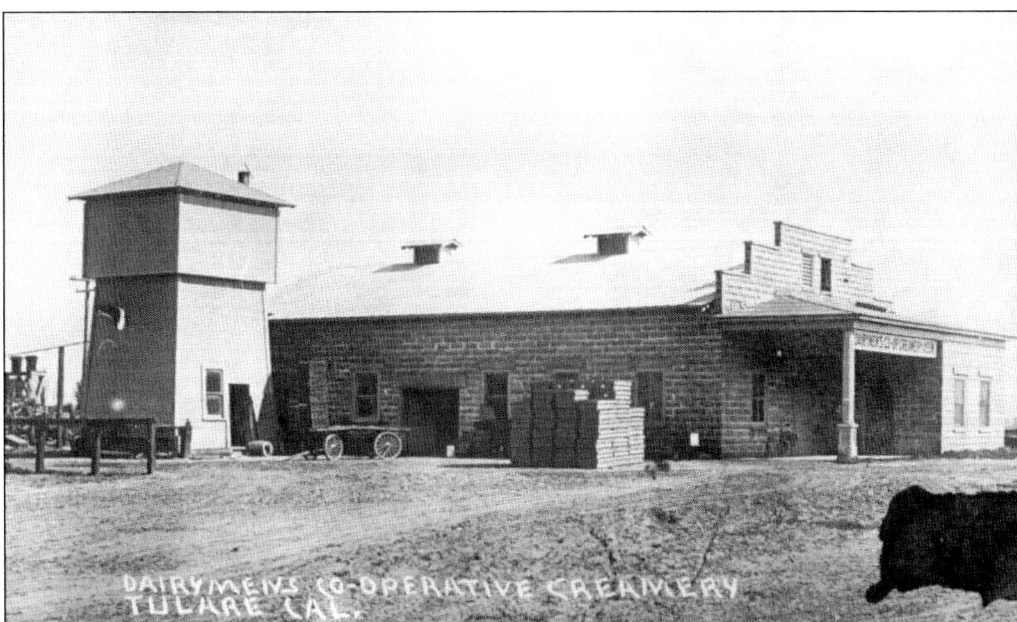

The Tulare Board of Trade, part of the chamber of commerce, helped organize the Dairyman's Cooperative Creamery Association with Wooster Cartmill as its manager. Within eight years, it was nearly bankrupt and was sold to a Los Angeles firm. In 1909, Joseph LaMarche, resident of the National Bank of Tulare, assisted in the organization of a new, wholly-owned farmers' cooperative, which opened in November of that year. (Tulare County Library.)

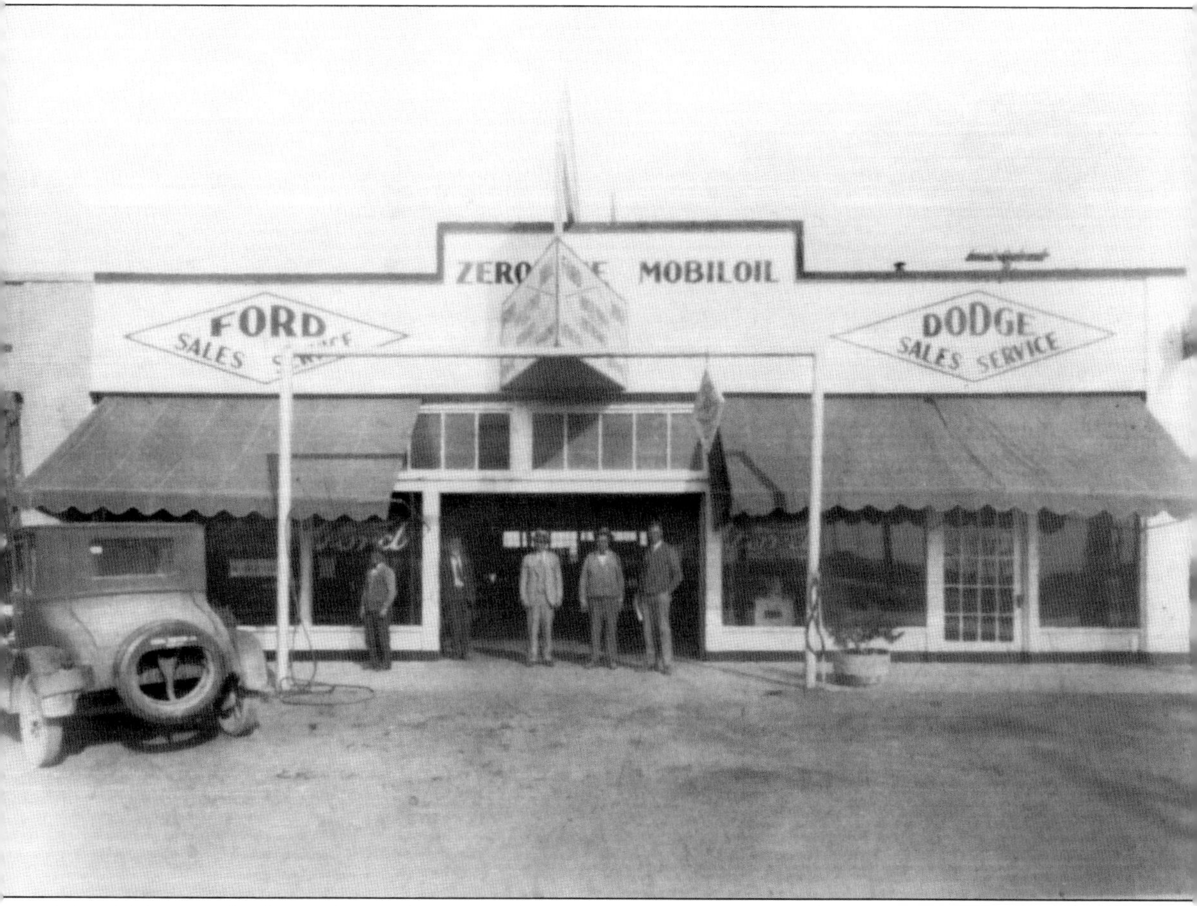

This Tulare dealership sold Fords and Dodges in the 1920s, the first full decade in which cars gained widespread popularity. (Tulare County Library.)

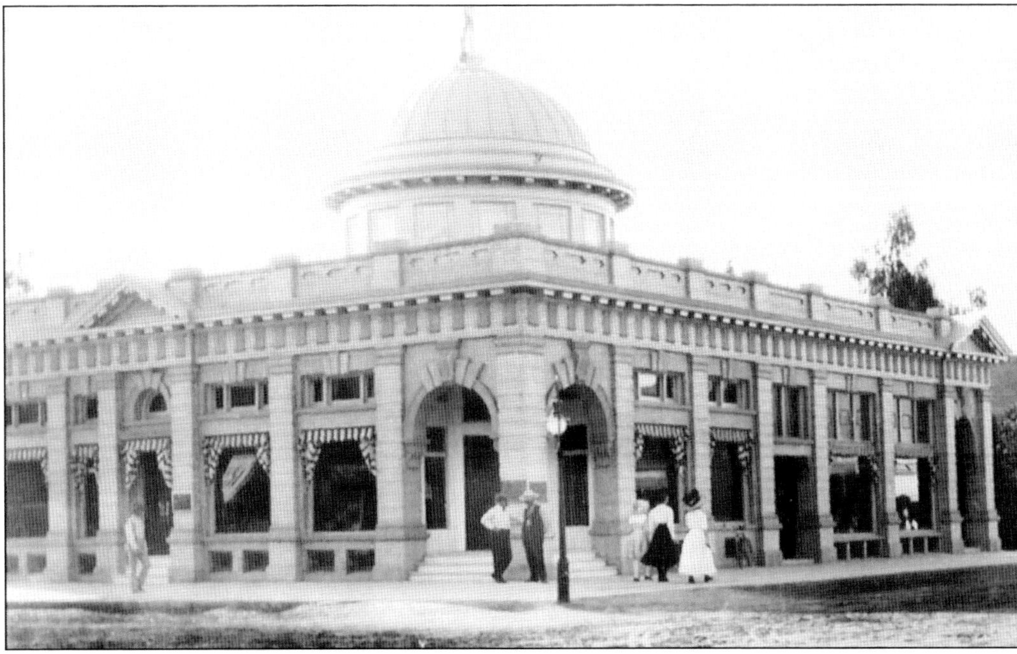

The First National Bank of Tulare was located at the corner of Kern Avenue and K Street in the early 1900s. Note that the cupola on the bank building was still intact at the time (it was removed in the 1940s), and there was a gap between the bank building and the first city hall. (California History Room, California State Library.)

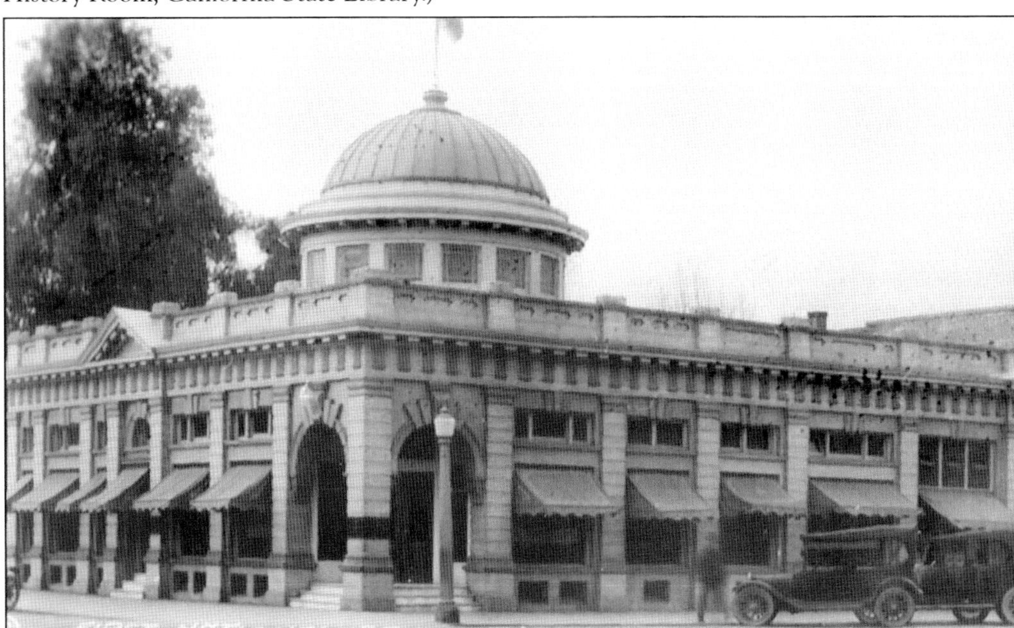

The First National Bank of Tulare still had the cupola on its roof in the 1920s. The structure is the last remaining between Kern Avenue before the razing of what was then Front Street. A vintage streetlamp stands at the corner near the 1920s automobiles parked at Kern Avenue and K Street. (California History Room, California State Library.)

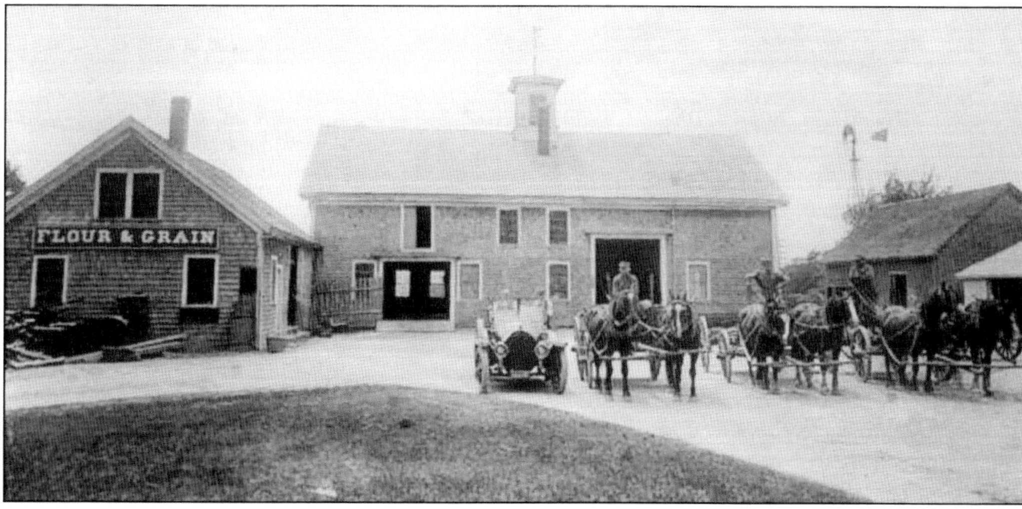

Tulare Flour and Grain is pictured in the early 1900s. Note the three teams of horse-drawn wagons, along with an early automobile. (Tulare County Library.)

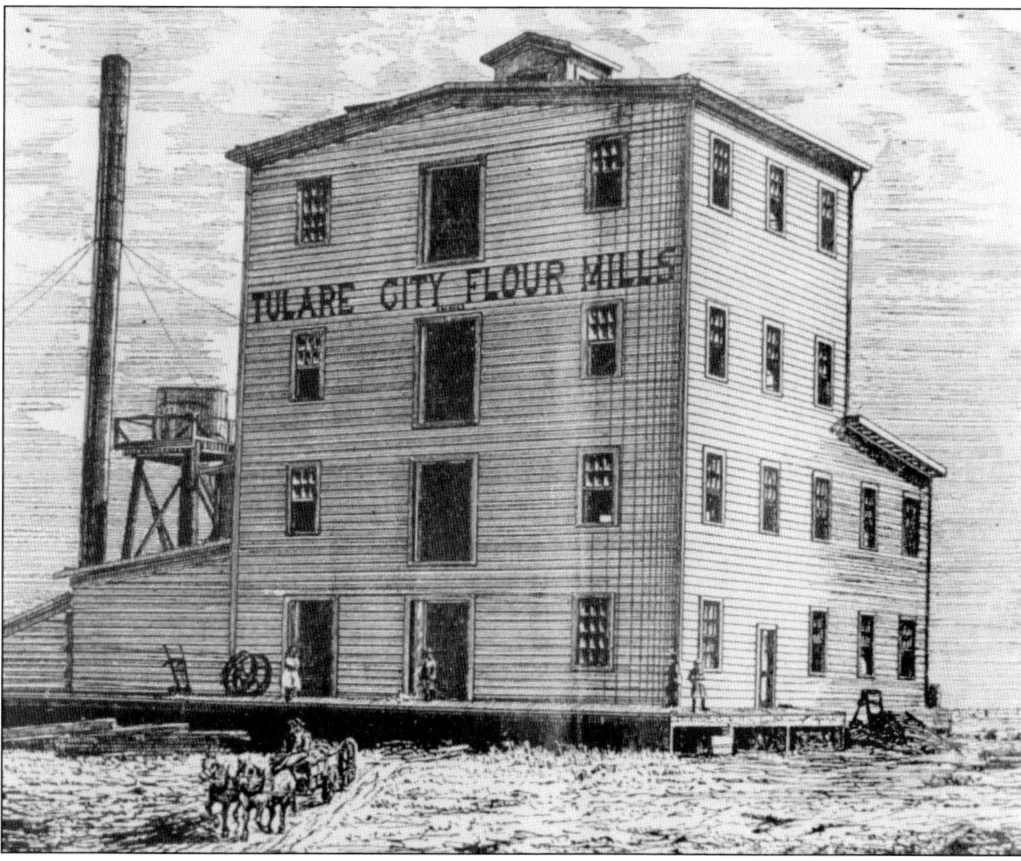

The Fox and Williams Flour Mill, operated by steam and water, is pictured in 1887. Israel Ham's mill was located on Mill Street, which later became South I Street. During its time of operation, the mill produced 200 barrels per day. It was located on the same site as J.D. Heiskell and Company until a fire destroyed it in 1887. Tulare did not have another flour mill for 10 years. (Tulare County Library.)

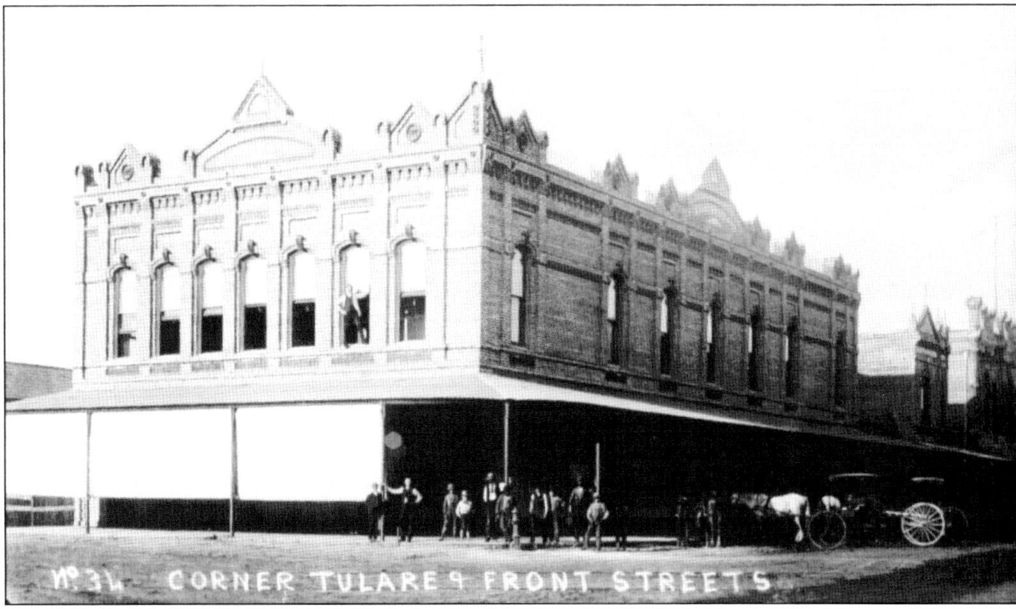

The J. Goldman and Company Building and Social Hall occupied 34 Tulare Street at the corner of Front Street about 1900. It was Goldman's second building; the first, a one-story structure, was destroyed in the 1886 Tulare fire. Today, a Carl's Jr. occupies the site where this imposing structure stood. (Tulare County Library.)

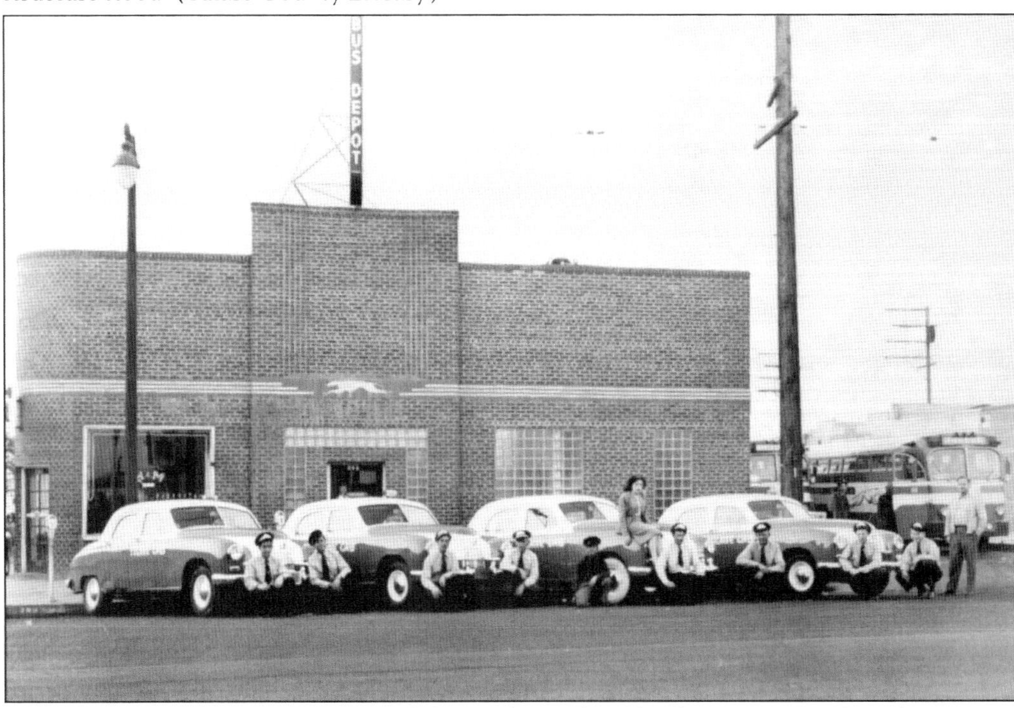

Tulare has had at least three railroad depots, but it has also been a center for other types of transportation. In the 1950s, a Greyhound depot stood at the southwest corner of Kern Avenue and L Street. Identified are Walter Frank, right, Greyhound agent; Skeeter Newson, second from right; and J.D. Kilgore, on the taxi fender. The others are unidentified. (Tulare County Library.)

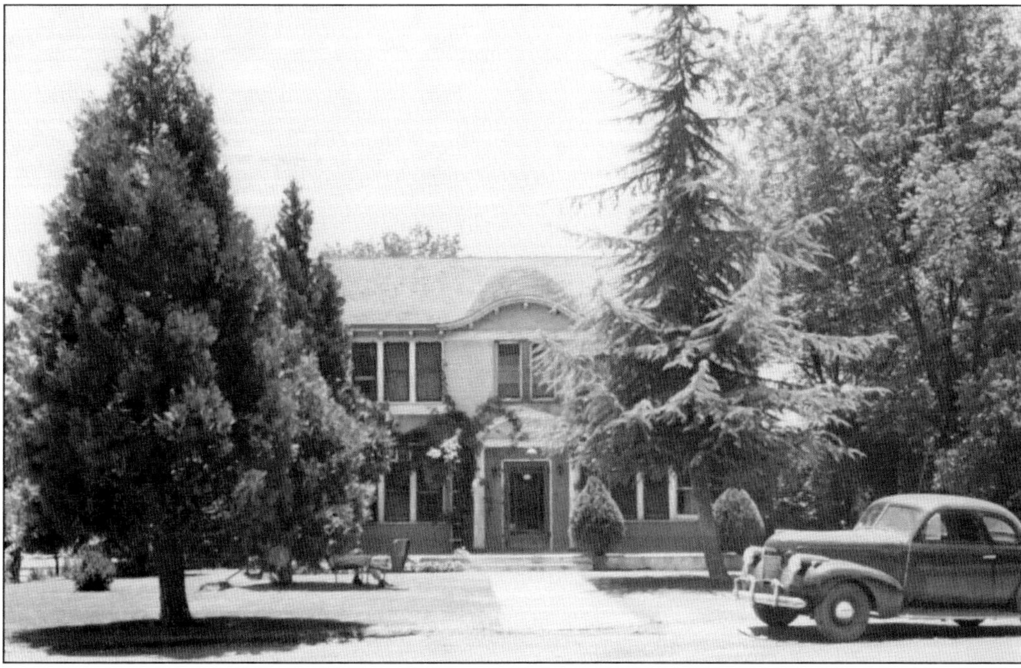

The East Tulare Hospital began as the Bellevue Hospital, just east of Blackstone Street, where US Highway 99 is today. It later became a maternity hospital, but was closed when the Tulare District Hospital opened in 1951. The building was one of the casualties of the construction of Highway 99 in the early 1950s. (Tulare County Library.)

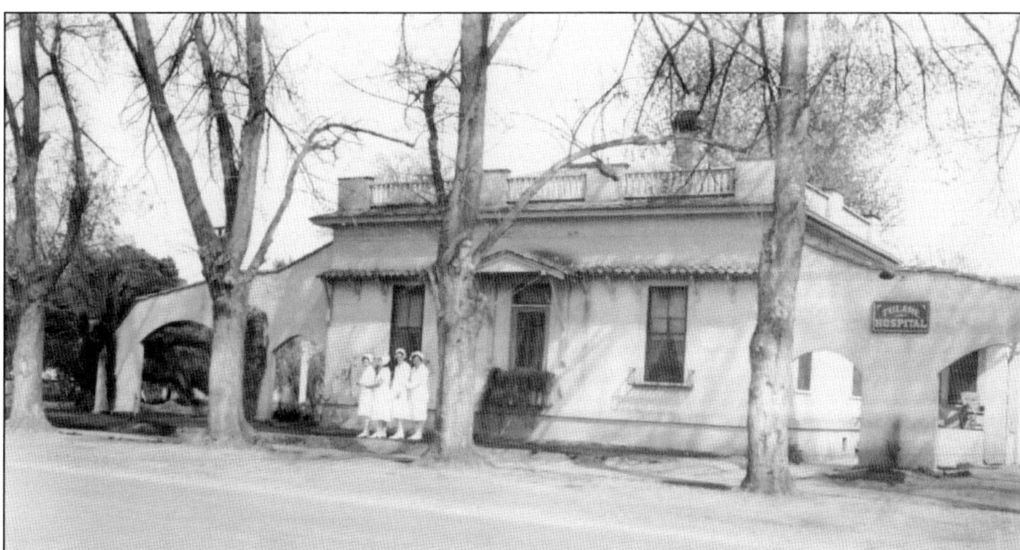

The West Tulare Hospital was located on North G Street at Tulare Avenue. In 1934, Bernice Harris, who had opened the East Tulare Hospital, leased property at 134 North G Street and opened the West Tulare Hospital as well. It operated until 1951, when the Tulare District Hospital started admitting patients. The building continued on as an apartment complex until 2012, when it was torn down. (Tulare County Library.)

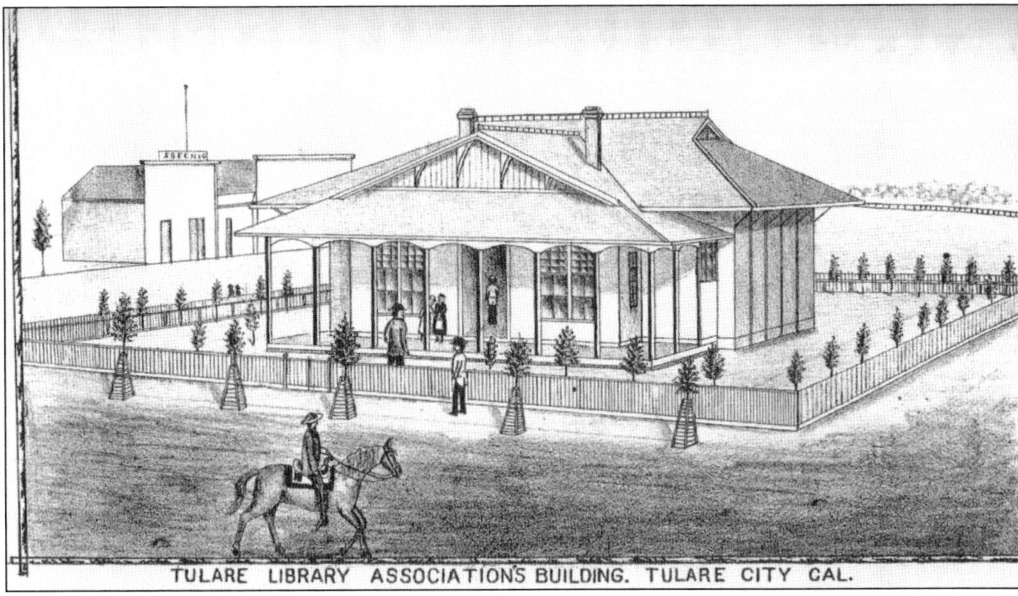

The first Tulare Library Association Building was constructed by the Southern Pacific Railroad in 1882 at I Street and West Tulare Avenue as a meeting and recreation center for railroad employees. It opened in May of that year with a grand ball with many of Tulare's prominent citizens in attendance. By 1896, it was used primarily as a library. The railroad transferred ownership of the building to the city that year, and it continued to serve as a library until the Carnegie library was built in 1905. (Author's collection.)

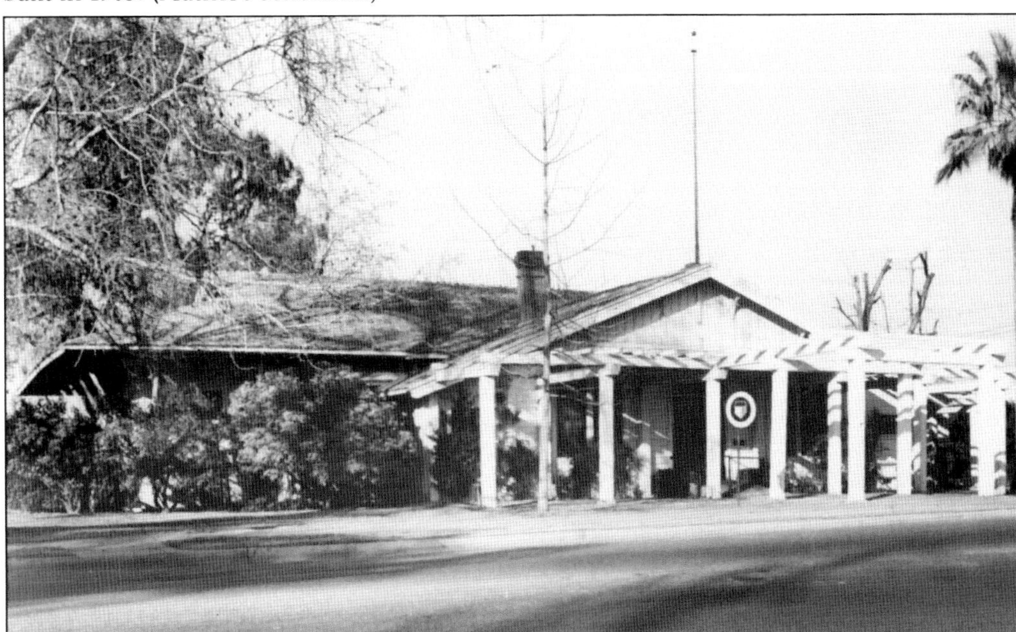

The Tulare Women's Club building has served many purposes over the years. It was initially a library hall, then became a women's club in 1912. It became a senior center in the 1970s until a new senior center was built behind the library on F Street, previously the site of the Central Grammar School. (Tulare County Library.)

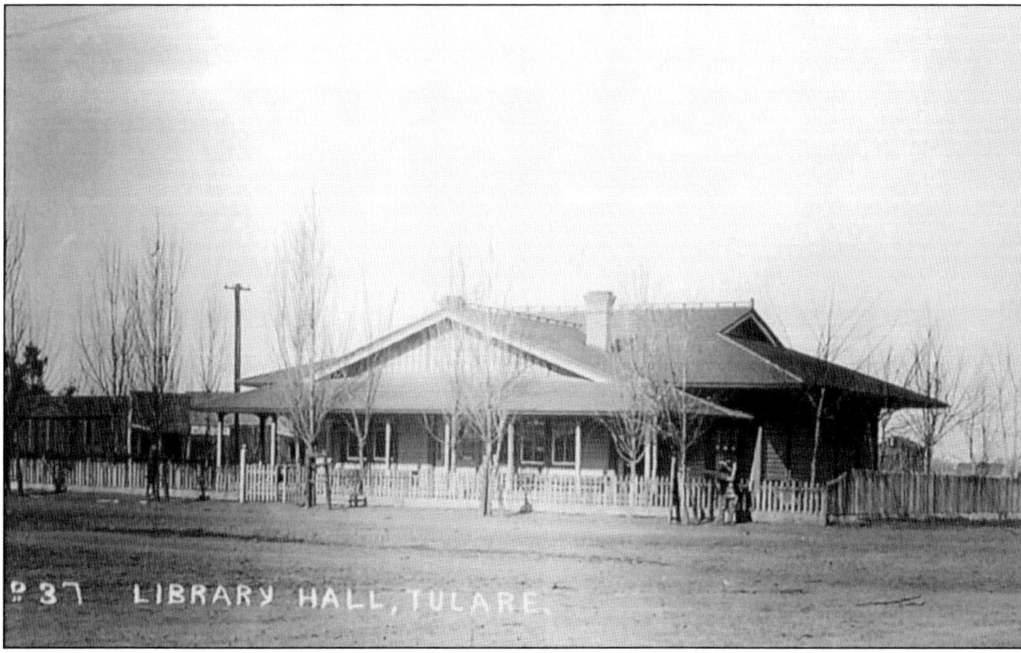

The building now known as the Women's Club was the city's first library. It has always been at 88 West Tulare Avenue, at the corner of I Street. Note that the trees in this 1888 photograph are barely saplings. Many patrons stand in front of the library hall and on the left is the corner house, which is still in use today. (Tulare County Library.)

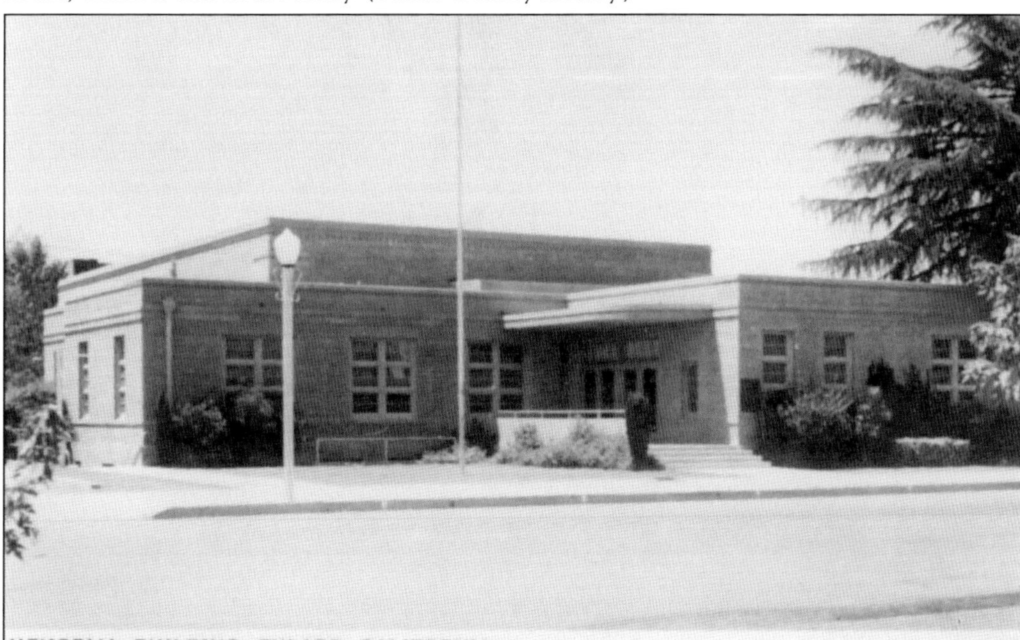

The Tulare Memorial Building, seen here in the 1930s, was at 131 South M Street and was known as the Civic Memorial Building. It had a stage at the rear for community productions. The building was used for city council meetings until a new building went up on Cross Street in 2010. (Author's collection.)

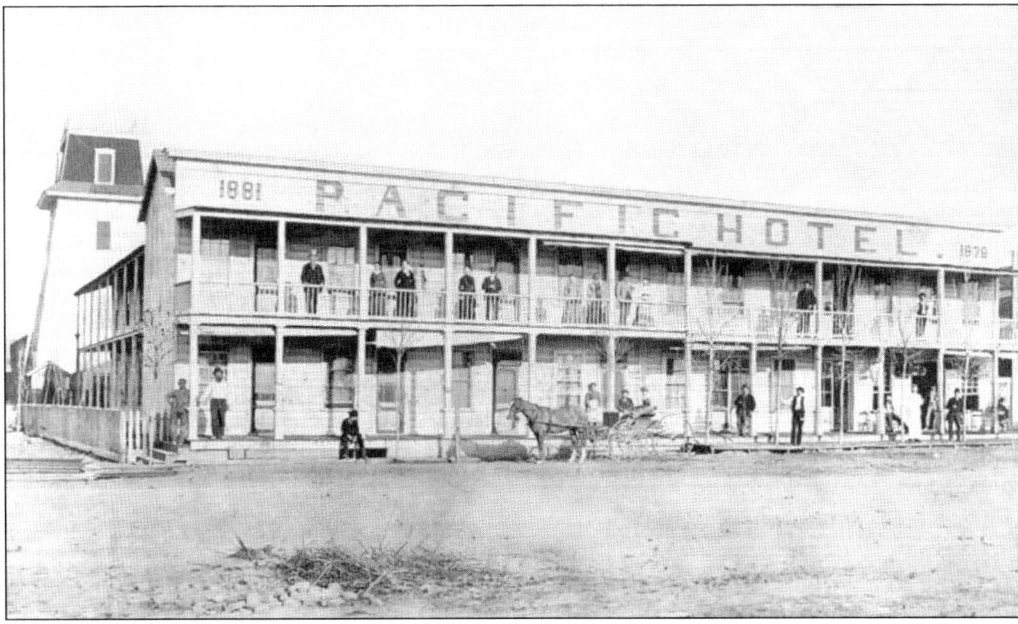

David W. Madden started the original waterworks to provide running water to the city. He opened the waterworks on the east side of O Street between Tulare and Kern Avenues. Later, he drilled a well on his property to provide water to the Pacific Hotel in the 100 block of North J Street. Other businesses joined, and the first running water system was in business. His water tower and the hotel were destroyed during the fire of 1886. (Author's collection.)

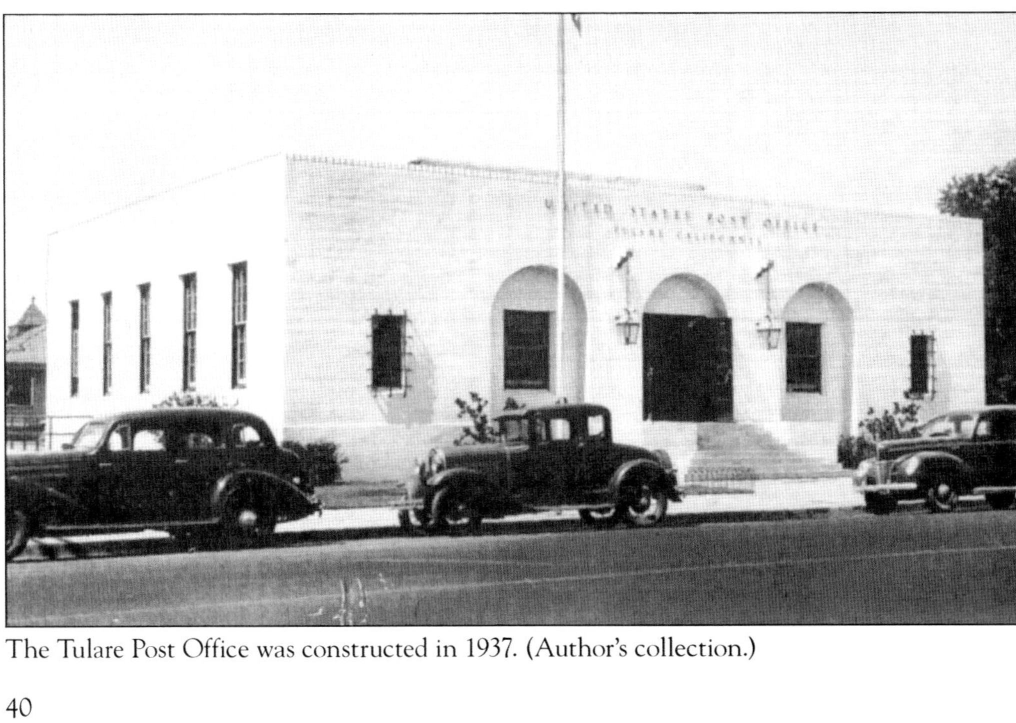

The Tulare Post Office was constructed in 1937. (Author's collection.)

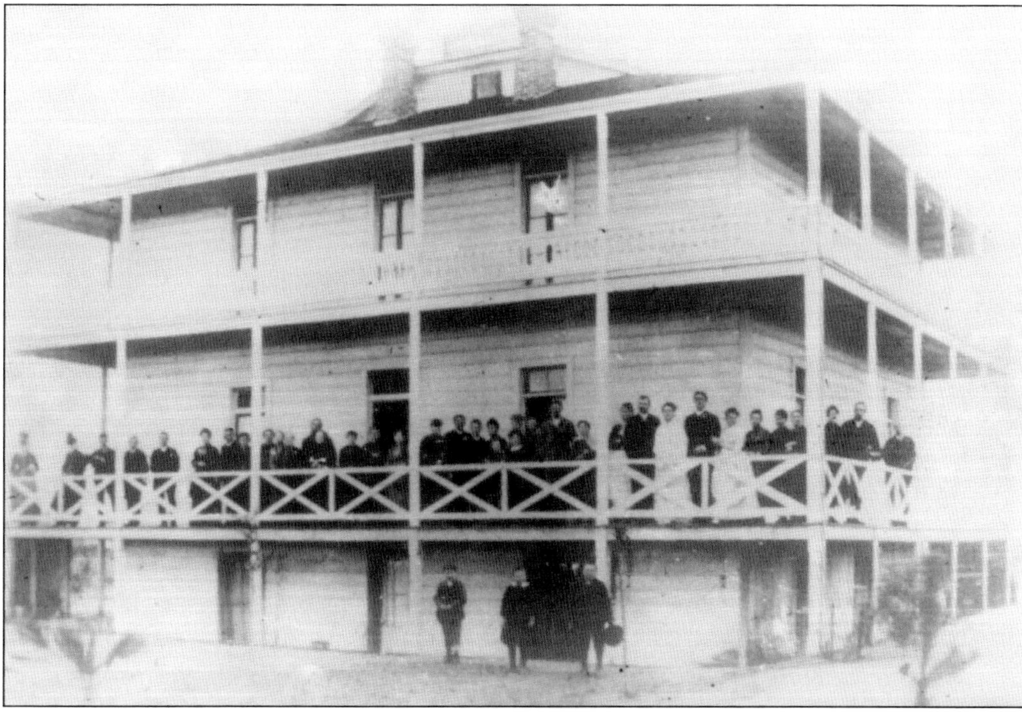

Smith College was founded in 1885 at Elm and D Streets. It was built on land donated by Dr. William T.F. Smith. The three-story building was 80 by 100 feet. In appreciation for the gift, it was named for Dr. Smith. The first floor included two classrooms, a dining area, and a kitchen. The second floor included a 50-seat chapel, and the third was a dormitory for female students. In about a decade, economic problems forced the school's closure. The building was sold and moved to Armona, near Hanford, where it was used as a hotel. (Tulare County Library.)

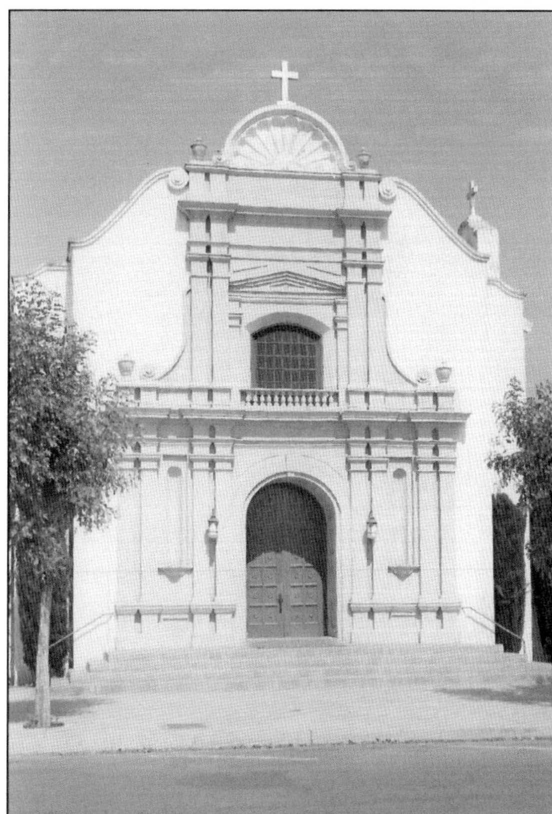

This beautiful California Mission Revival–style church replaced the old wooden chapel of St. Aloysius in 1925. It served the parish community until 1970, when the new church was built on J Street at Pleasant Avenue. St. Aloysius became a freestanding parish in 1905 and was assigned a permanent pastor and staff. (St. Aloysius Archival Collection.)

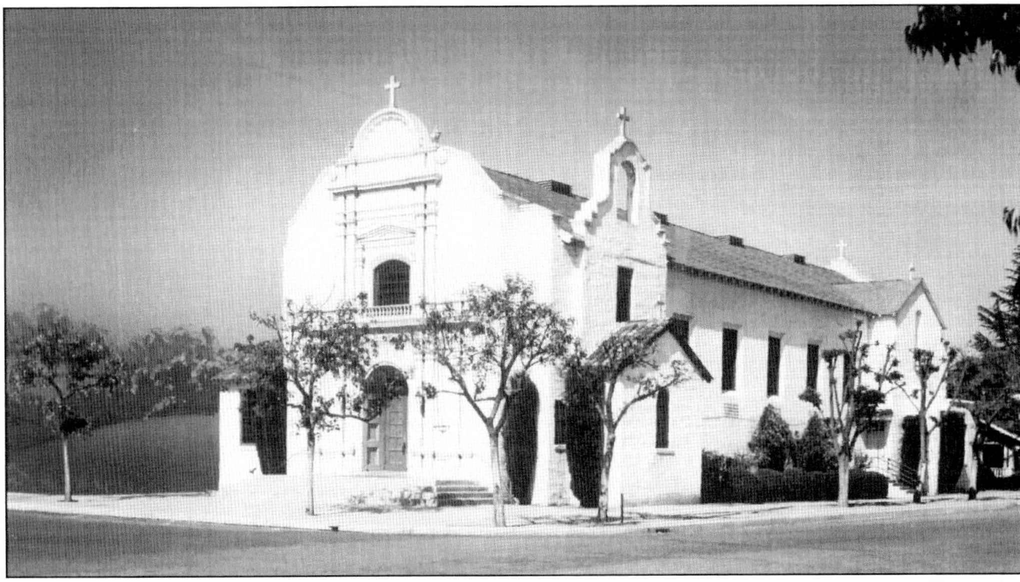

This view of St. Aloysius gives a good perspective of the church along Kern Avenue. From this vantage point, the four crosses on the roof are clearly visible, as are the side entrances on Kern Avenue and the main entrance to the church on F Street. It was replaced by a new church in 1970. (St. Aloysius Archival Collection.)

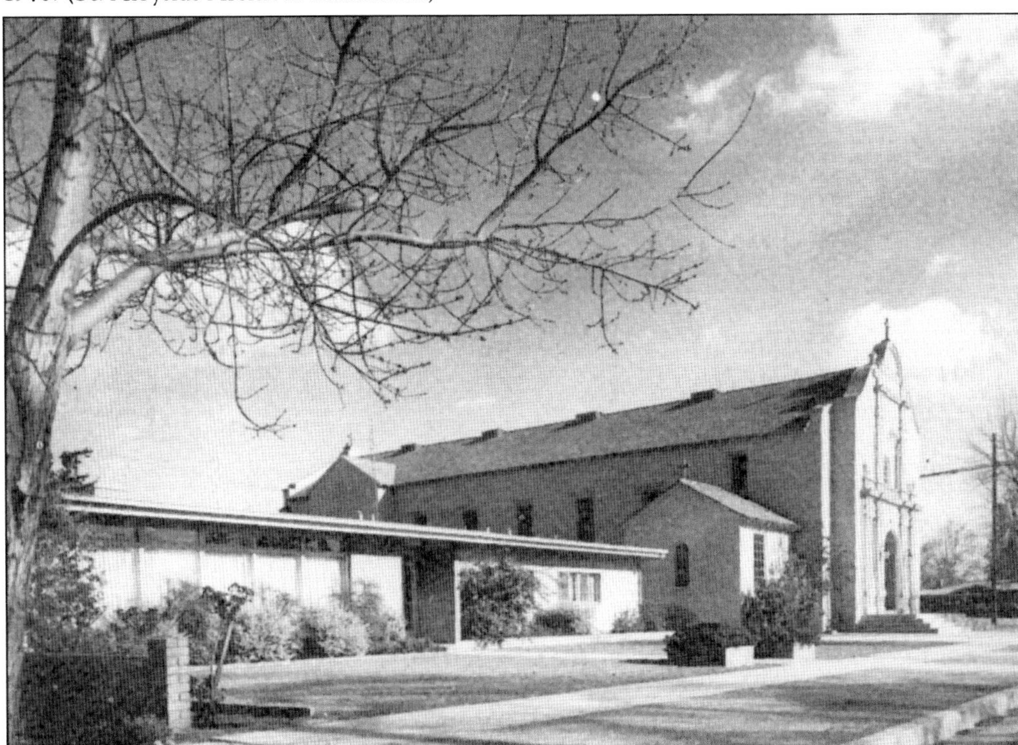

This view looking toward South F Street and Kern Avenue shows St. Aloysius Church and the convent. The entire property took up about a third of the eastern portion of the block. (St. Aloysius Archival Collection.)

St. Aloysius Church is pictured in the 1950s with the neighborhood encroaching on it. (St. Aloysius Archival Collection.)

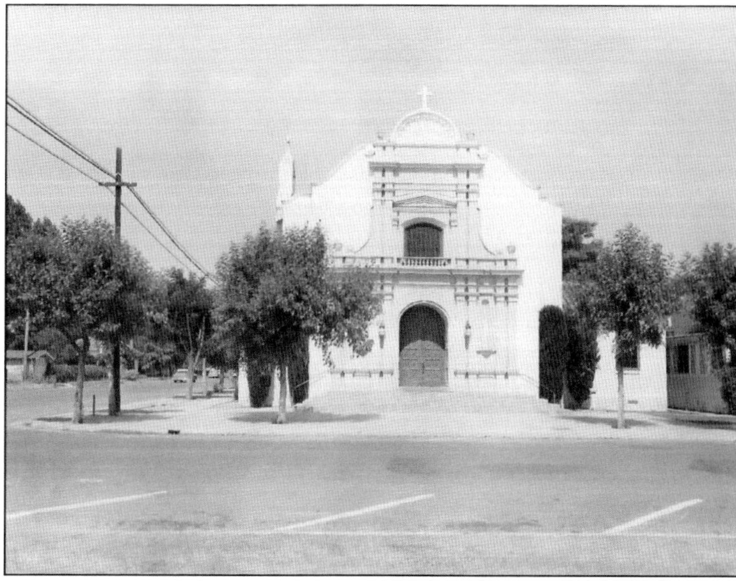

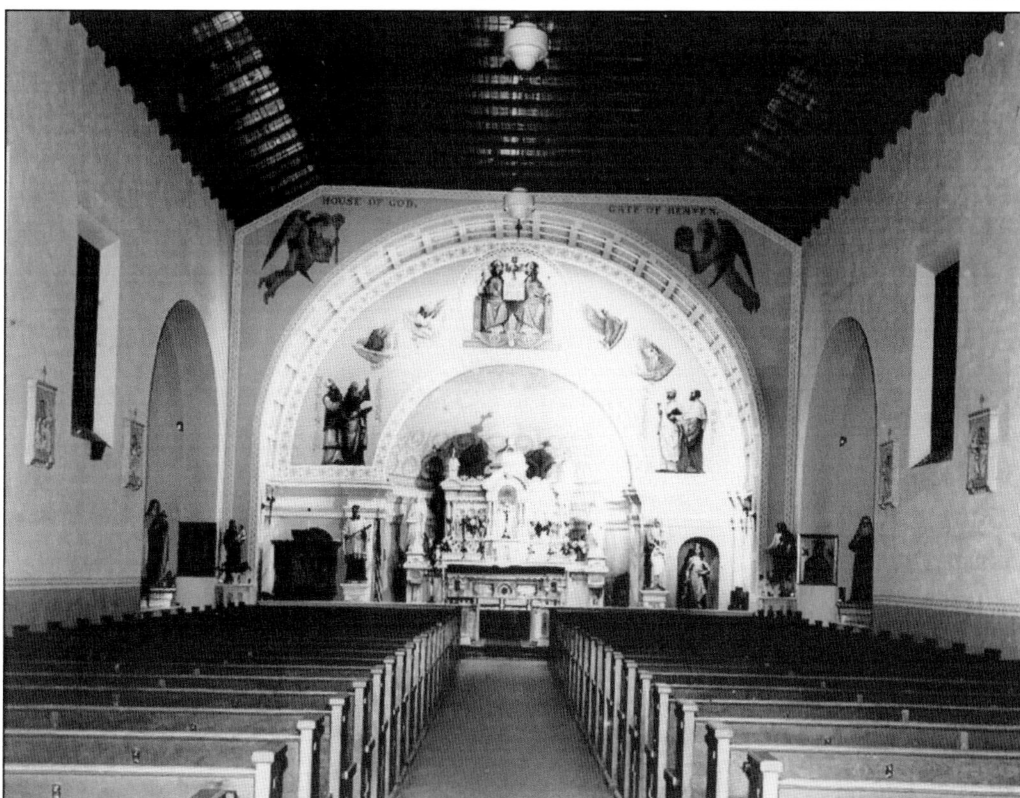

The interior of the original St. Aloysius Church contained wooden pews that led to the altar. The altar had a tabernacle in the niche, along with a variety of images of saints on either side. On both sides are images of the Virgin Mary. Painted on the walls above the altar are the words "House of God" and "Gate of Heaven." The building also had an open-timber ceiling. (St. Aloysius Archival Collection.)

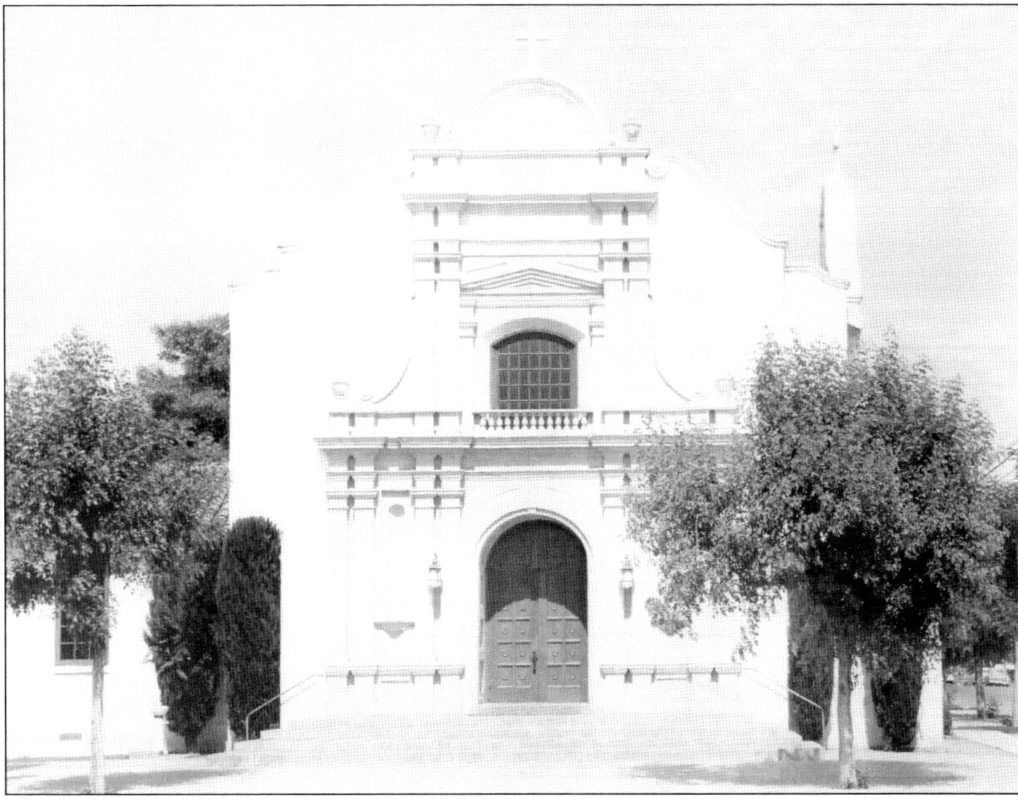

This is a 1950-era close-up of the corner of Kern Avenue and F Street in which Kern is clearly visible. The main entrance to St. Aloysius had Moorish features and a large, wooden door with four steps that led to it. At left are a sacristy and a baptismal font. (St. Aloysius Archival Collection.)

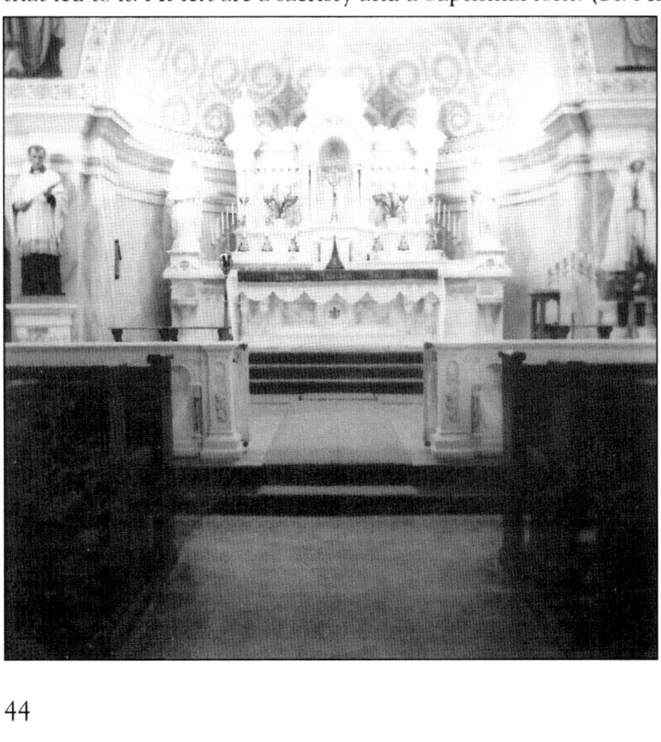

An interior view of the second St. Aloysius Church in the 1940s reveals a simpler look with far less wood than in the original chapel. Note that the tabernacle is deep inside a nice, which is characteristic of pre–Vatican II style. The new interior also shows taller pews, ornate posts, and fewer statues. At right is an image of the Virgin Mary; on the left, a statue of St. Aloysius holding a cross. The altar had the Latin word *sanctus*, which means "holy," written three times on the front of it. (St. Aloysius Archival Collection.)

The new St. Aloysius was opened in 1970 adjacent to the school grounds. Here, the parish hall is on the left. The school, which opened in 1948, had used the hall as a cafeteria as well. (St. Aloysius Archival Collection.)

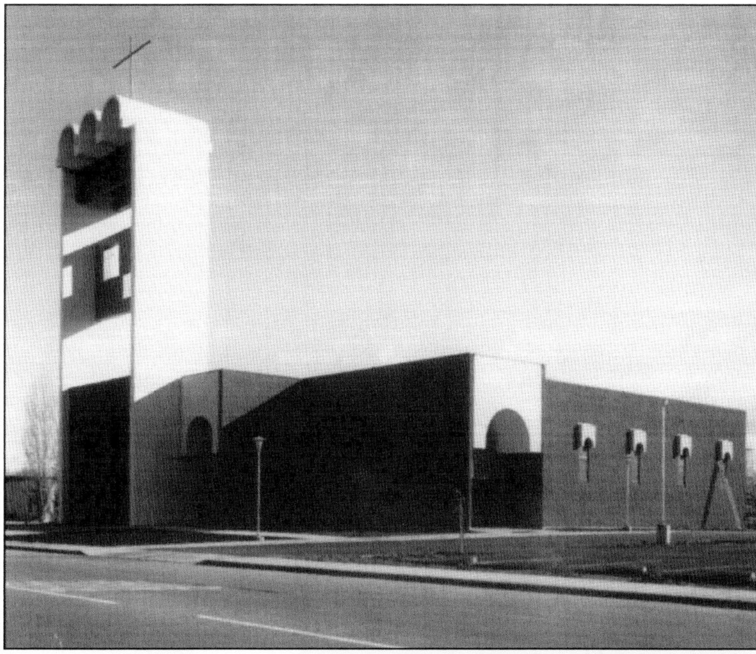

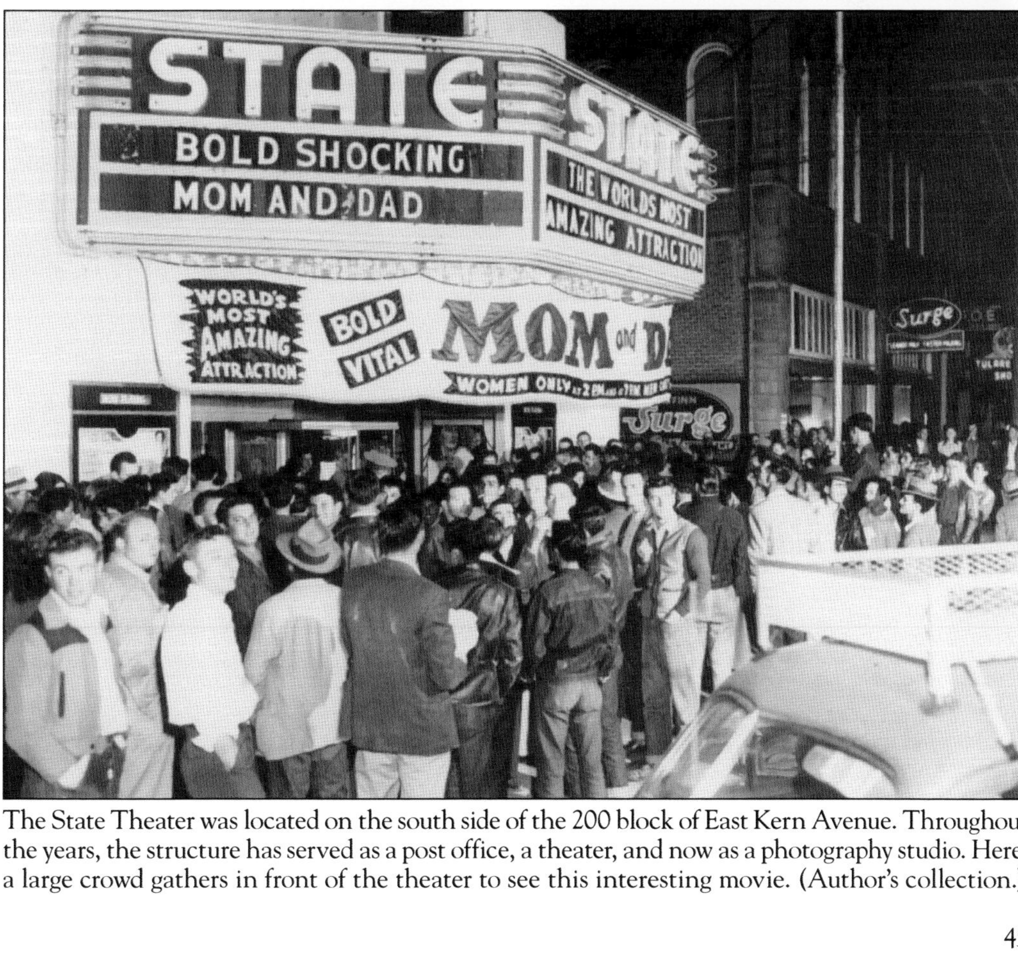

The State Theater was located on the south side of the 200 block of East Kern Avenue. Throughout the years, the structure has served as a post office, a theater, and now as a photography studio. Here, a large crowd gathers in front of the theater to see this interesting movie. (Author's collection.)

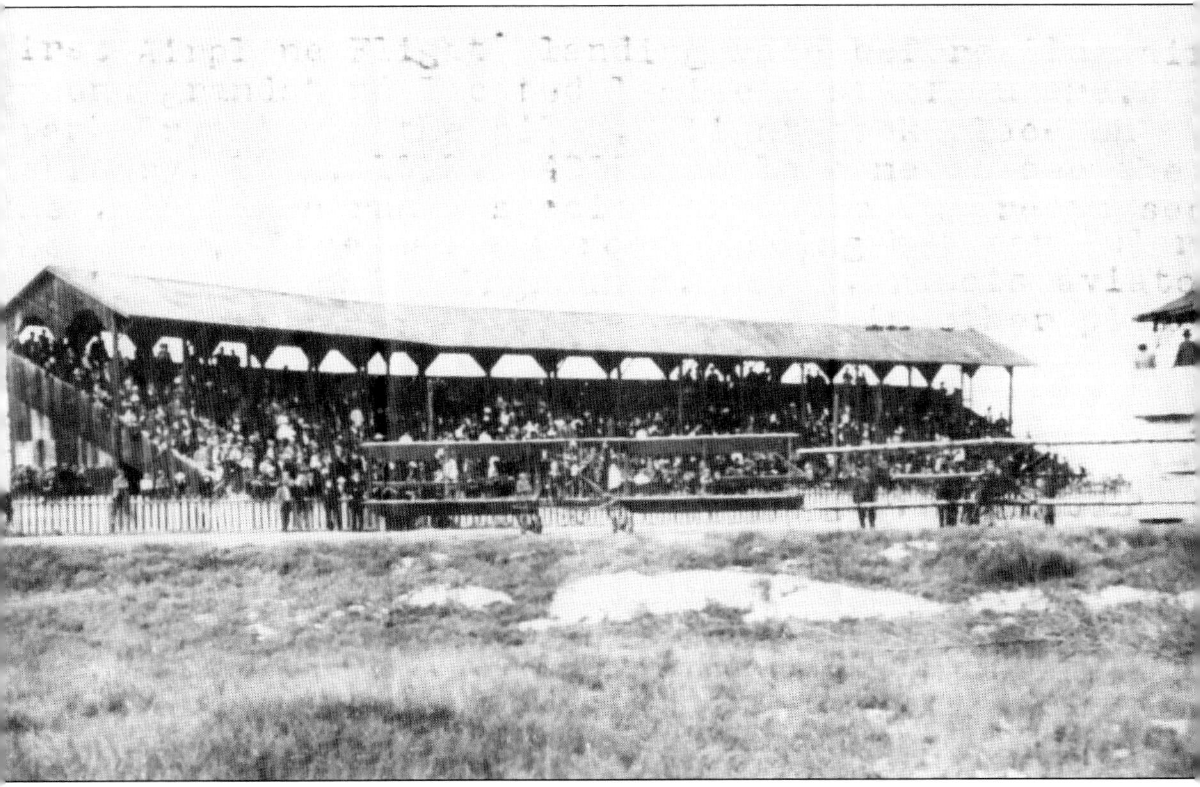

February 10, 1912, was an exciting day for 4,000 Tulare County residents who showed up for the area's first airplane landing. It was scheduled at the fairgrounds, a mile east of the city. Pilots Frank Bryant and Roy N. Frances were to land their planes there, while the Santa Fe Railway ran a special train between the site and downtown Tulare. Bryant was forced to make an emergency landing just a half mile from the site (today, the site of the Veterans Memorial Building), but Frances landed at the fairground. (Tulare County Library.)

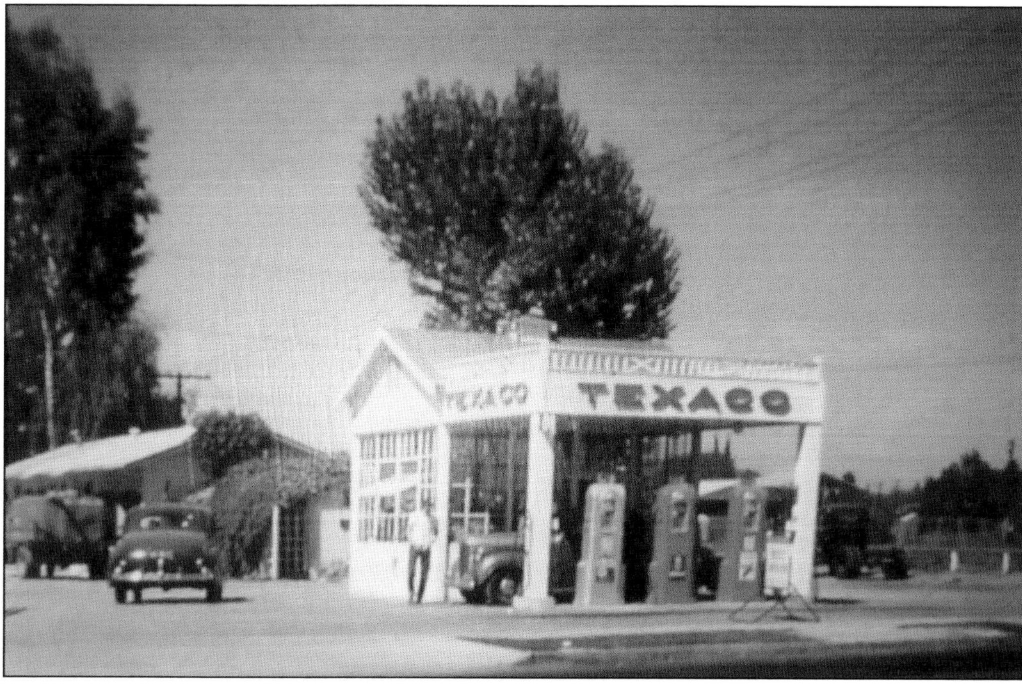

In the 1940s, the Texaco station near the Motor Lodge Inn on K Street was bustling. Today, the abandoned building is a haven for criminal activity. The pumps are gone, and all the signs have been removed. (Author's collection.)

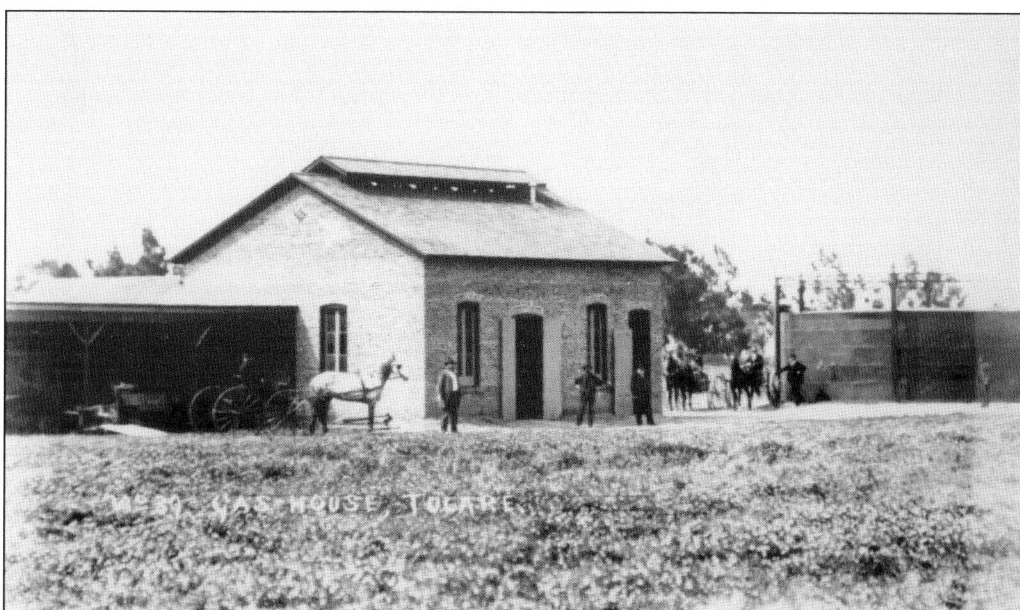

This gashouse, photographed in 1888, provided Tulare with gas before electricity became commonplace. Ezra Lathrop incorporated the company in January 1884 and became its president the following year. (Tulare County Library.)

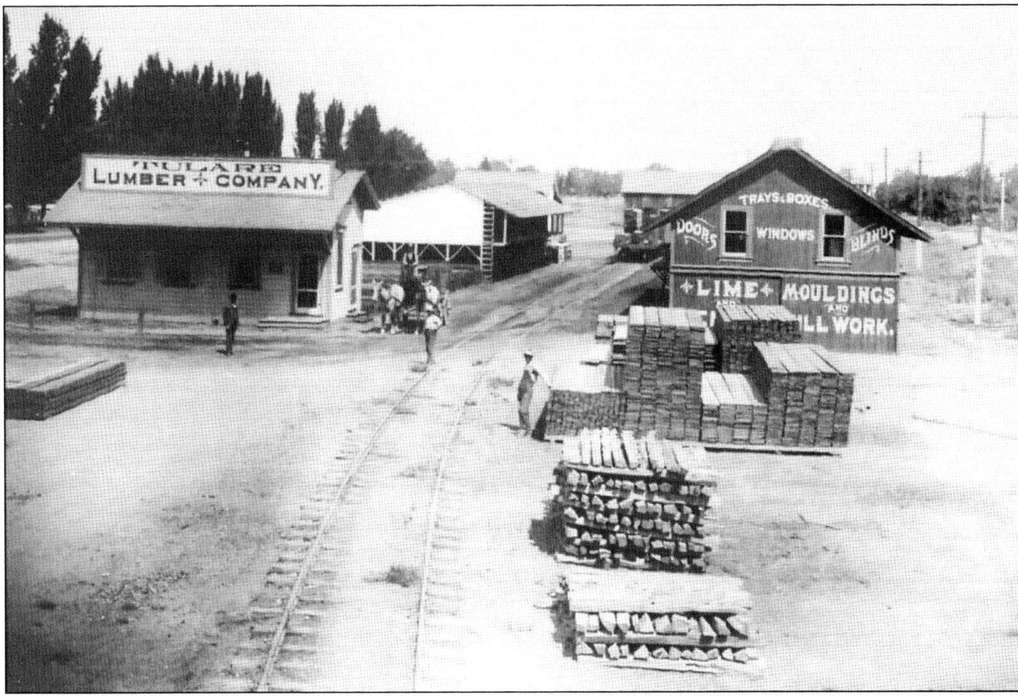

The original Tulare Lumber Company was in business for many years before being succeeded by the E.M. Cox Lumber Company in 1910. (Tulare County Library.)

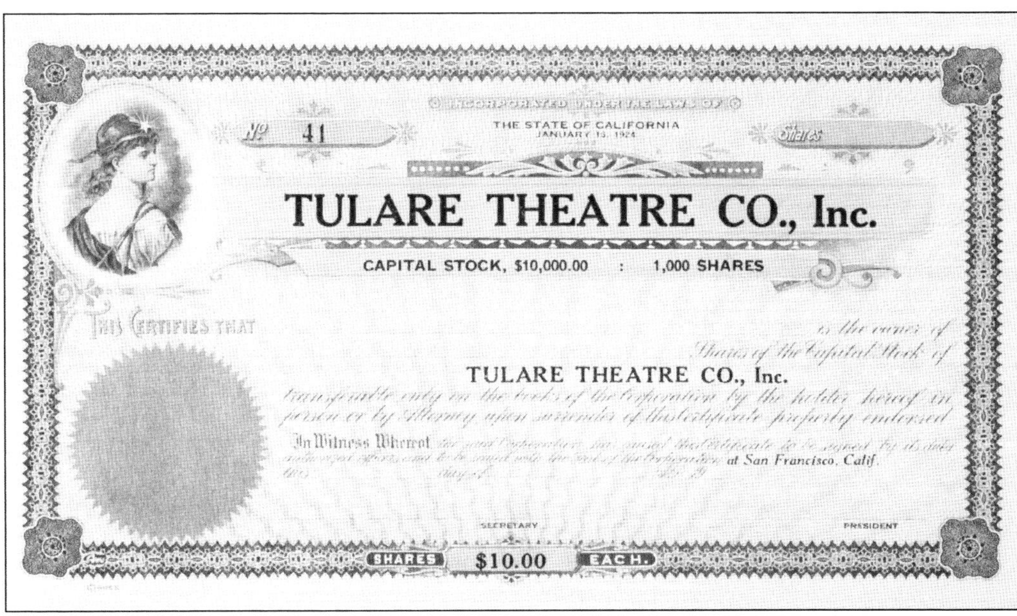

The 1,400-seat Tulare Theatre opened at 229 East Tulare Avenue at L Street on March 18, 1927, to large crowds of moviegoers. It remained open until 1975. The building was demolished in 1980 to make way for a Wells Fargo Bank. This $10 stock certificate is one of 1,000 issued to raise funds for the theater. Owners had hoped to raise $10,000 to build the theater. (Author's collection.)

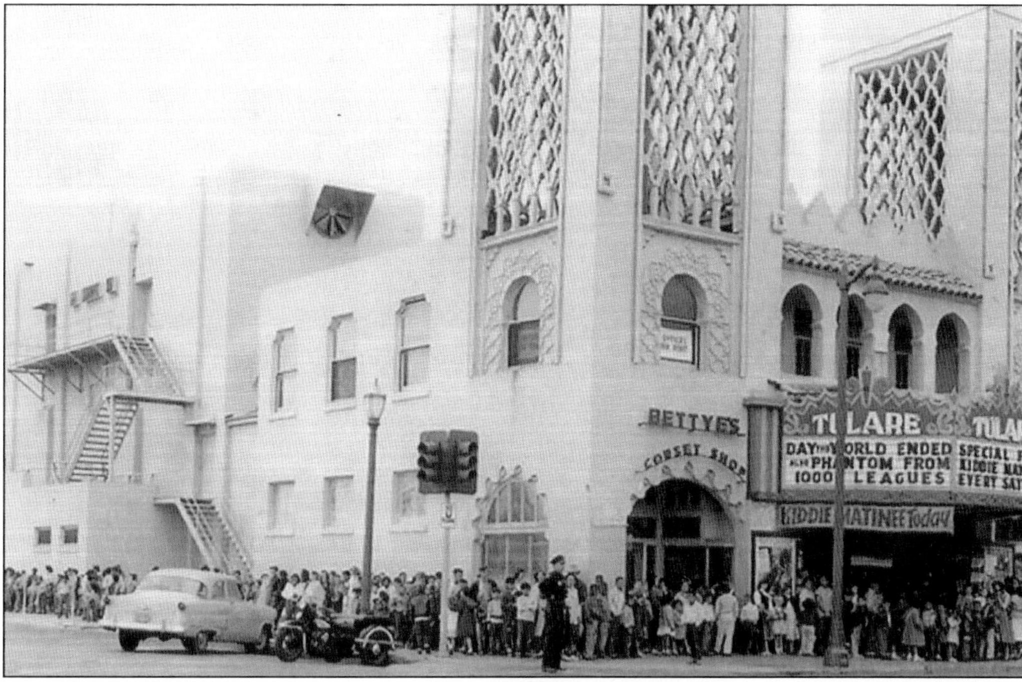

The Tulare Theatre featured motifs based on the Ishtar Gate of Babylon. Designer Timothy Pflueger included zigzag patterns in the twin-towered facade, trimmed in neon accents. He also brought Streamline Moderne, a late kind of Art Deco, to the interior via sweeping curves in steel banister railings and Mayan-style touches in the stepped mirrors. The final cost of the construction was $250,000. This view from the north side of Tulare Avenue shows the theater and its towers in 1955. (Author's collection.)

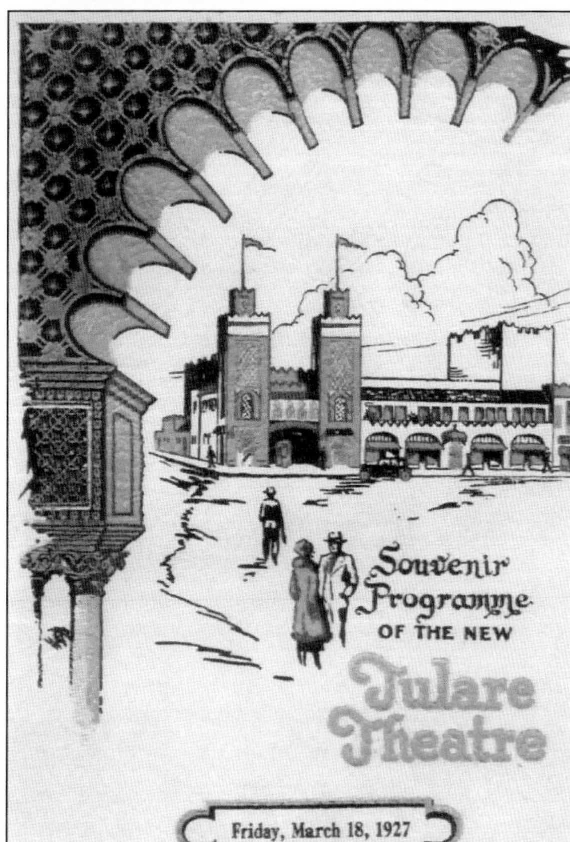

The program for the opening night at the Tulare Theatre featured a vaudeville show and a silent film. The next day, *Hills of Kentucky*, featuring Rin Tin Tin, a hugely popular trained German shepherd, was shown. The theater offered vaudeville shows every Sunday—a matinee and an evening performance. On April 15, the theater had its first live production, *Castles in the Air*, by Edward D. Smith. Lower-floor seats were $2.75, and last-row balcony seats were $1.10. (Author's collection.)

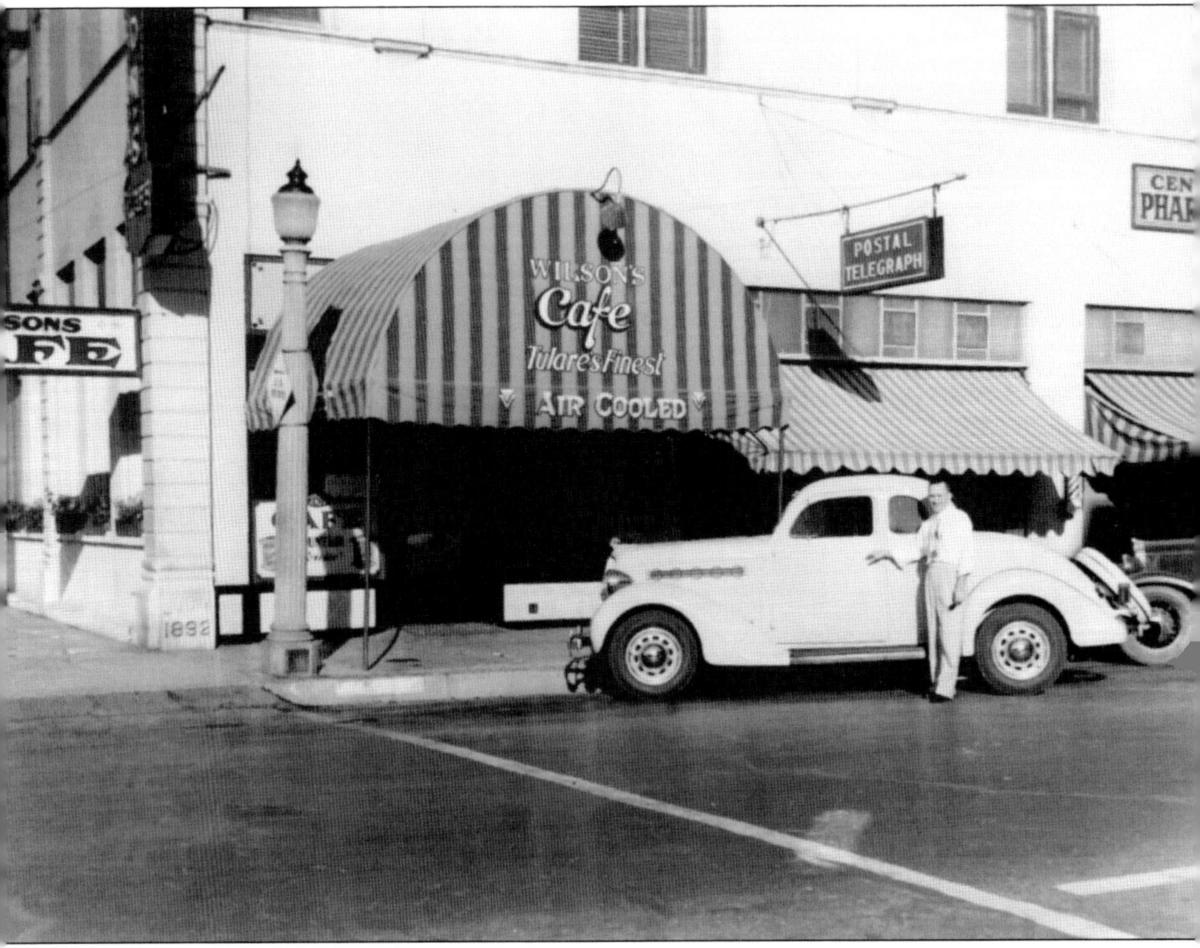

Wilson's Café claimed to offer Tulare's finest food in air-cooled comfort in this 1930s photograph. (Tulare County Library.)

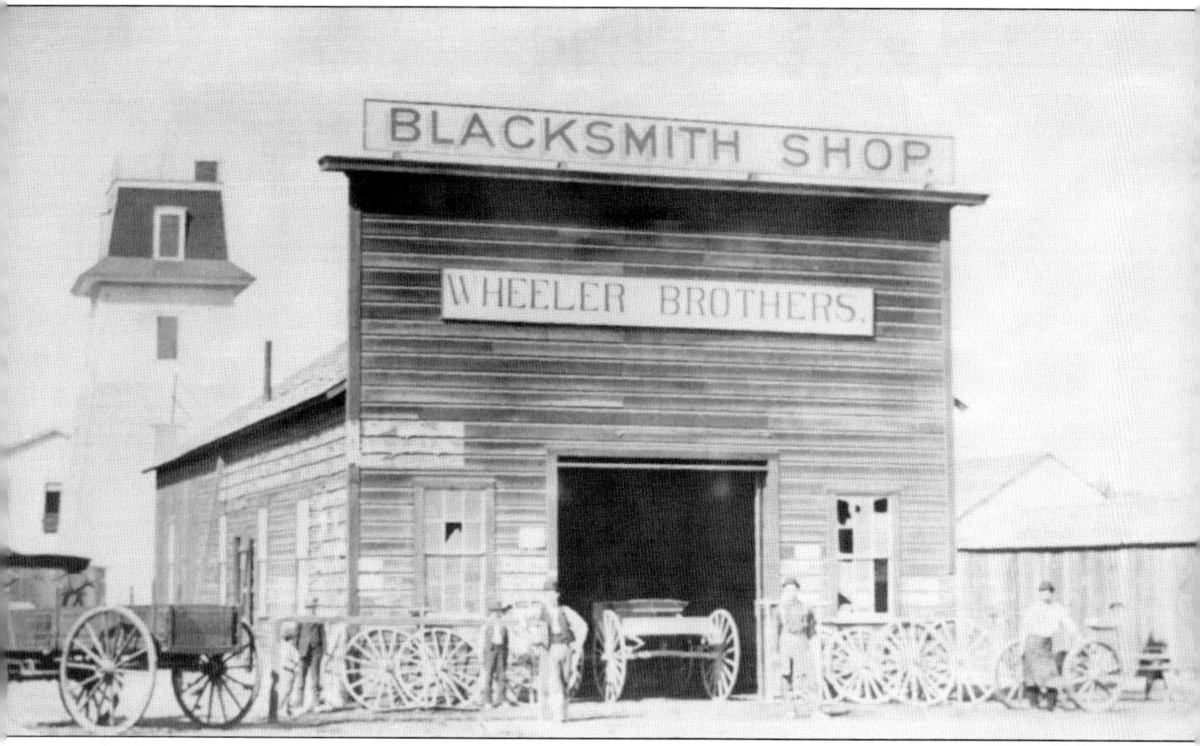

In the late 1800s, the Wheeler Brothers blacksmith shop was located on the north side of the 100 block of East Tulare Avenue and D Street. The water tower for D.W. Madden's Palace Hotel is on the left. Fred and Alexander Wheeler came to Tulare in 1882 from England, founded their business, and 18 months later, went their separate ways. Later, Alexander "Alec" opened a furniture store in a rented building at the southeast corner of Tulare Avenue and K Street, next door to the Thomas Calvert Carruthers funeral home. The Wheeler furniture store eventually became the site of a Woolworth five-and-dime store. Fred in the meantime partnered with George W. Zartman and continued in the carriage and blacksmith business. (Tulare County Library.)

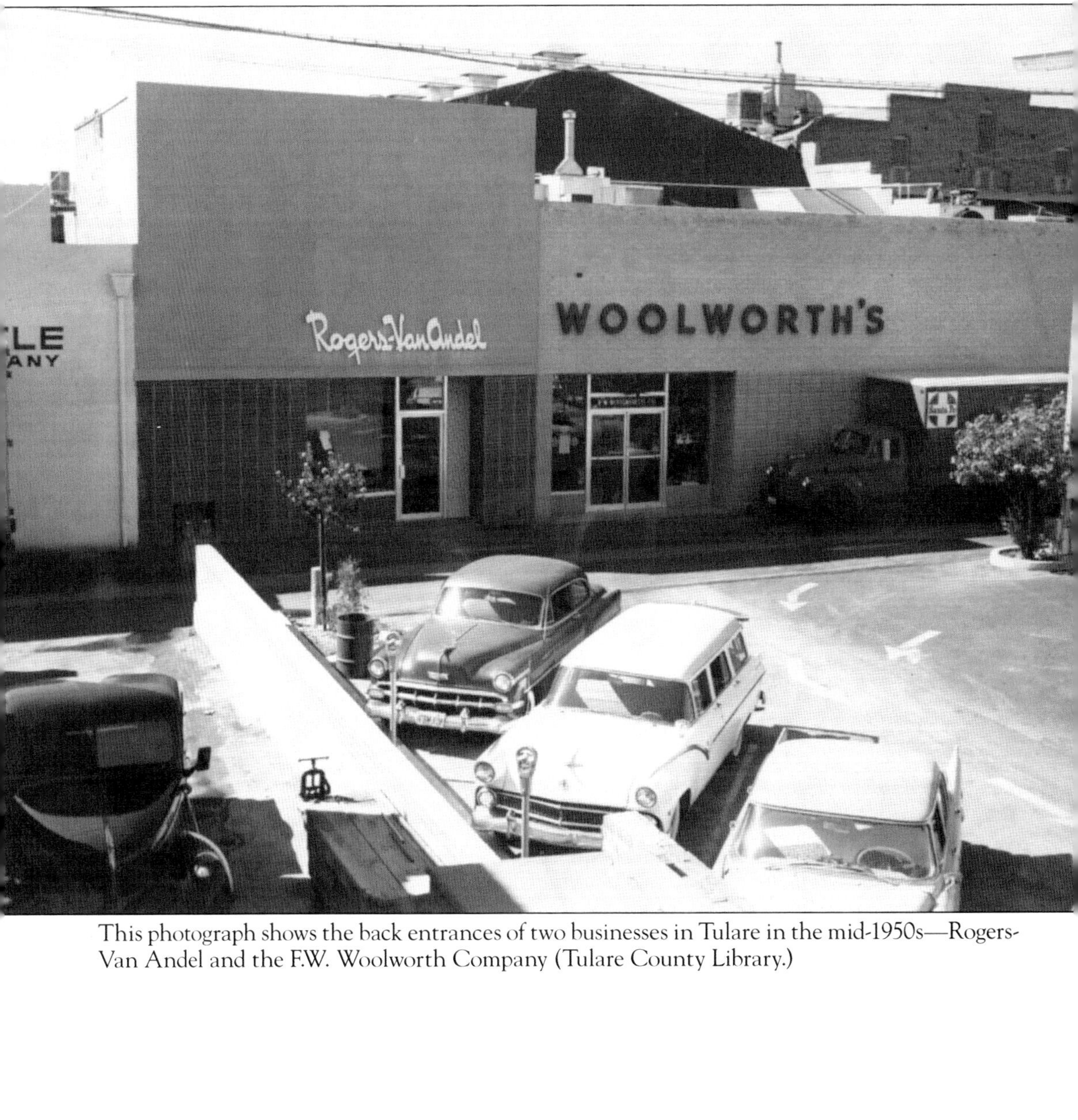

This photograph shows the back entrances of two businesses in Tulare in the mid-1950s—Rogers-Van Andel and the F.W. Woolworth Company (Tulare County Library.)

Three

Railroad

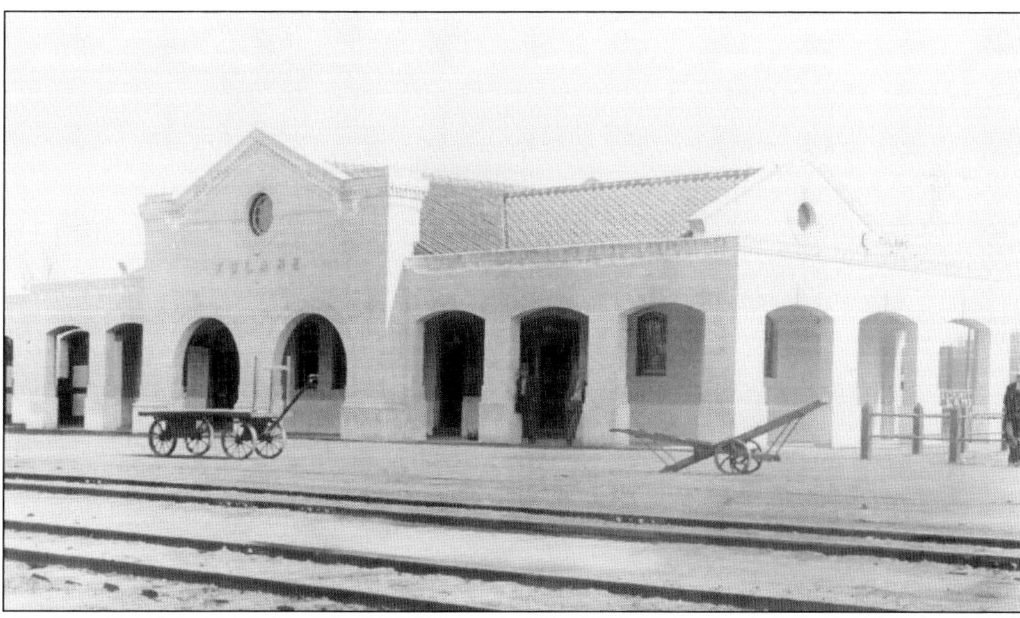

The Southern Pacific Railroad built this Mission-style depot to accommodate the heavy passenger traffic. The depot was built across from where the original dual-purpose passenger and freight station had been. The hope was that Tulare could be really considered a railroad town with a separate passenger depot and freight station. The depot was built in 1914 and destroyed by arson in 1983. The depot had a red tile roof and beautiful arches in the entranceways. (Author's collection.)

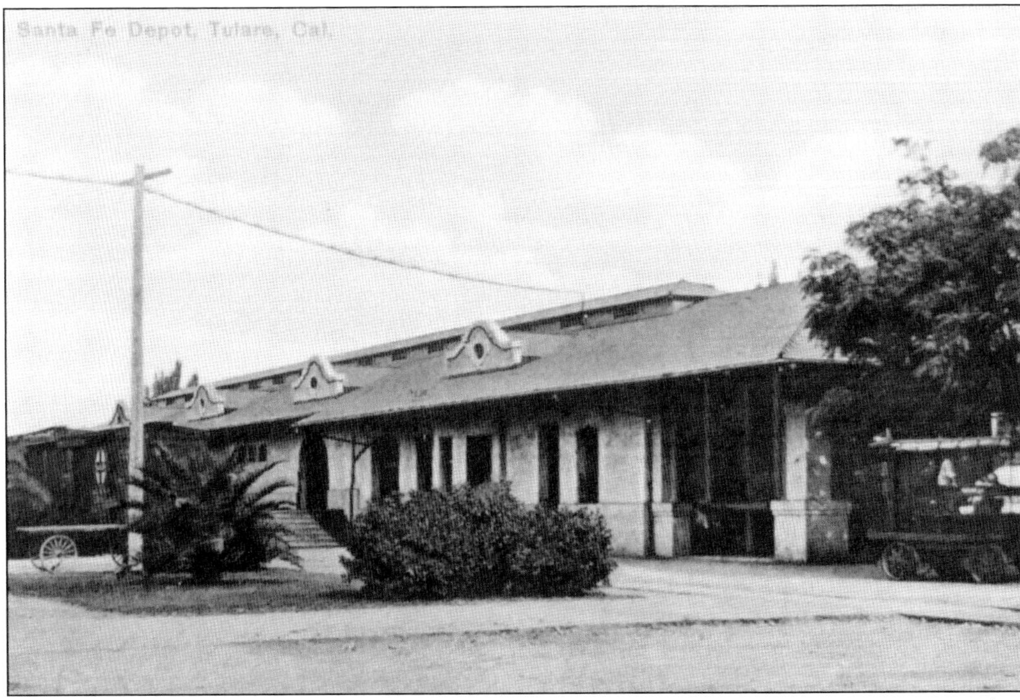

The Santa Fe Railway was a latecomer to Tulare, arriving in 1900 and constructing a line connecting through Tulare to Visalia then on to Corcoran. The basic rail line ran along San Joaquin and Cross Avenues. The depot was erected in 1895 and razed by the railroad in 1973. (Author's collection.)

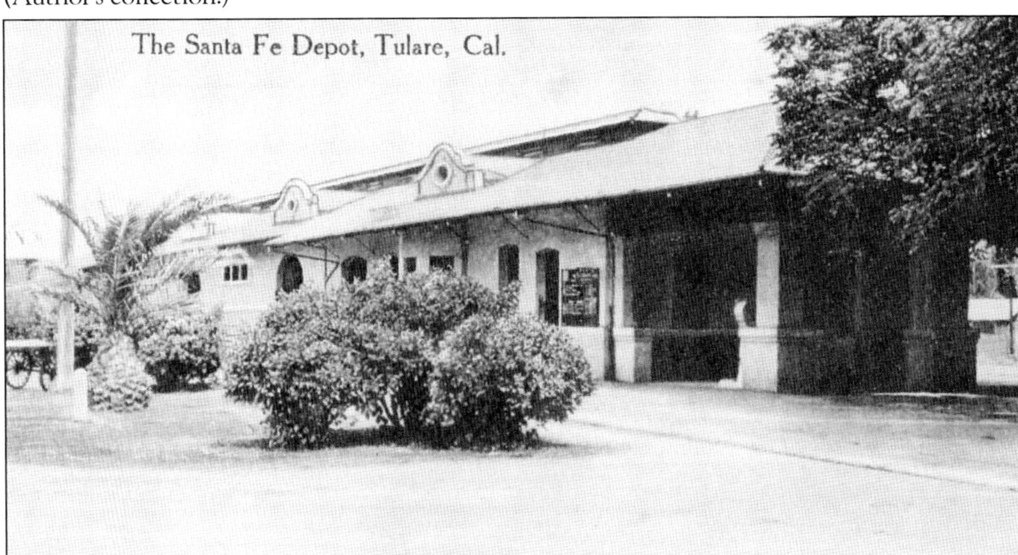

The Santa Fe Depot was erected some time in early 1895, thus making Tulare a three-railroad town. Since the older railroad had the right of way, the Santa Fe erected a wooden tower near Cross Street to control train traffic. This tower had to be staffed at all times so the signals could be raised to avoid a Santa Fe train colliding with a Southern Pacific train. (Author's collection.)

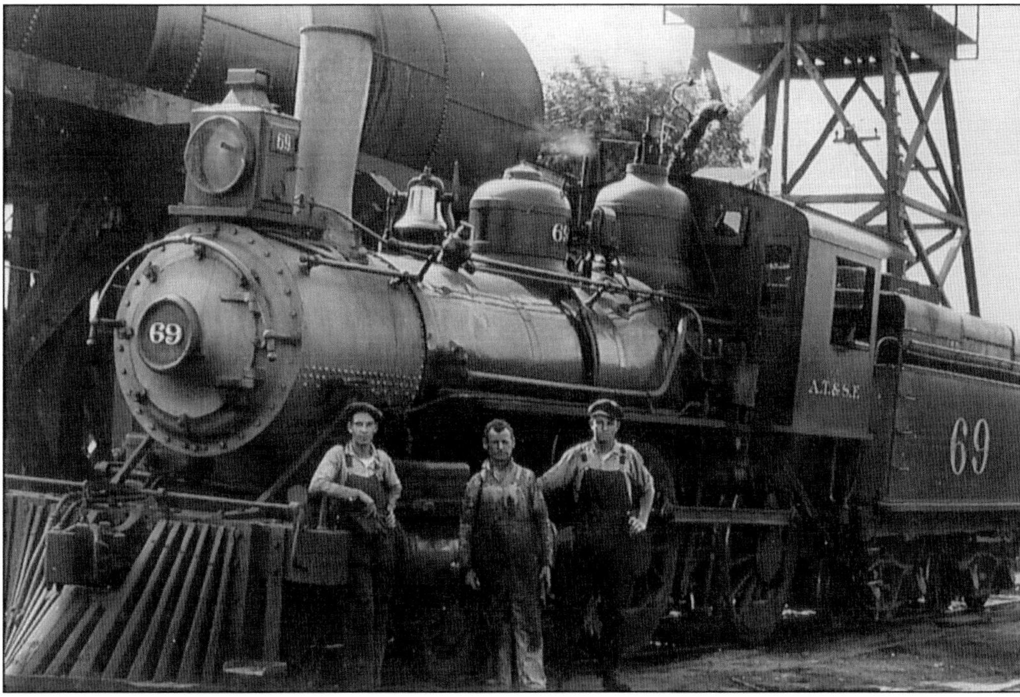

Here is a Visalia and Tulare train at the Tulare Depot in 1890 with Arch Turner (center), who was the fireman, and later engineer, of the Atchison, Topeka & Santa Fe Railway engine. (Tulare County Library.)

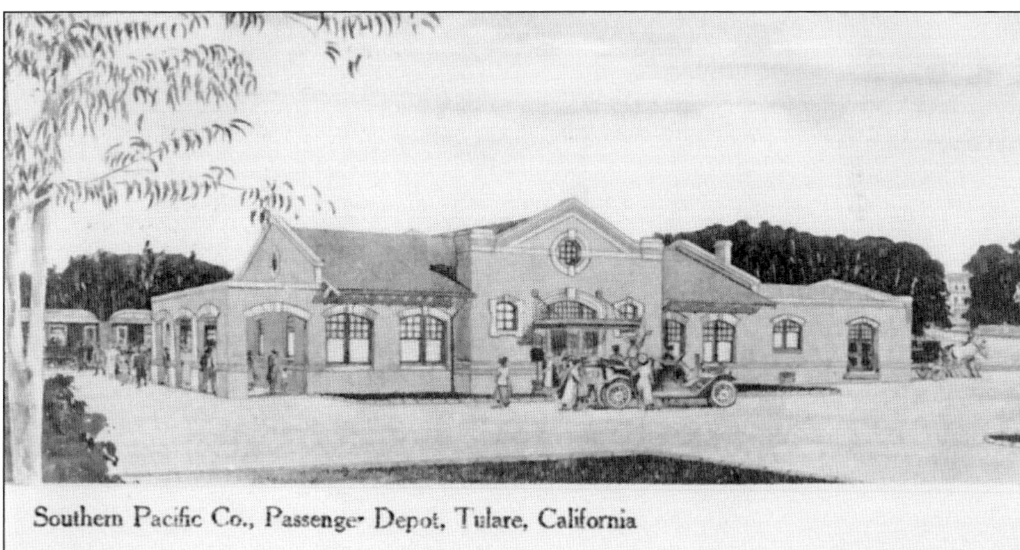

The oldest railroad facility in Tulare was the Southern Pacific Depot and freight station. Then the Southern Pacific Railroad but this passenger station in 1914 to alleviate the demand for passenger service. The depot was a victim of arson in 1983. The remaining old wooden one was left exclusively for freight traffic. Today, the depot has been replaced by Jack's Git-N-Go market. A remnant of the depot remains just behind the A&W Restaurant and is still used as a signal yard. (Author's collection.)

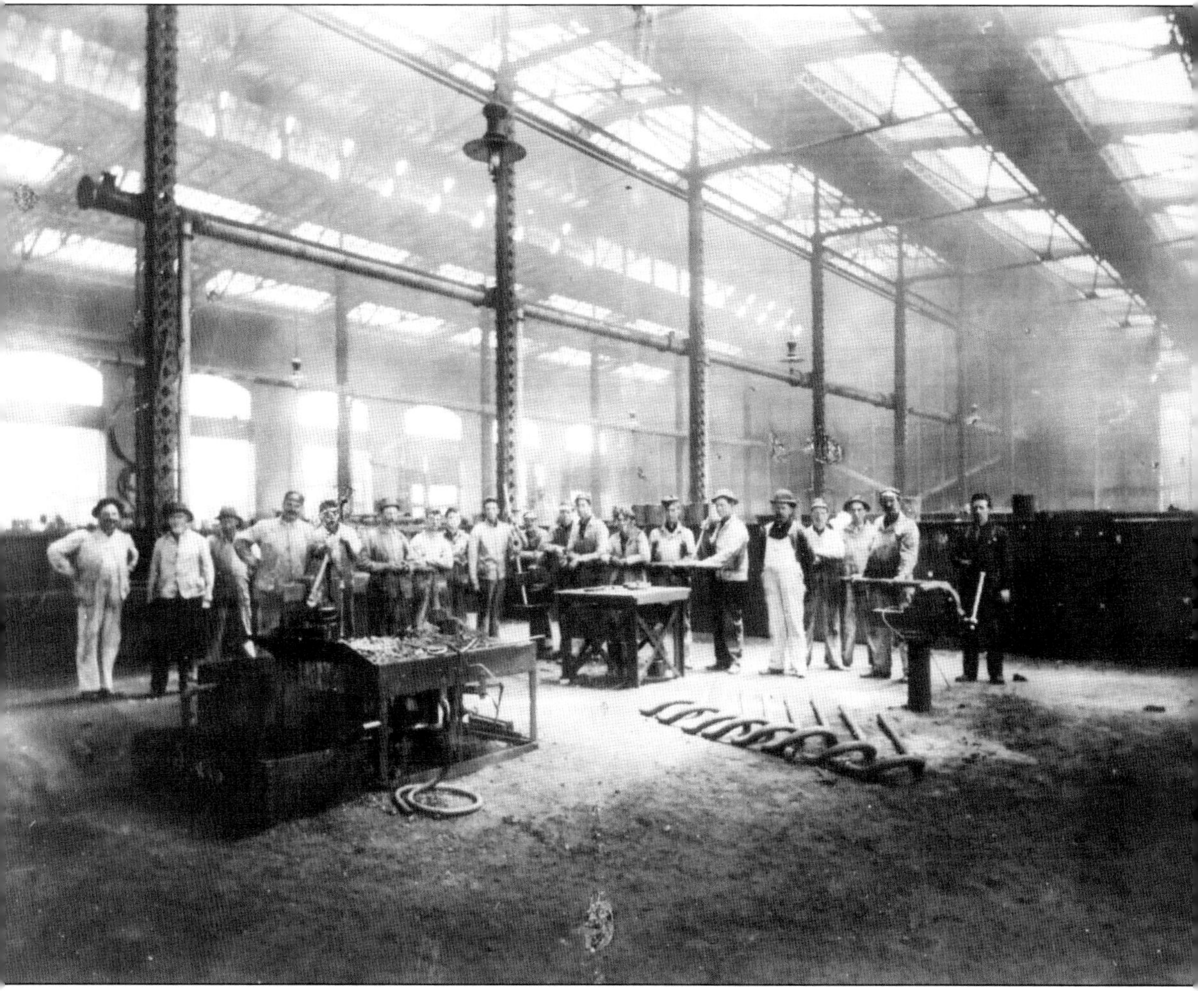

Before 1891, the Southern Pacific Railroad had a huge presence in Tulare that included workshops, building, a roundhouse, and as many as 20 engines. The Southern Pacific Railroad could be called the father of Tulare since it founded the town as the end of the San Joaquin Valley Division in 1872. In 1875, the engine house was expanded to accommodate 13 stalls. In 1876, it built extensive machine workshops and in 1878 put in one of the largest turntables at the time. (Author's collection.)

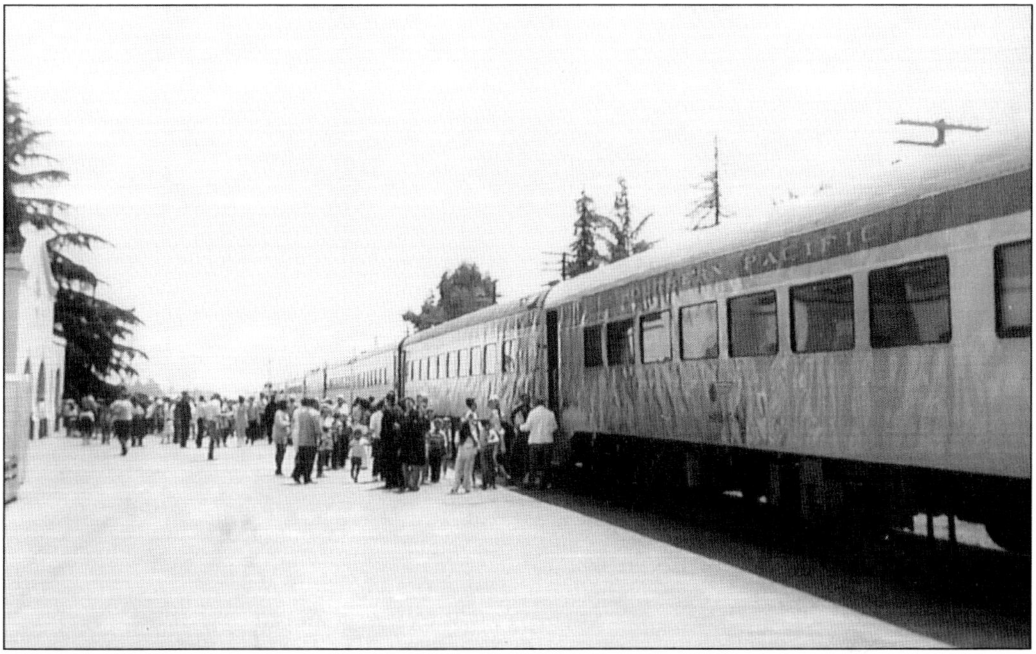

A Southern Pacific Railroad passenger is ready to board a train at the depot in the 1950s. At left is the Tulare Southern Pacific Depot that was built in 1914 and destroyed by fire in 1983. To the north of the depot is a large evergreen tree that is no longer there. Today, a gas station is located where the depot had been. (Tulare County Library.)

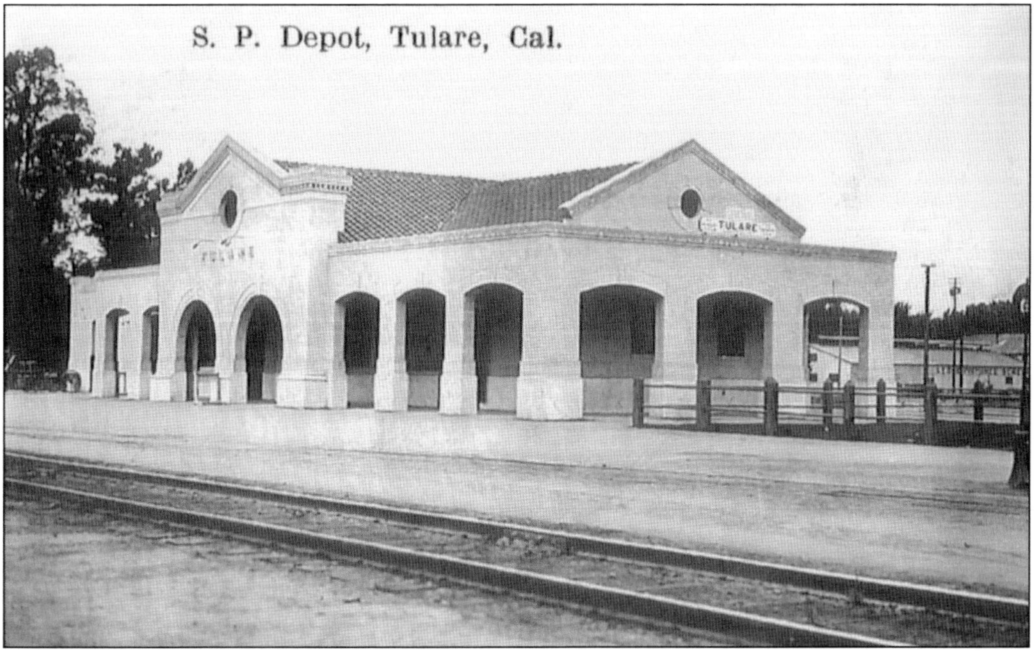

The Southern Pacific in 1914 built this ornate depot for its passengers. The depot had four signs with the name Tulare in large letters, including those on the side facing the tracks and on the west side facing J Street. To the left of this picture is a group of large trees near the depot, and to the right are buildings on J Street. (Tulare County Library.)

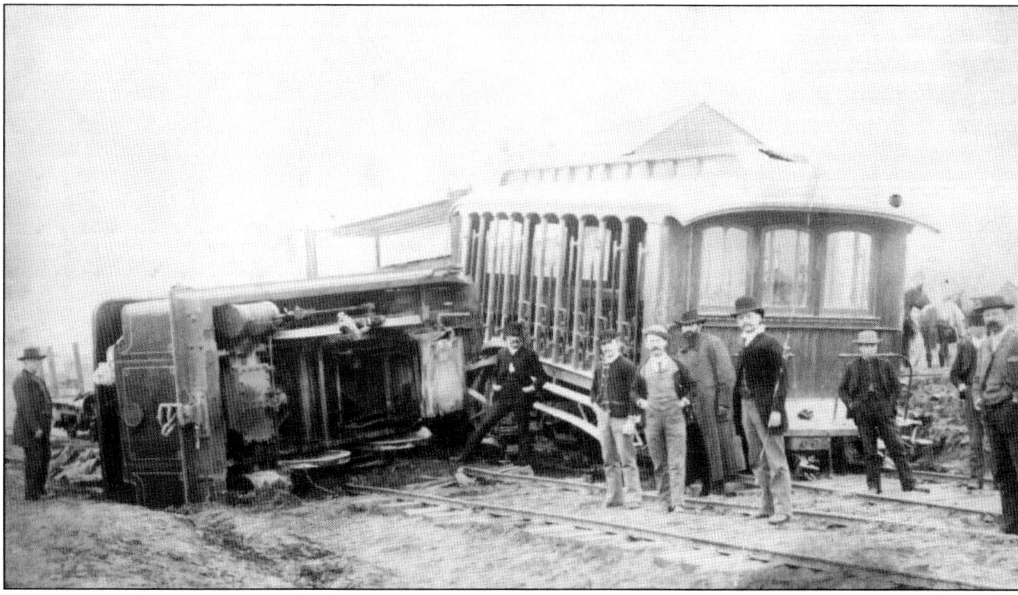

A wreck occurred on May 5, 1900, on the Visalia–Tulare line at Watson and Tulare Avenues. The accident took place when the train ran into a cow that had strayed onto the tracks. This image shows the aftermath of the accident, where one of the cars is overturned and the others are piled up. As a result of this collision, 34 were injured and the railroad soon ceased operations. (Tulare County Library.)

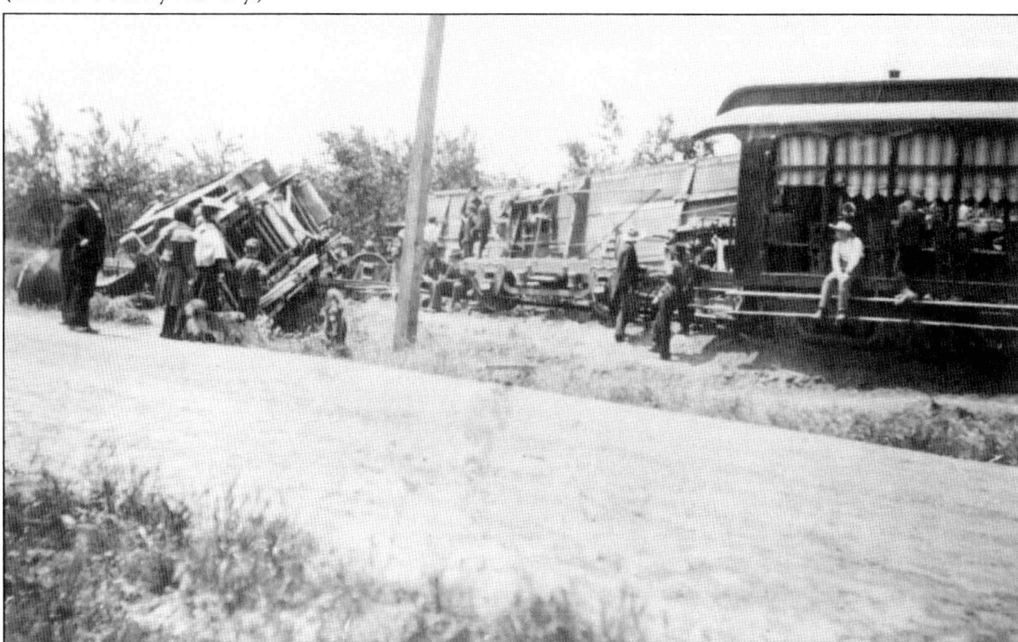

The Visalia and Tulare Railroad was considered by many in Tulare the easiest and most convenient route to Visalia. That all changed on May 5, 1900, when the small engine ran into a cow, thus destroying the engine and the railroad line. Soon after this, the rails and rolling stock were sold. The line had operated for about 10 years before its demise. The site of the accident is referred to as Caldwell's Corner and is about three miles south of Visalia. (Tulare County Library.)

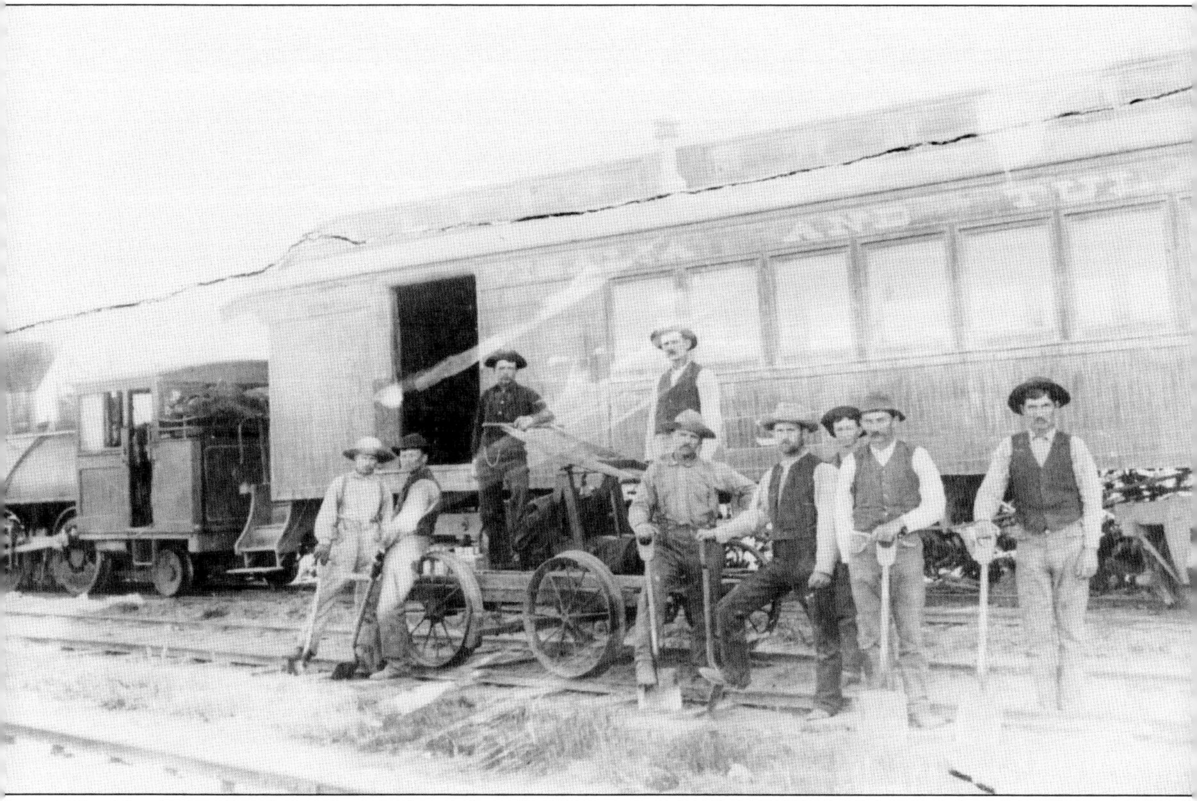

The Visalia and Tulare Railroad was founded by a group of businessmen who sought a quicker route to the county seat. The small engine made three trips in each direction daily. Passengers boarded the train at Tulare Avenue and J Street. The small engine and the rolling stock are pictured here with a group of men standing in front the car. Note the name Visalia and Tulare near the top of the railcar. (Tulare County Library.)

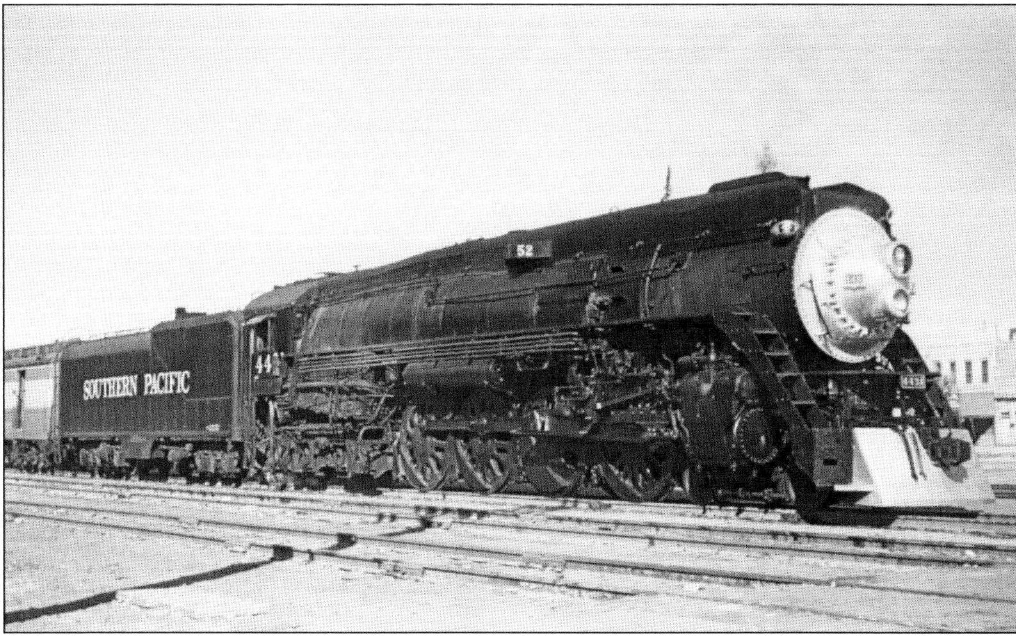

The Southern Pacific's General Service, 4-8-4 steam locomotive No. 4431 heads south toward Los Angeles at the depot on October 23, 1955. To the right of the engine, the old headquarters for the Tulare Fire Department is visible on J Street. (Author's collection.)

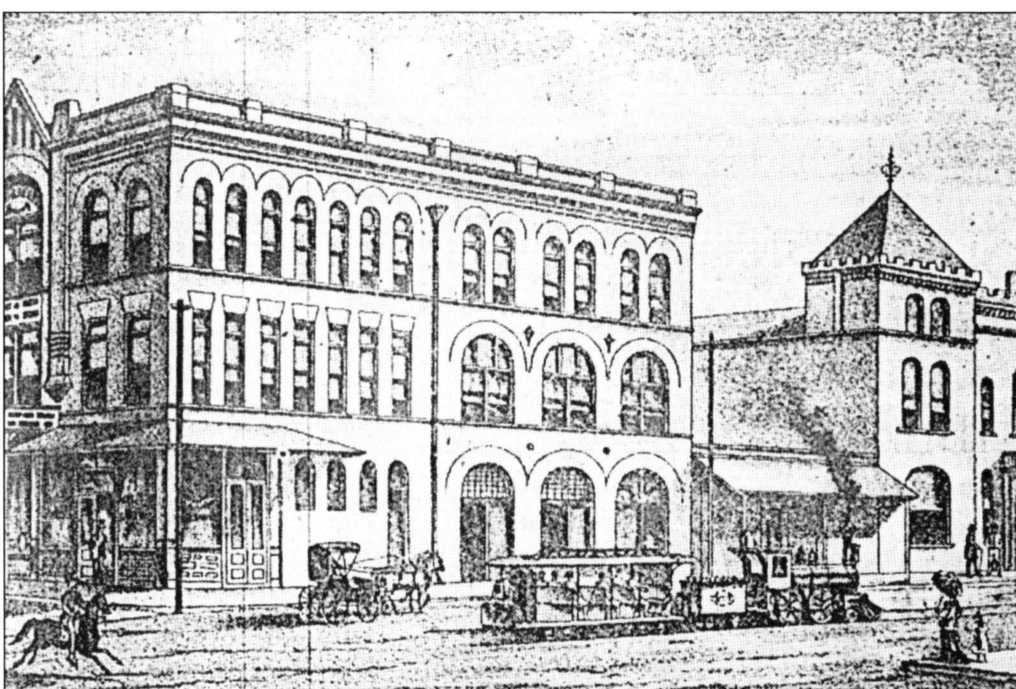

This illustration from a local newspaper shows the small engine that was used on the Visalia and Tulare Railroad in Visalia passing the J. Harrell Bank in Visalia in the 1890s. (Author's collection.)

Four

SCHOOLS

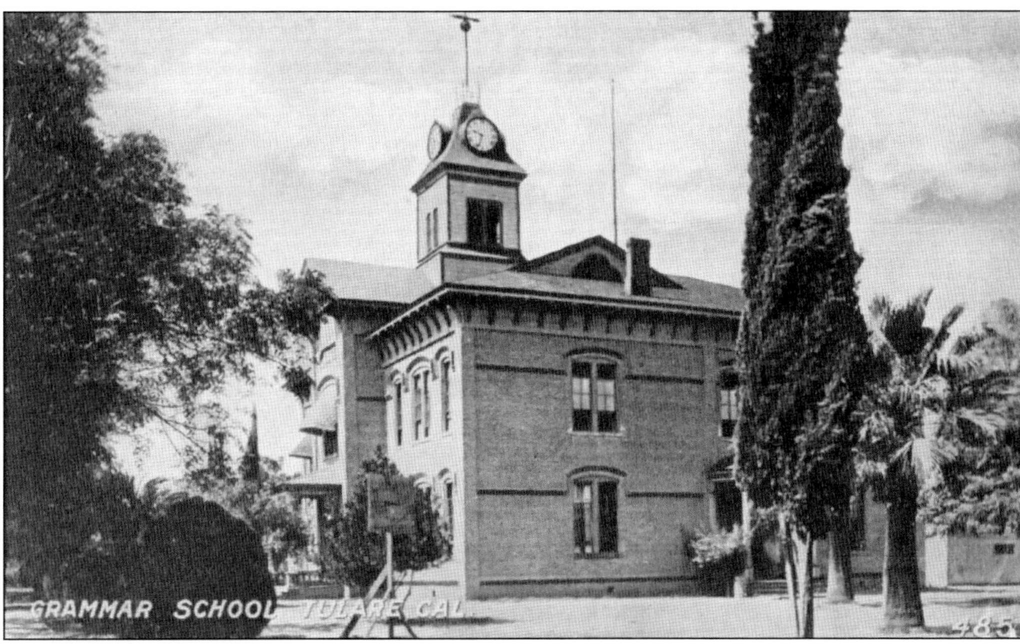

In 1873, community leaders purchased a school site consisting of an entire block on West Tulare Avenue between E and F Streets. They constructed a simple two-room frame building at the cost of $1,700 on the southeast portion of the lot. The first two Tulare teachers were Victoria Wright, daughter of Isaac Wright, and Thalia Houston. (Author's collection.)

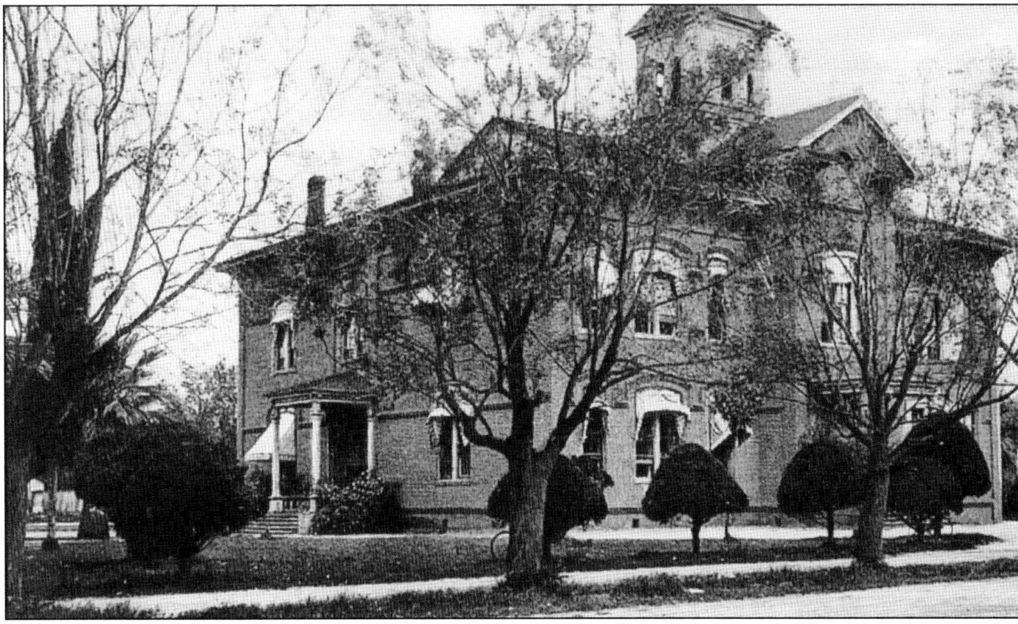

Central School as it was known in the early years was built to accommodate the growing population of the small town. In 1884, voters passed a 10-year, $20,000 bond to build the city's first comprehensive school. It was two stories tall and constructed of red brick with a beautiful belfry and a large, four-faced clock. The clock become a local landmark and could be heard quite a distance away when it struck the hours. A high school was added in 1893. (Author's collection.)

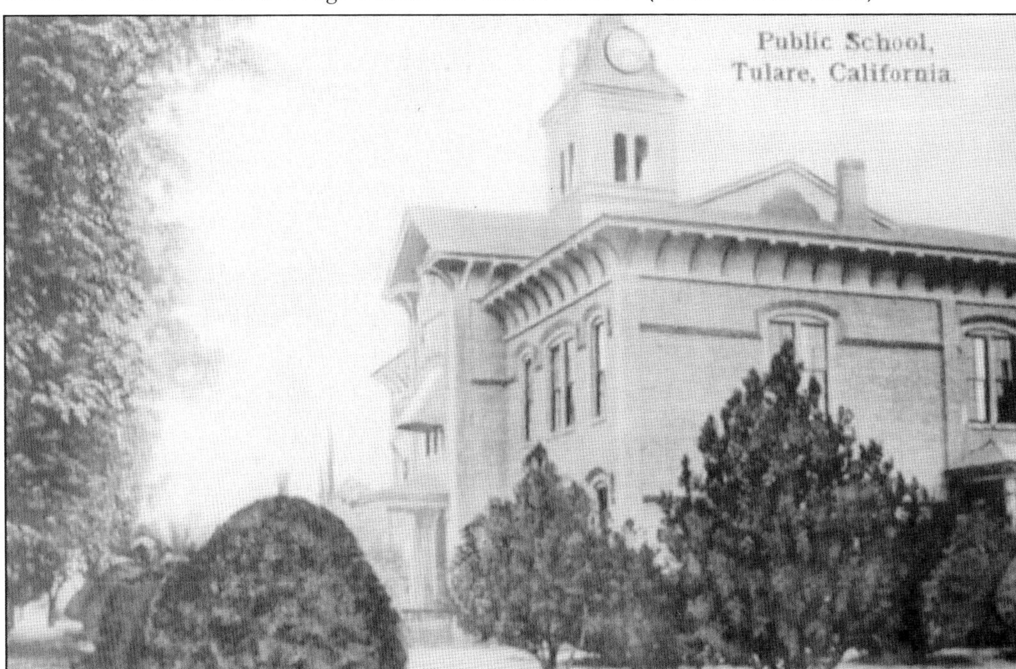

This view looks eastward from the grammar school, showing a well-kept front lawn with flower beds. The rear of the building was used as a playground. Later, the school district asked the city to shut down King Street so it could enlarge the playground area. (Author's collection.)

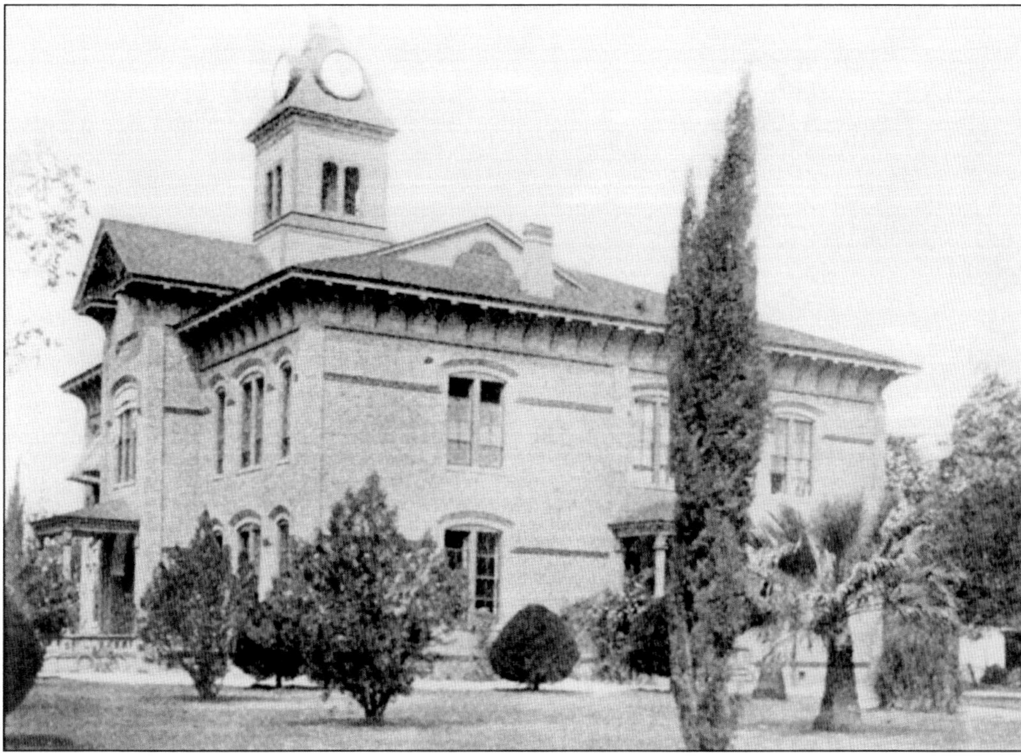

Tulare's first high school was housed in the second floor of the grammar school from 1890 until 1908, when the new building on Tulare Avenue and South O Street was completed. Classes were initially small; in 1895, no one graduated, and in 1896, two students graduated. One, Gracie Linder, delivered the valedictorian speech. Soon, the population began to grow and the second floor was overwhelmed, necessitating the construction of an entirely new high school nearby. (Author's collection.)

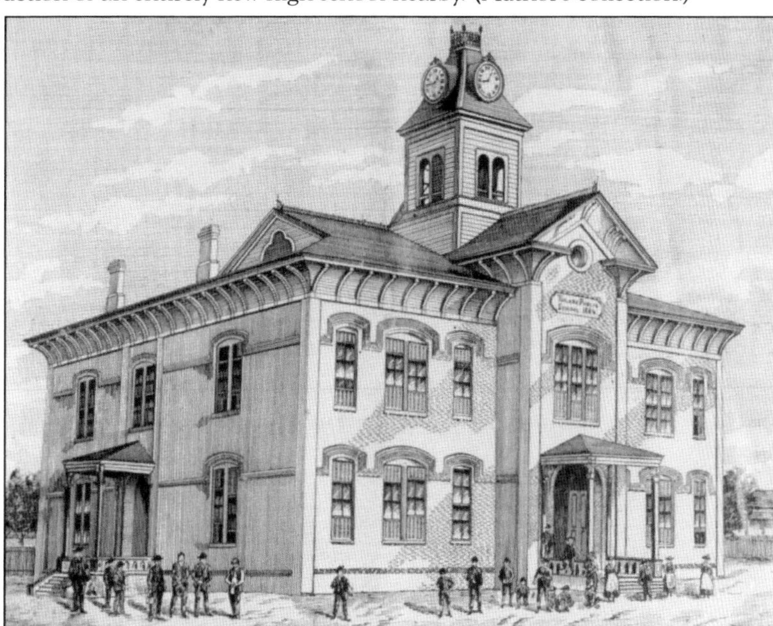

This drawing shows the Tulare Central Grammar School before class in the late 1890s. It seems odd that in the drawing, the majority of the students out front are mostly boys, and there is no landscaping. One of the best features of this school was the beautiful manicured lawns and flower beds. (Tulare County Library.)

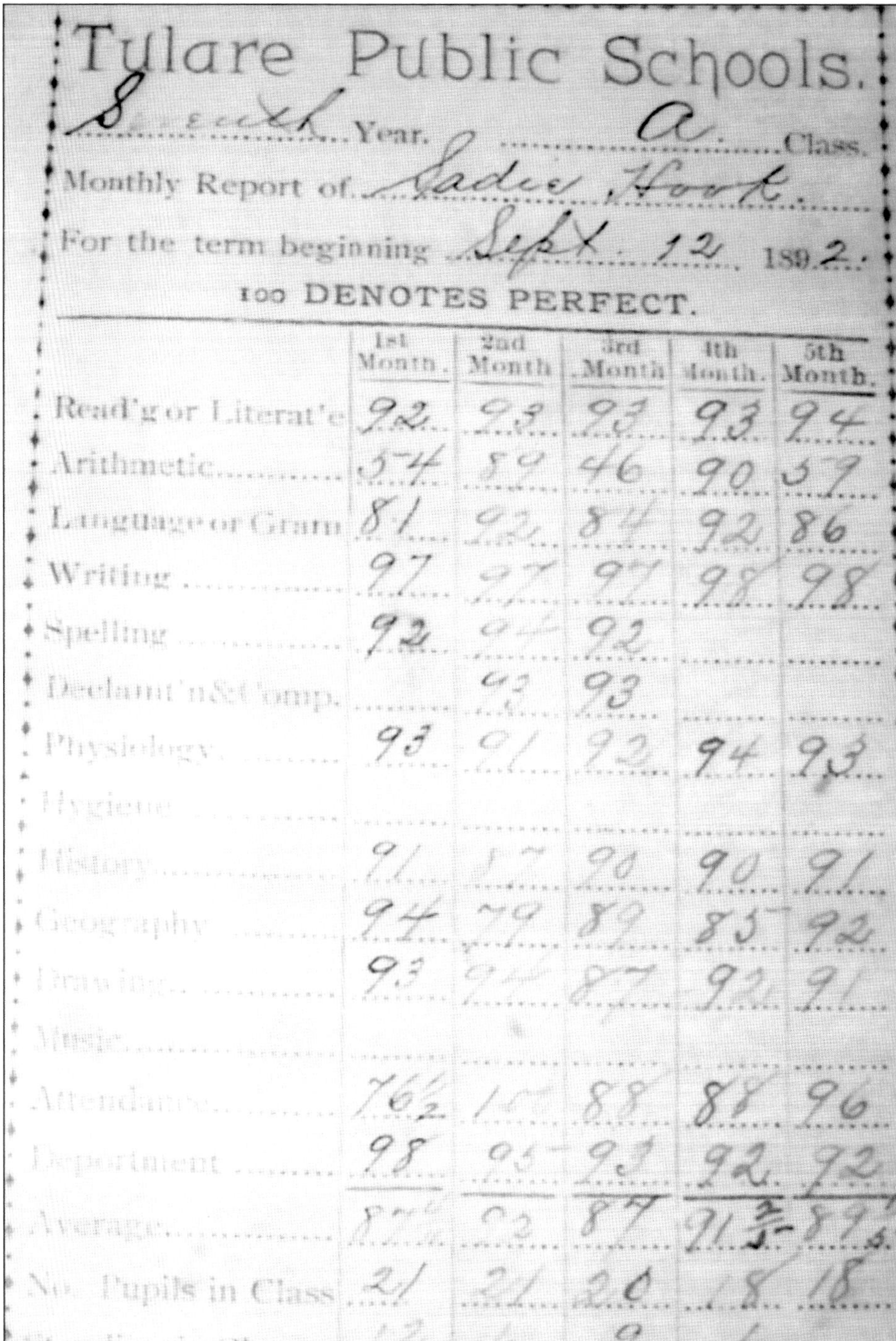

Tulare Public Schools.

Seventh Year. A Class.

Monthly Report of Sadie Hook.

For the term beginning Sept. 12 1892.

100 DENOTES PERFECT.

	1st Month.	2nd Month	3rd Month	4th Month.	5th Month.
Read'g or Literat'e	92	93	93	93	94
Arithmetic	54	89	46	90	57
Language or Gram	81	92	84	92	86
Writing	97	97	97	98	98
Spelling	92	94	92		
Declamt'n&Comp.		93	93		
Physiology	93	91	92	94	93
Hygiene					
History	91	77	90	90	91
Geography	94	79	89	85	92
Drawing	93	94	87	92	91
Music					
Attendance	76½	15	88	88	96
Deportment	98	95	93	92	92
Average	[illegible]	93	87	91 3/5	89 [illegible]/5
No. Pupils in Class	21	21	20	18	18
Standing in Class	12	6	9	6	

This is a Tulare Public School report card for Sadie Hook, a seventh-grade student, from September 12, 1892. Sadie's teacher was Ida Downing. Sadie excelled in writing, earning a 98, with a 94 in reading and a 96 in attendance. The report card also indicates how many students were in Sadie's class. At the beginning of the year, there were 21 students, and by the time this report card was issued, there were only 18. (Author's collection.)

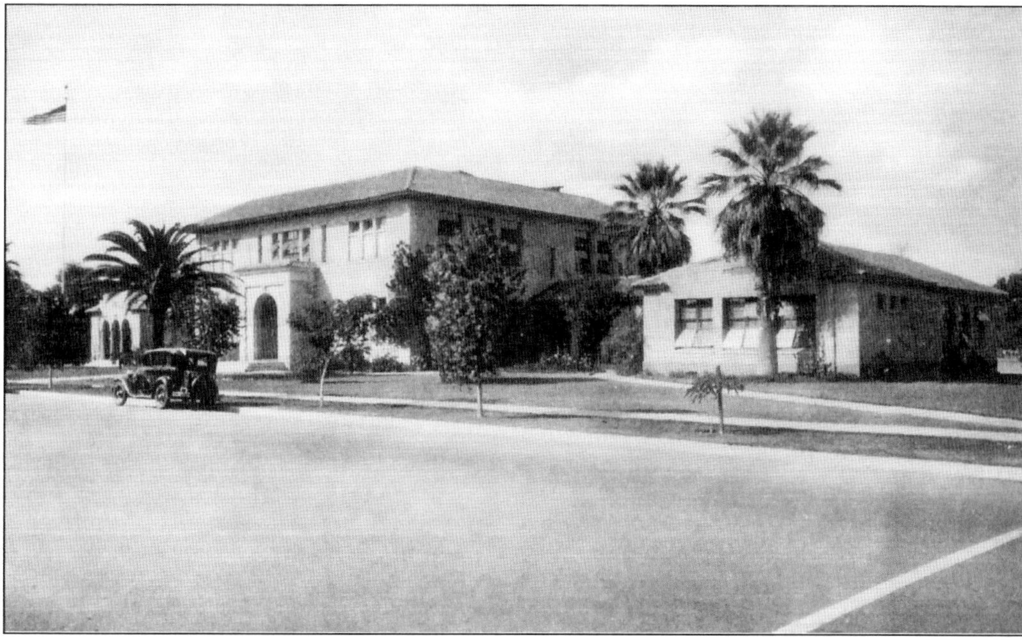

The Central Grammar School appears here after remodeling in the late 1920s. On the left is the auditorium with new landscaping in front, while on the right is the music and homemaking building. A comparison of old photographs with newer ones shows extensive remodeling. Note the modern look of the windows and the modernized entry. (Author's collection.)

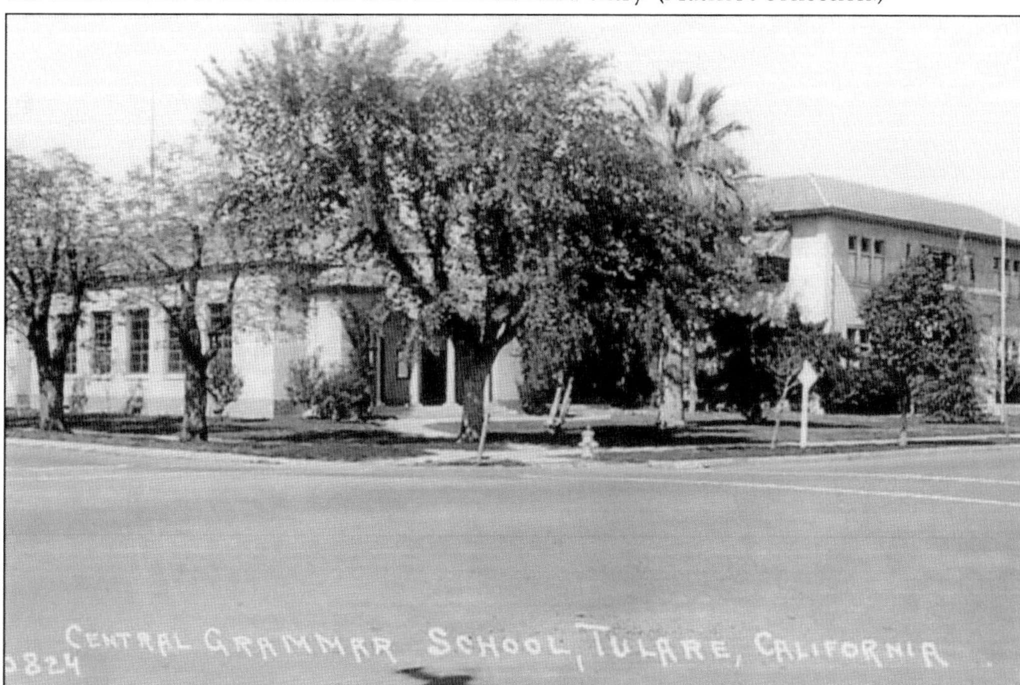

Central Grammar School is shown with the auditorium to the left side as it appeared in the 1930s. Today, the Tulare Historical Museum stands on the corner of E Street and Tulare Avenue. (Author's collection.)

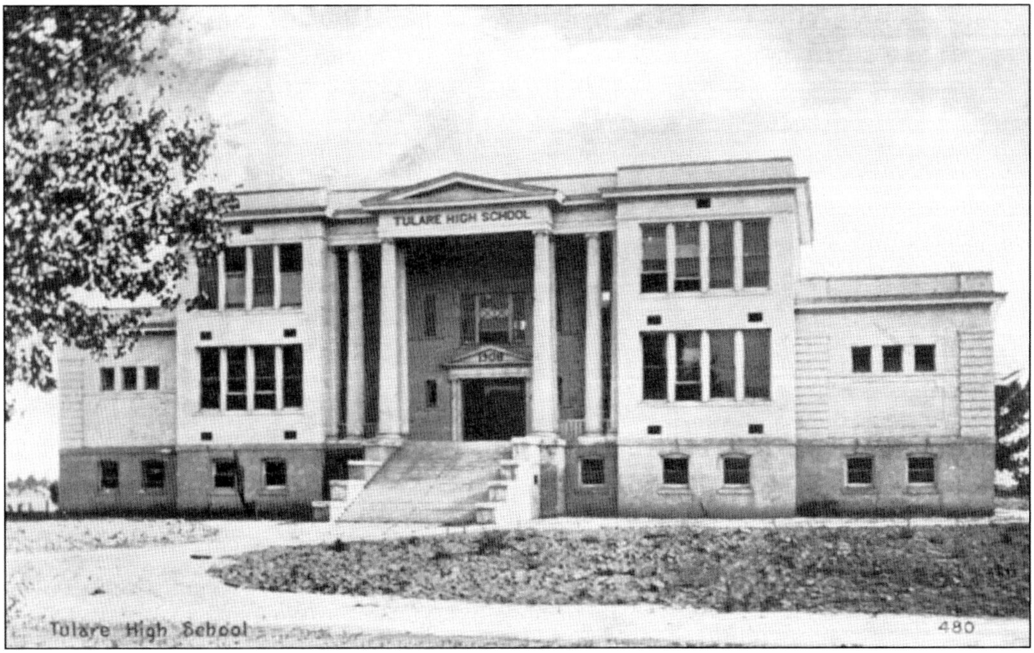

Tulare High School was built in 1908 and opened the following spring on a 10-acre plot of land that was purchased from David W. Madden at O Street and Tulare Avenue. At its outset, the new school was called Tulare High School and the name was later changed to its current version, Tulare Union High School. (Author's collection.)

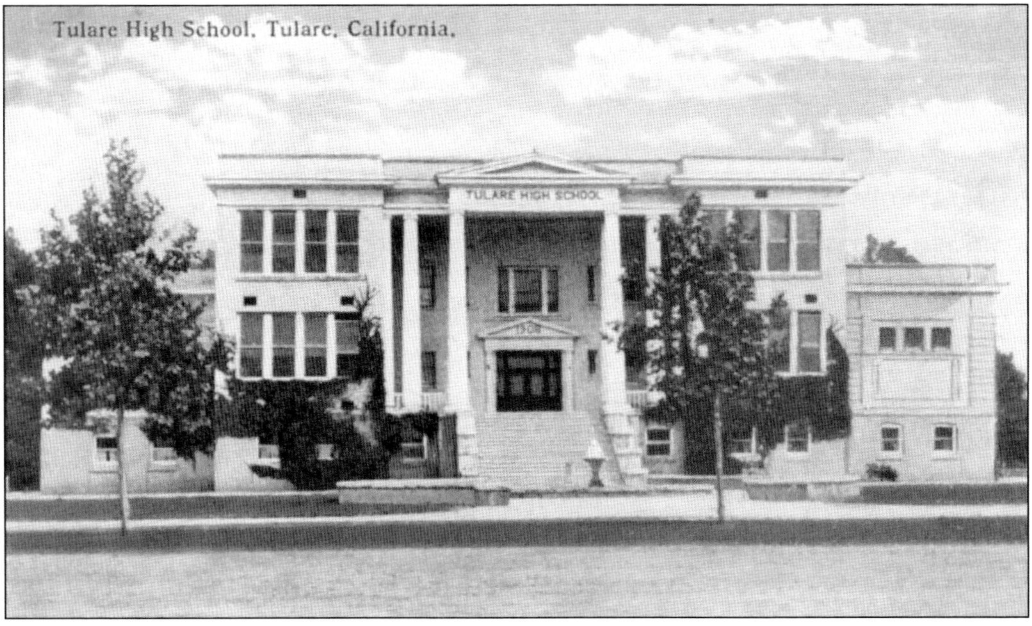

In 1908, school officials decided to pass a bond for $40,000 for the construction of a new high school building. The new edifice faced north on the south side of Tulare Avenue and was constructed toward the middle of the block because the David Madden family still lived on the corner of O Street and Tulare Avenue. Later, the high school expanded and eventually occupied the entire block between Tulare Avenue and King Street. (Author's collection.)

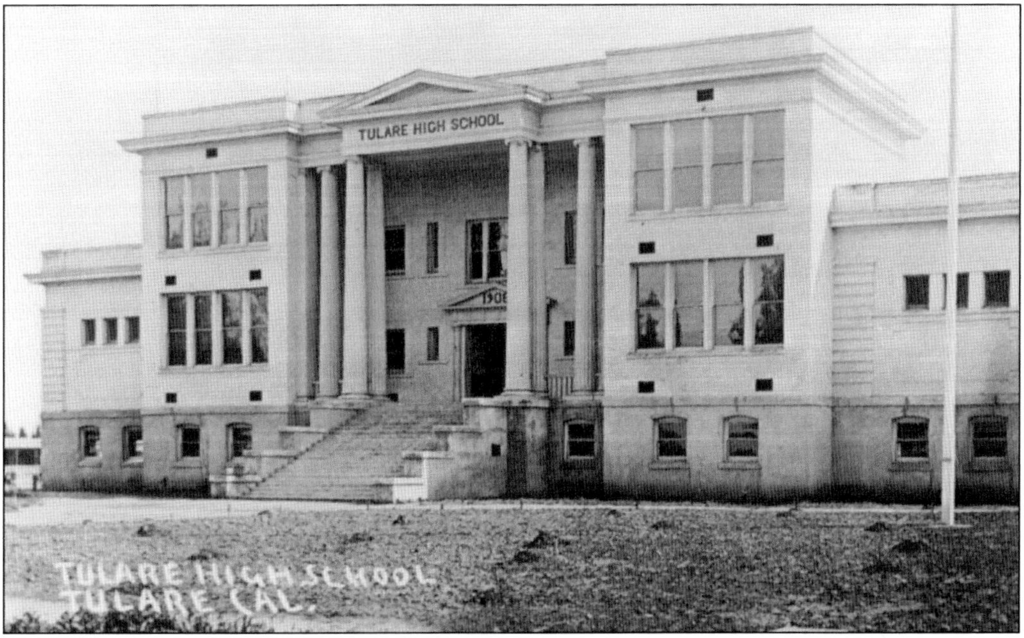

Tulare High School, built in 1908, was three stories tall and nearly 150 feet wide, with three two-story classroom wings extending rear to the south. A small gym was in the rear near Kern Avenue. In 1920, the high school district enlarged its boundaries and became the Tulare Joint Union High School District. (Author's collection.)

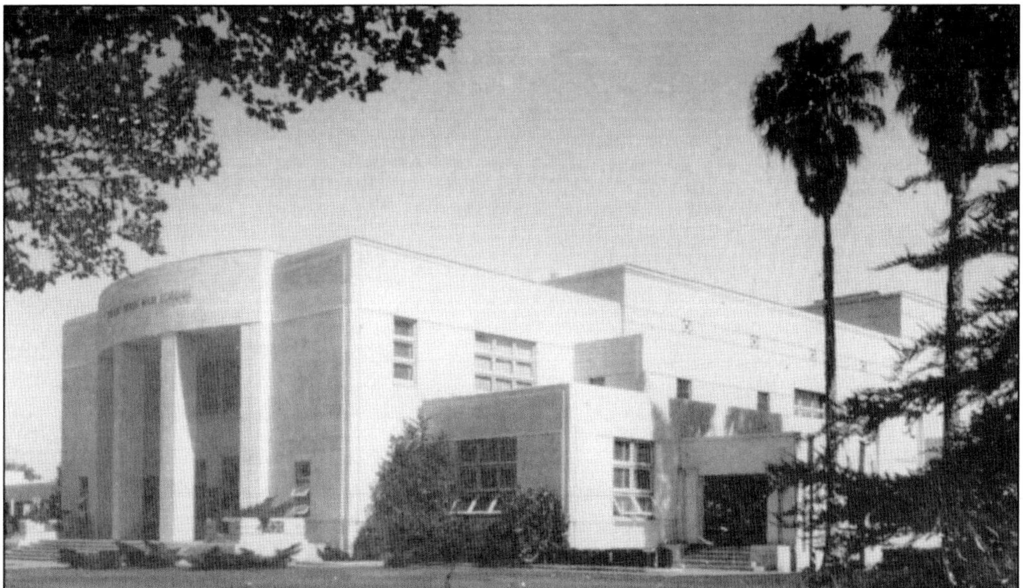

After the 1933 Long Beach earthquake, state lawmakers become alarmed at the danger posed by older brick buildings, and in 1935, the school board decided to replace the original high school campus with a new building with better seismic safety. The crown jewel of this construction was the Art Deco auditorium that could seat 1,400 people. Most of the $245,000 construction costs for the auditorium and classrooms were covered by the Works Progress Administration (WPA). (Author's collection.)

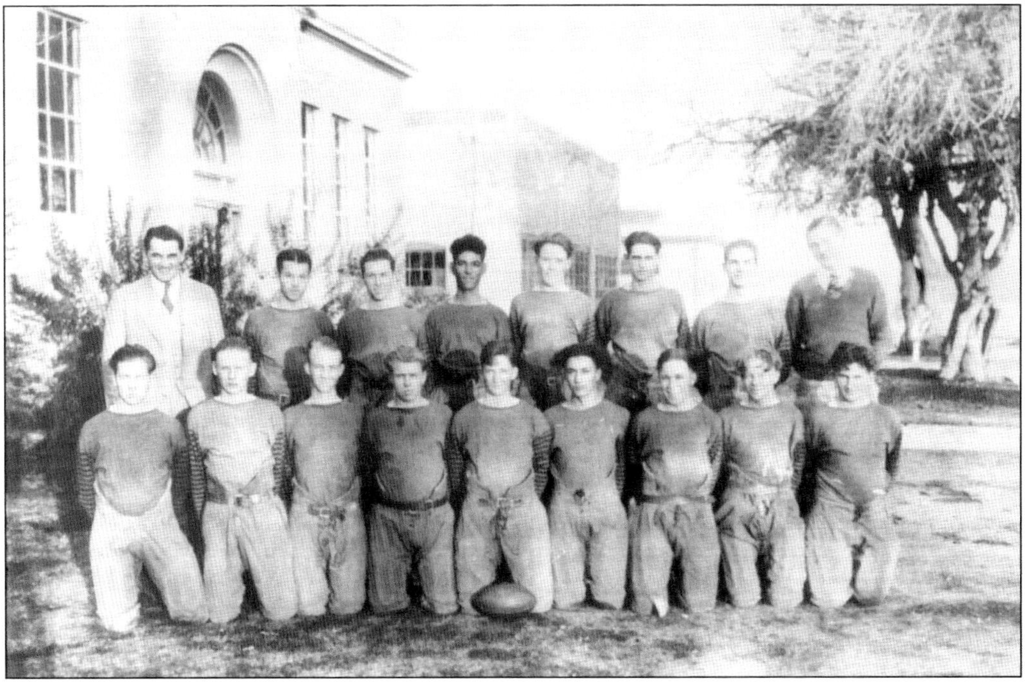

The Tulare Union High School football team in the early 1930s includes Charles E. King, second from the left in the back row. The King family ran King's Café at 322 South K Street until 1952. (Tulare County Library.)

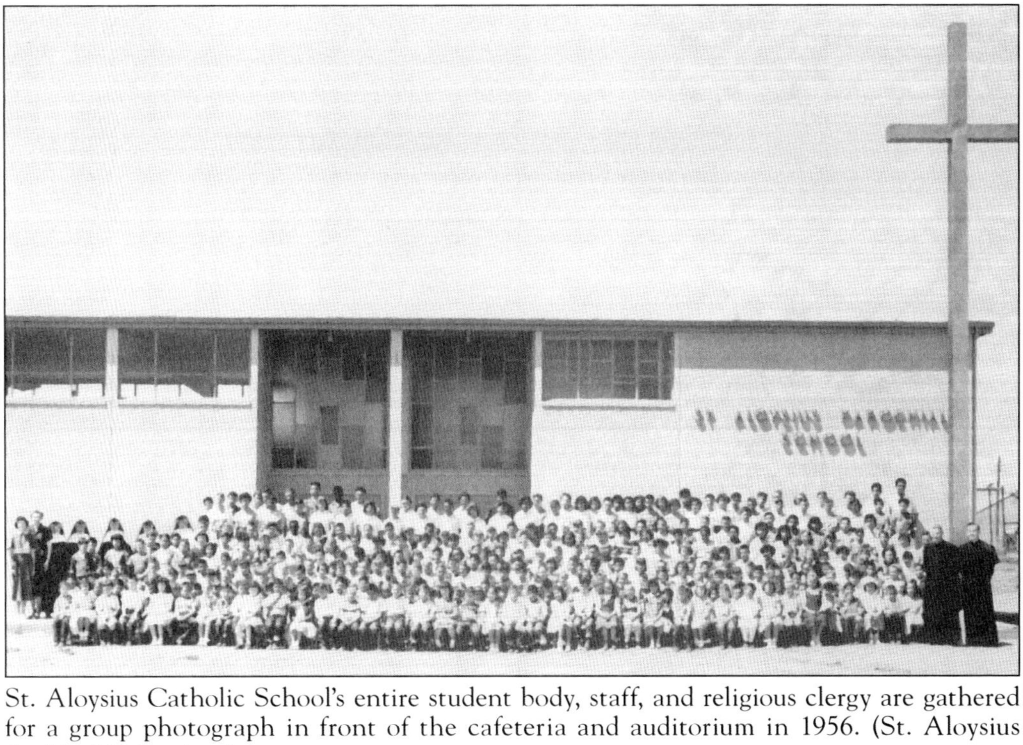

St. Aloysius Catholic School's entire student body, staff, and religious clergy are gathered for a group photograph in front of the cafeteria and auditorium in 1956. (St. Aloysius Archival Collection.)

The teaching staff of St. Aloysius School was comprised mostly of nuns from the order of the Sisters of Notre Dame in the late 1940s and 1950s. The sisters who comprised the teaching staff at St. Aloysius are gathered in the front primary wing, which includes first through fourth grades. The office is on the left. (St. Aloysius Archival Collection.)

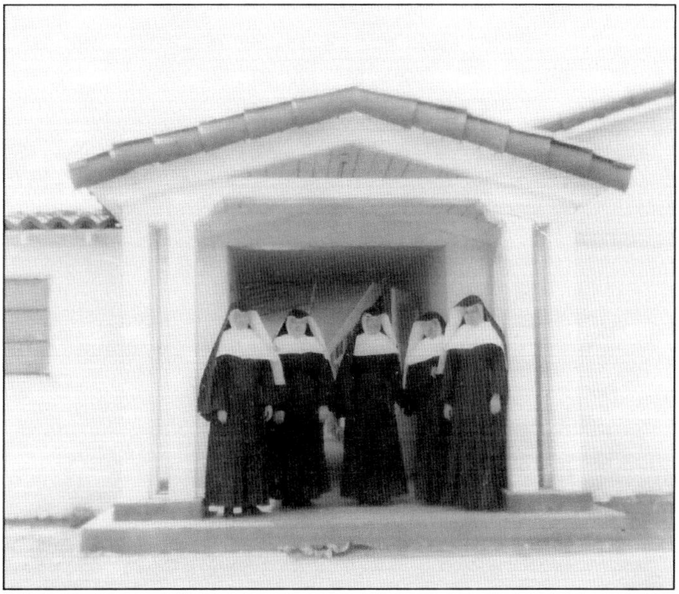

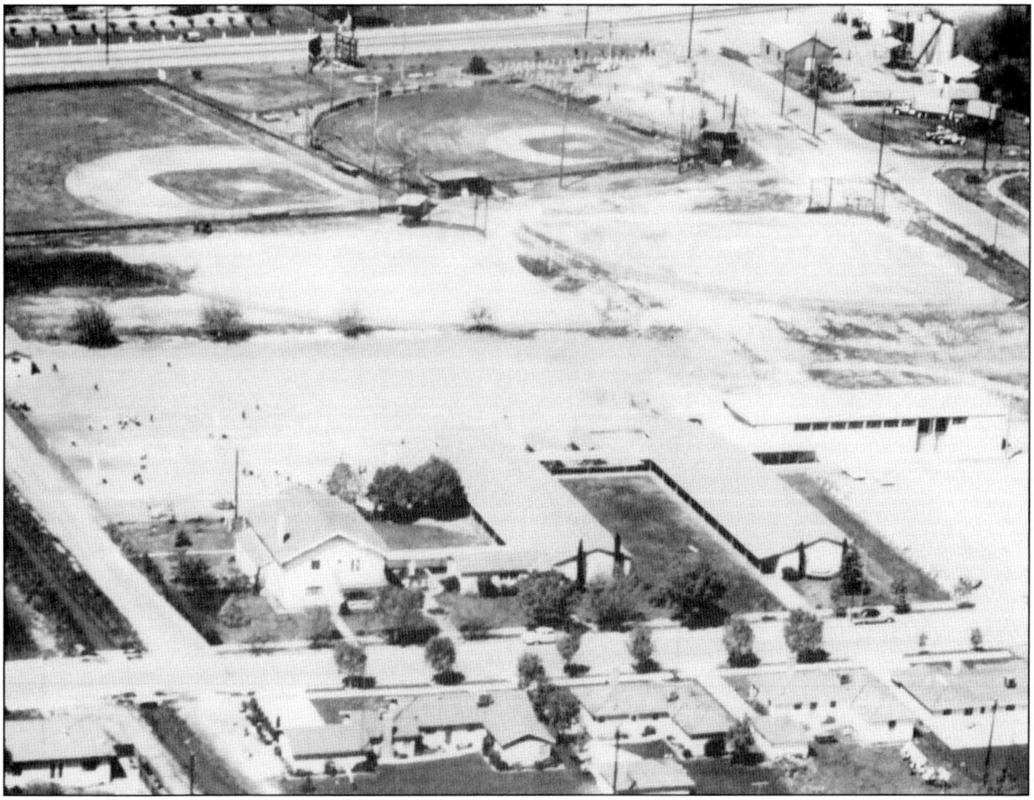

This is an aerial view of the St. Aloysius School grounds before the current church was built in 1970. At the top are J Street, running north, and Pleasant Street, which appears to be without curbs and gutters. The school grounds are similar today, except the convent is now used for day care and office space. The playground is somewhat the same, but with fewer baseball diamonds. (St. Aloysius Archival Collection.)

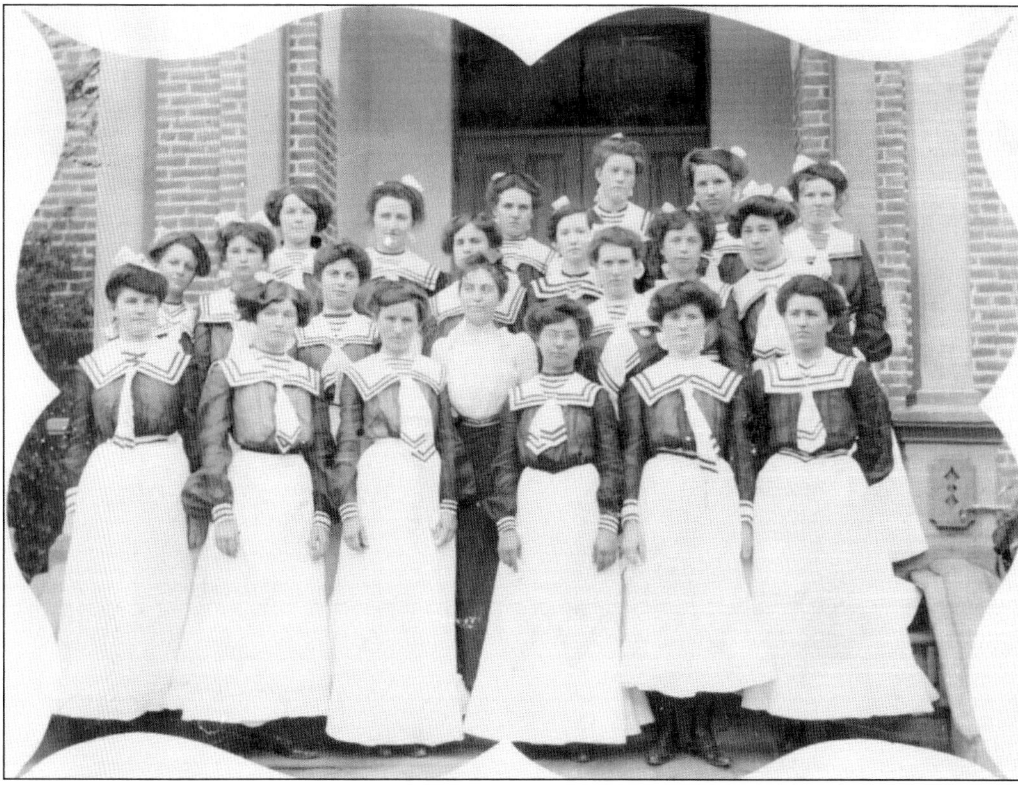

These grammar school girls are from the class of 1900. They are, from left to right, (first row) Nora Murphy, Margaret Hicks, Ella Falconer, Pearl Birch, Charlotte Murphy, and Hortense Fleming; (second row) Hazel Church, Mary Wharton Hastings, Margaret Pyle Howard, unidentified, Myrtle Weaver, Bertha Hamilton, and Jessie Farrar; (third row) Myrtle Falconer, Bertha Griffles, Myrtle Allen, Susie Gillum, Edna Hall, Ethel Peck, and Esther Fisk. (Tulare County Library.)

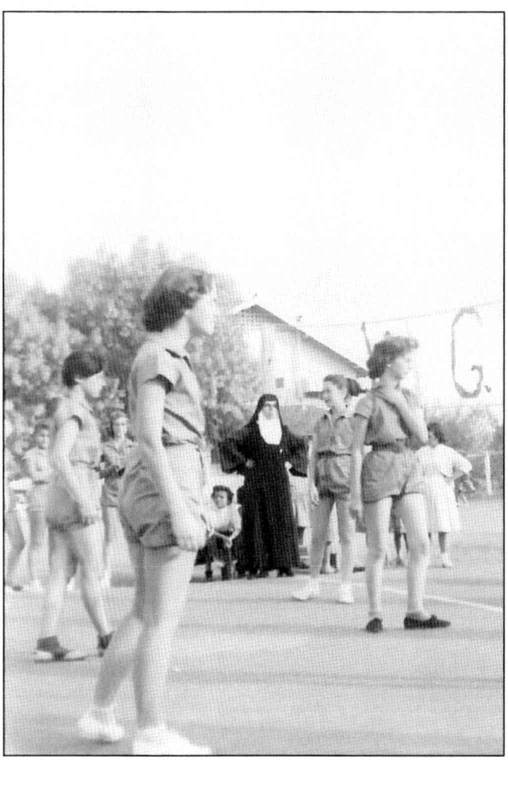

The St. Aloysius girls' volleyball team is playing against an unknown opponent in this 1959 photograph. Note the convent in the background and the nun coaching in her habit, the customary dress of Catholic nuns at the time. (Author's collection.)

Five

Houses

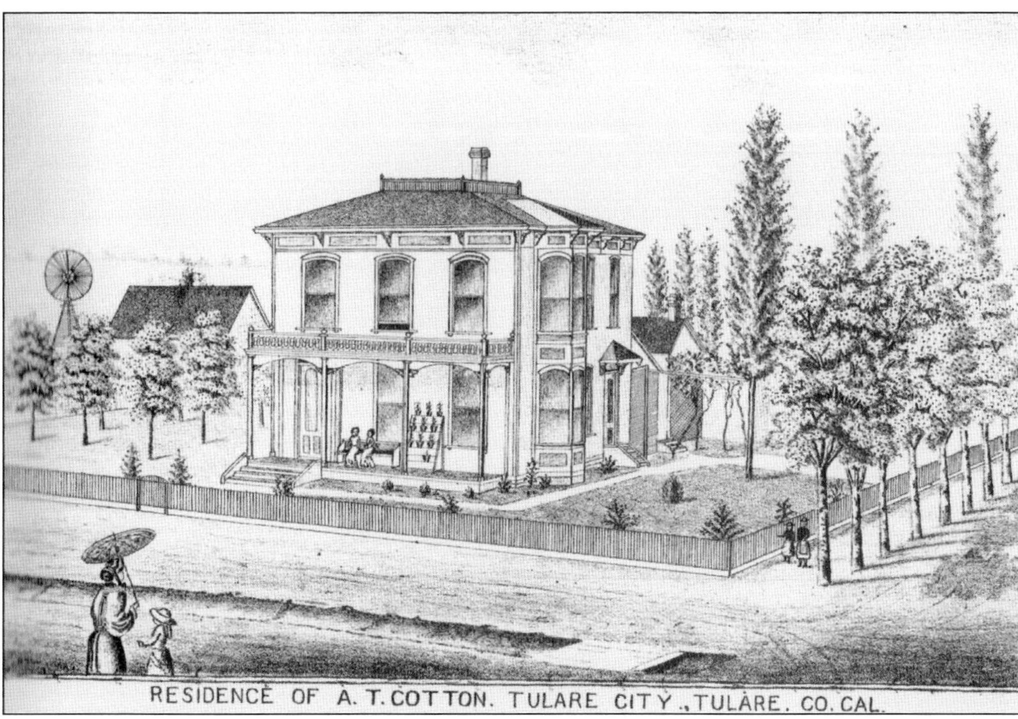

The Cotton House belonged to A.T. Cotton, who came to Tulare County in 1871 and began a well-boring enterprise. In 1873, he opened a tin shop in Tulare. Soon, he expanded the business to include stoves, hardware, and home furnishings, making it into one of Tulare's most thriving enterprises. (Author's collection.)

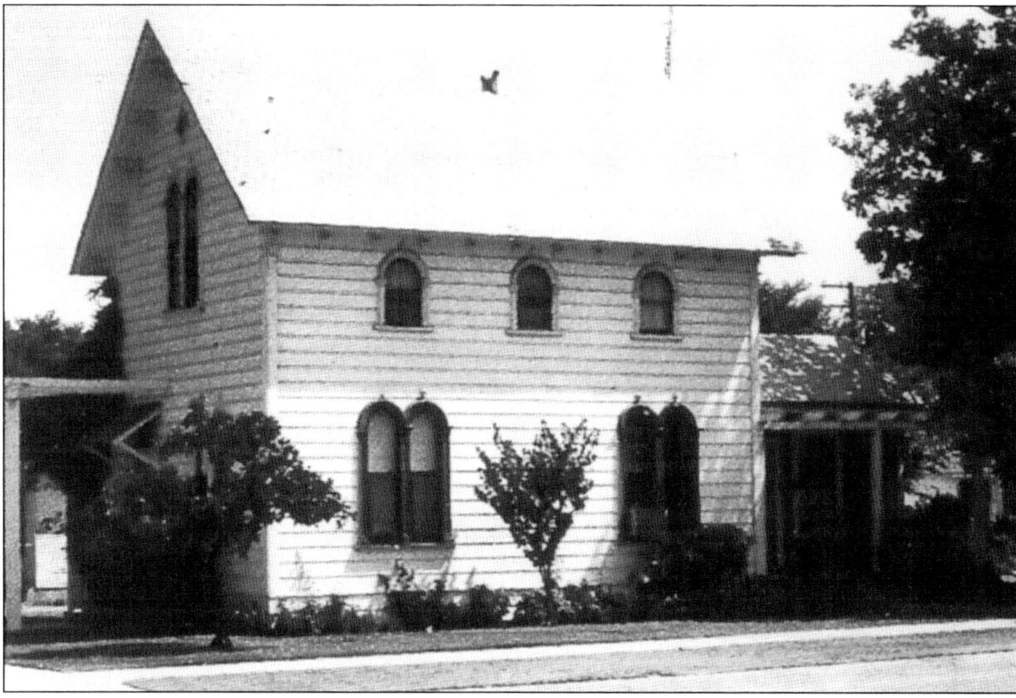

This house is on the corner of Tulare Avenue and H Street opposite the Congregational church and the Masonic Temple. It has undergone little change since it was built in the late 1800s. The most prominent owner of this house was Seymour Johnson, who was a master mechanic for the Southern Pacific. (Author's collection.)

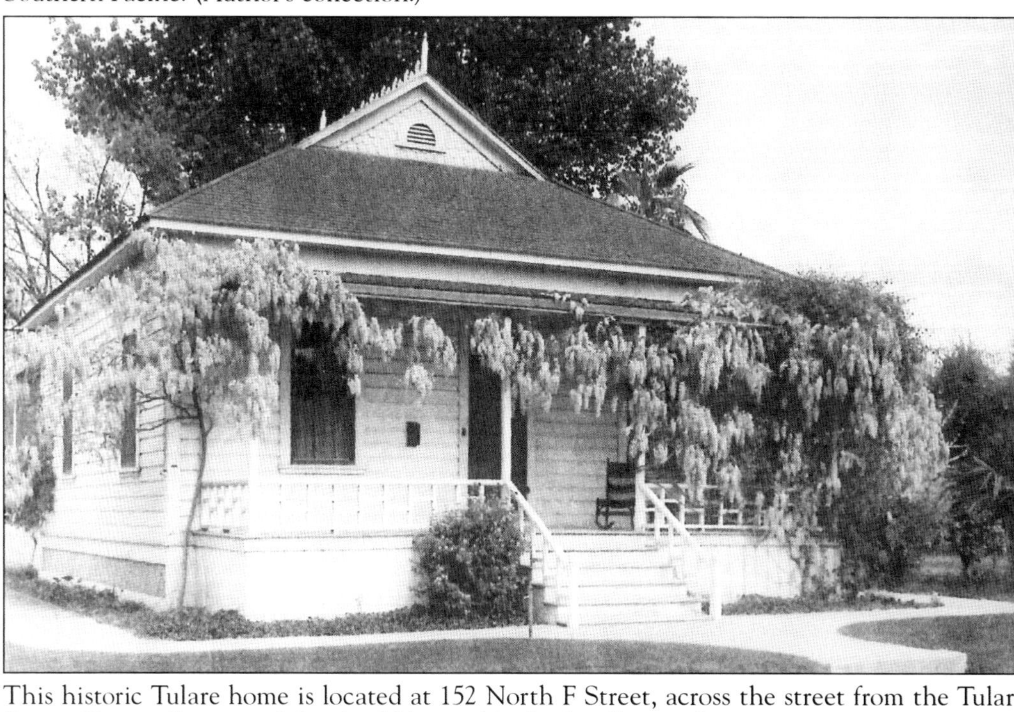

This historic Tulare home is located at 152 North F Street, across the street from the Tulare Senior Citizen Center and the third library. (Author's collection.)

A typical Tulare house from the early 1900s was rather simple. It included a porch, a living room, two or three bedrooms, and a small kitchen. As with most houses of this era, the plumbing was located on the outside rather than inside. (Author's collection.)

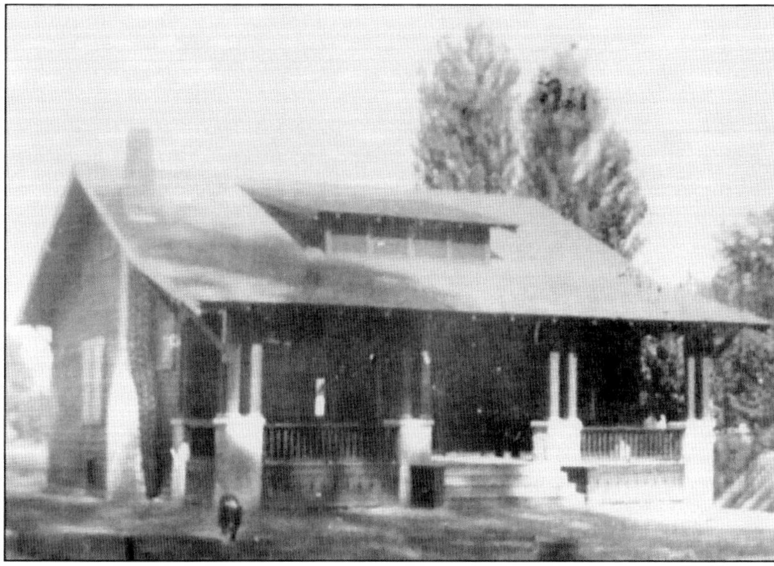

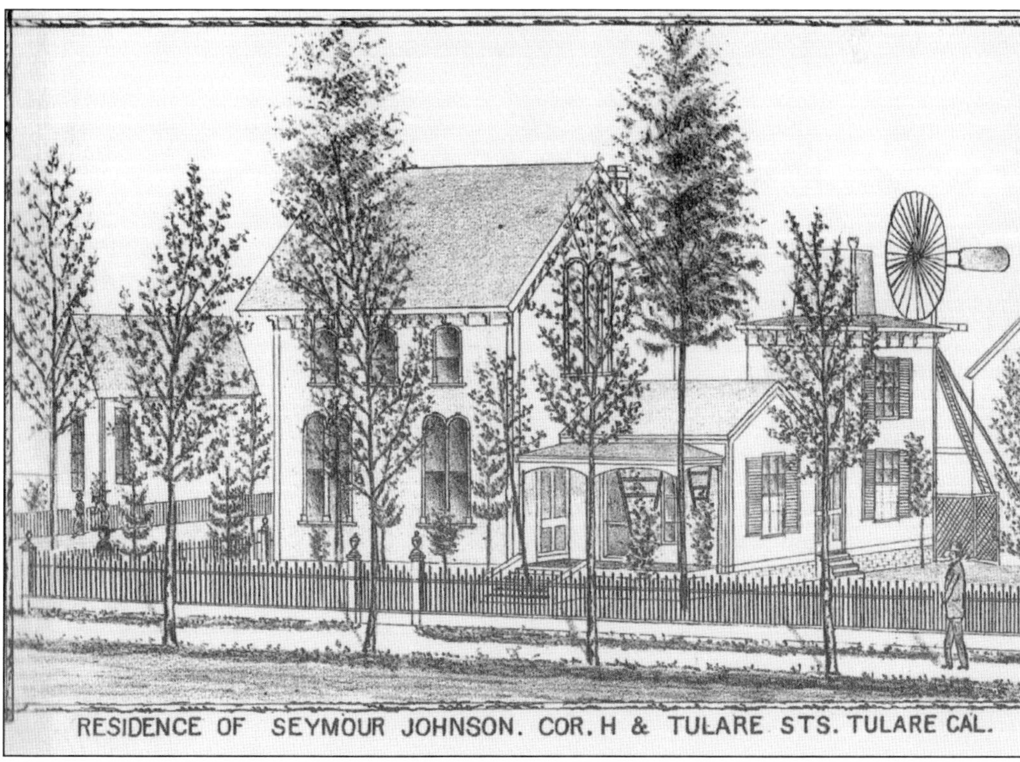

The Seymour Johnson house is at the corner of H Street and Tulare Avenue. Johnson was a division master mechanic for the Central Pacific Railroad, which was presided over by Leland Stanford. Johnson came to Tulare in 1875, when there was little but the dry plains to see, and expressed a strong belief in the future of the town. The railroad shops were the most important between San Francisco and Los Angeles. Later, Johnson was president of the library association. (Author's collection.)

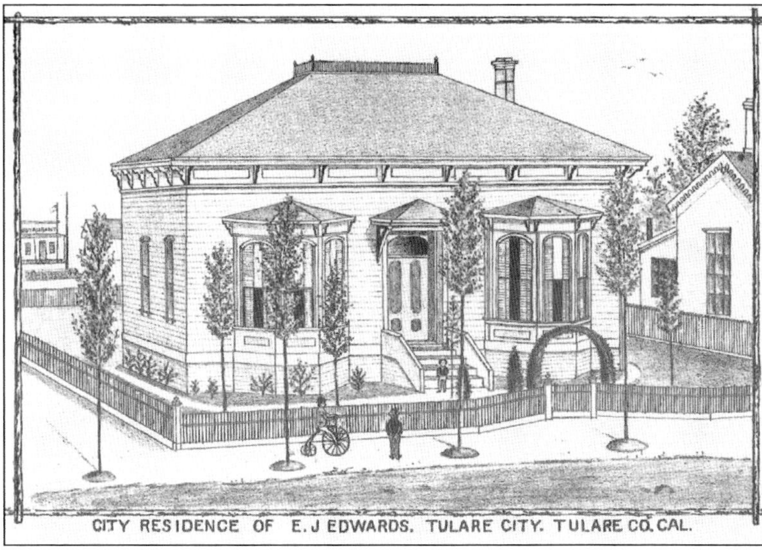

E.J. Edwards had a home in Tulare when he served as district attorney for Tulare County from 1877 until 1882. (Author's collection.)

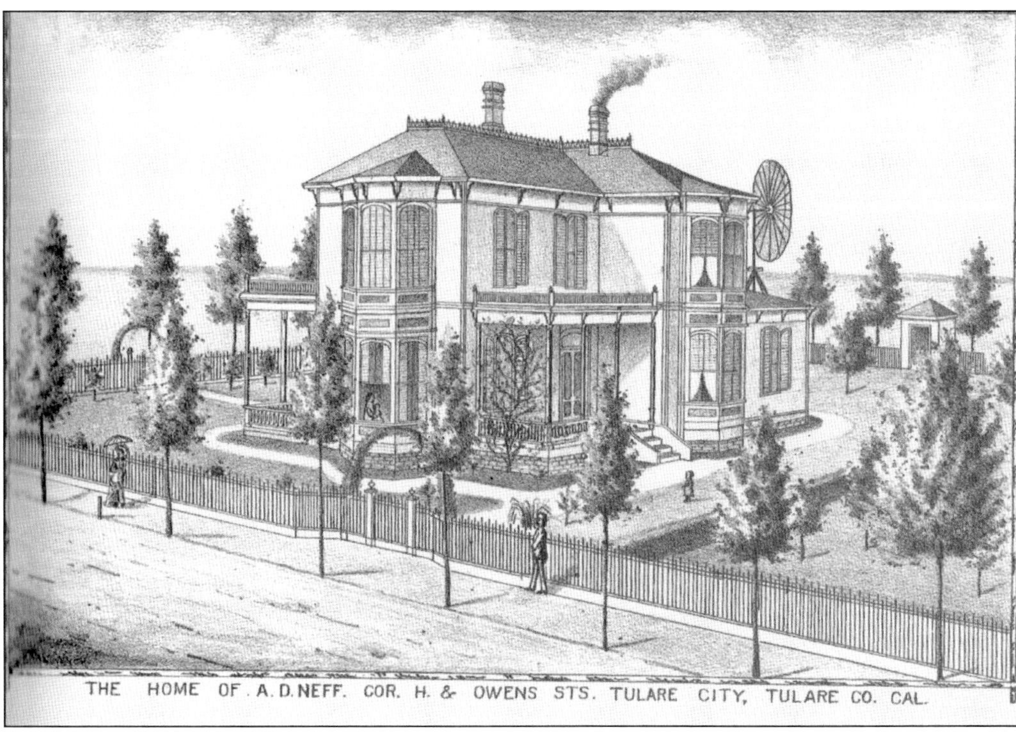

Built in 1888, the Andrew D. Neff residence was located at 457 South H Street at Owens Street. Neff was the engineer of the first train that came into the new town of Tulare in 1872. He quickly became a prominent Tularean, marrying Victoria Wright, the daughter of Isaac Wright. The Wright family already had a farm and home, but the Southern Pacific traded its acreage for a large tract of land, which the Wright family then occupied. When the Southern Pacific left town, so did the Neff family, which sold its home to Turner Nelson. (Author's collection.)

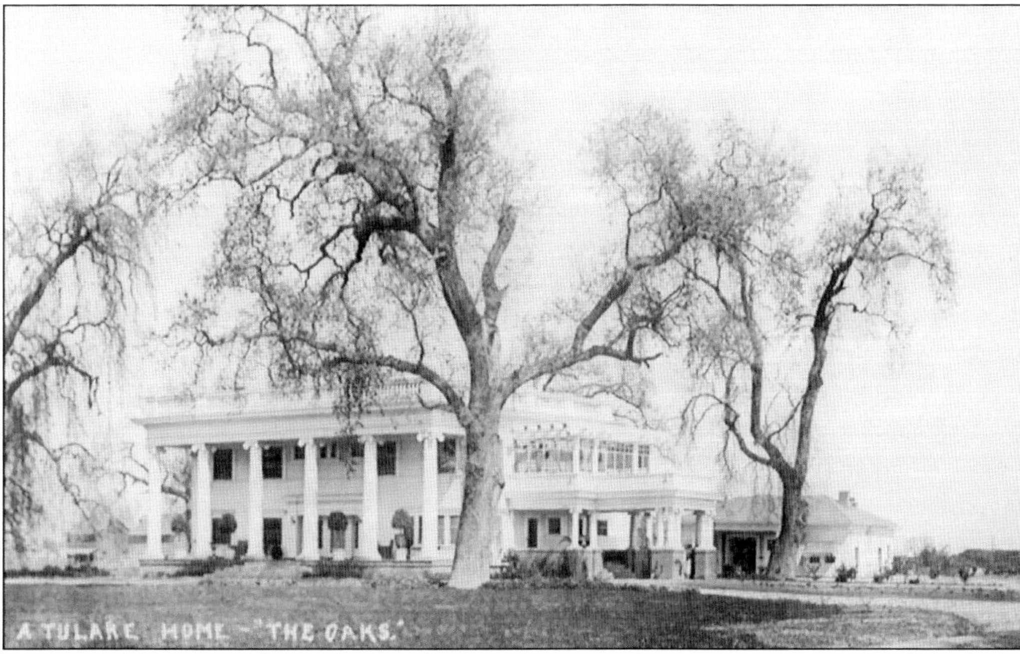

This once beautiful house was at the corner of Oaks Street and Merritt Avenue. The manager of the Paige and Morton Ranch built the home in 1912 and referred to it as The Oaks because of the oak trees that surround the area and the residence. The original owner was P.J.S. Montgomery, but by the 1920s, Hulett C. Merritt, who owned the Tagus Ranch, purchased it and renamed it Hulett Manor. In 1959, it was razed to make way for an upscale subdivision, The Elks, at the southeast corner and occupying the surrounding 32 acres. (Author's collection.)

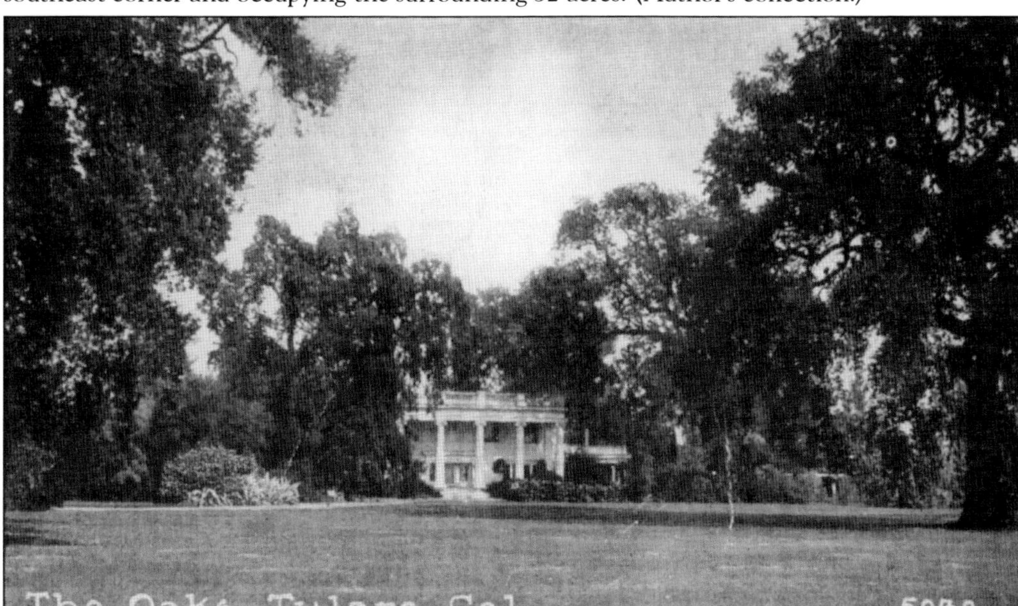

The Oaks mansion, partially hidden behind a thicket of oak trees, was razed in 1959. When Hulett Merritt bought the home, he had the interior remodeled with imported Italian woodwork. (Author's collection.)

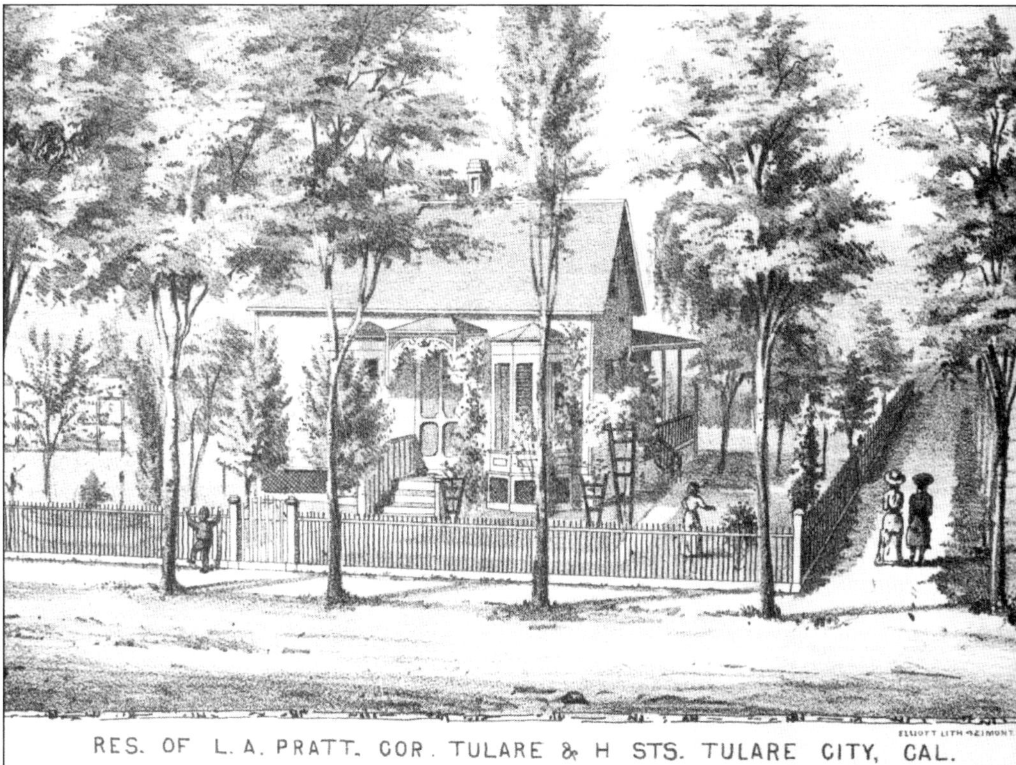

The L.A. Pratt residence was the home to Tulare's earliest undertaker—and later contractor and builder. His business was located in what today is the Masonic Temple, which came to be known as the Pratt Block. Pratt arrived in Tulare in 1870 with Isaac Wright, and in 1874, he was one of the original founders of the Congregational church. In 1882, he also helped build the Methodist church. Pratt was also a town constable, policeman, and tax collector. (Author's collection.)

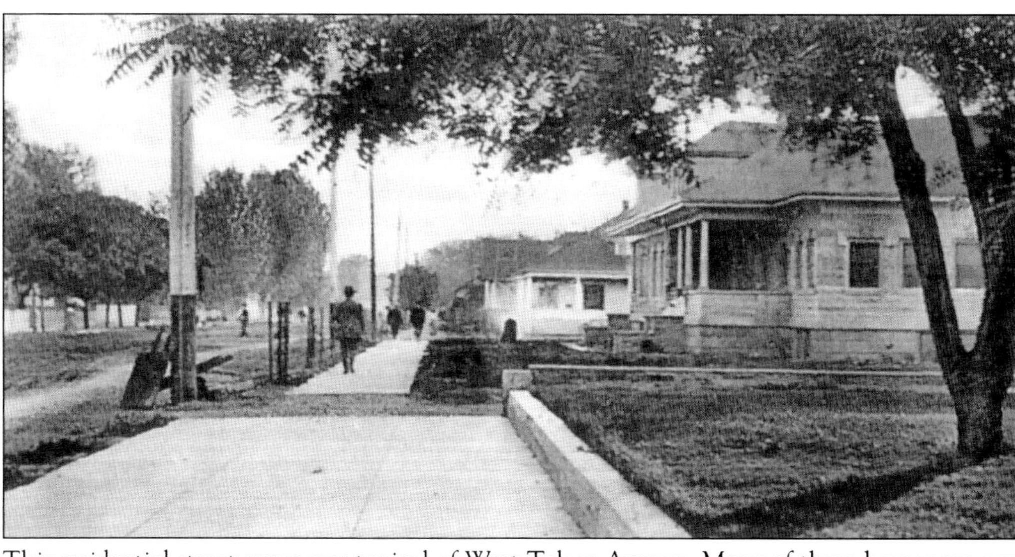

This residential street scene was typical of West Tulare Avenue. Many of these homes are now gone, as are the trees. (Author's collection.)

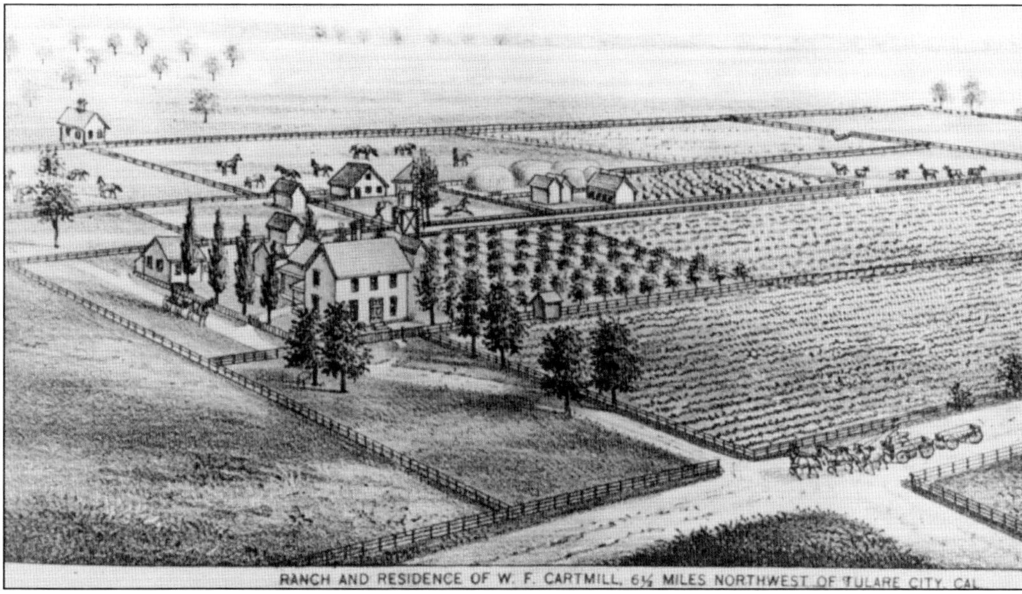

The W.F. Cartmill home was 6.5 miles north of what is now Tulare. He initially ran a cattle business and then raised sheep, with a peak of 6,000 head at one time. He built a home at 304 West Tulare Avenue so that his children could be closer to school. (Author's collection.)

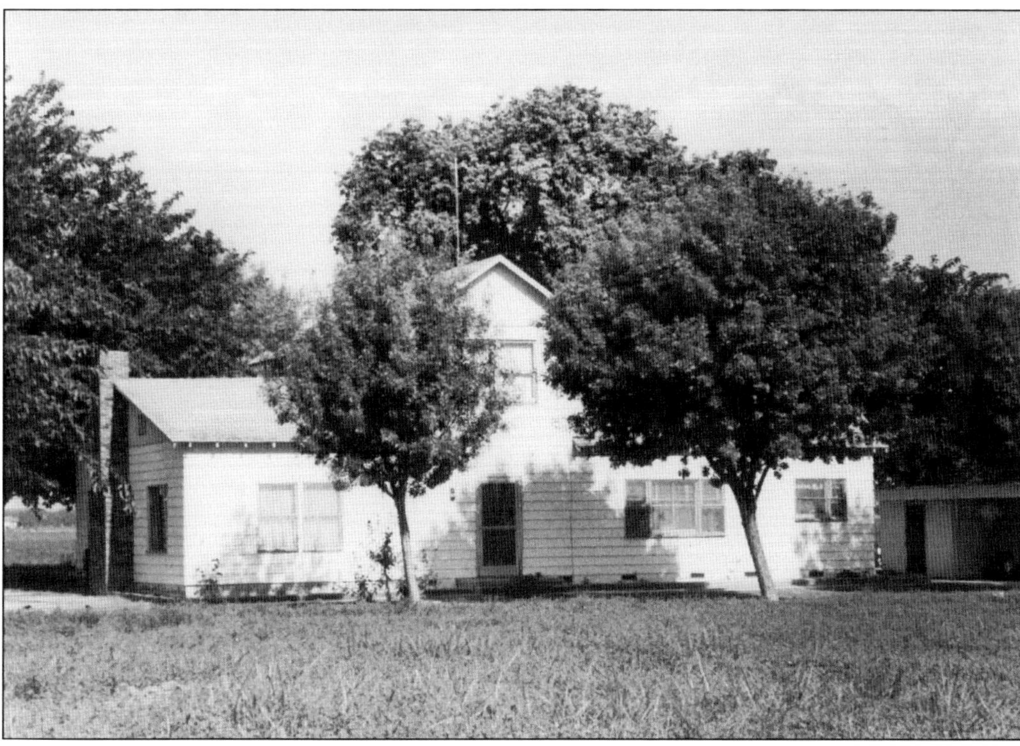

Old Cartmill house near Oak Valley Elementary School is pictured here in 1972. Cartmill later built a home in Tulare so his children could attend school. In 1900 his son Wooster Cartmill established the first creamery in Tulare, an enterprise on North J Street, where the Adohr sculpture stands today. This first creamery had an output of 500 pounds of butter daily. (Tulare County Library.)

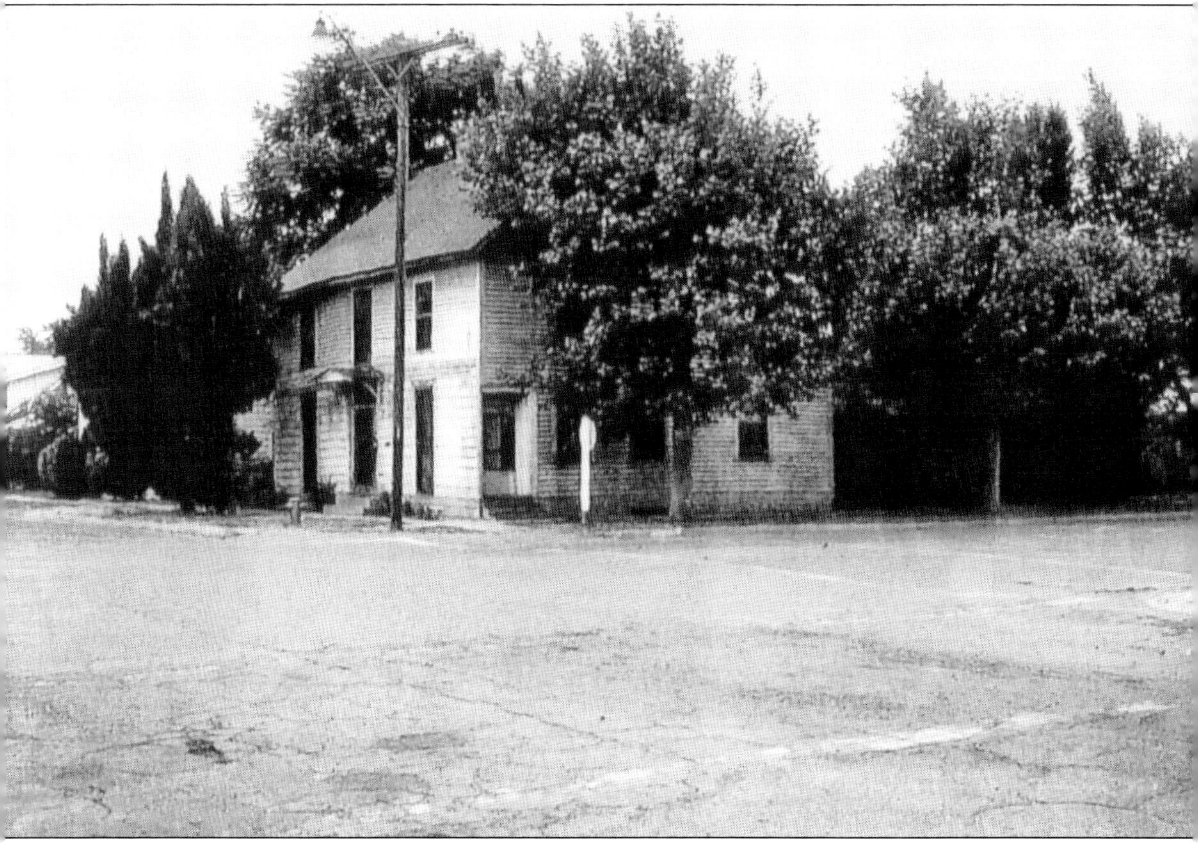

The Lovejoy house, pictured in 1955, was at the southwest corner of Kern and I Streets in Tulare. It was the first house built after the 1872 founding of the city. The residence cost $10,000. It was razed in the late 1950s or early 1960s. (Tulare County Library.)

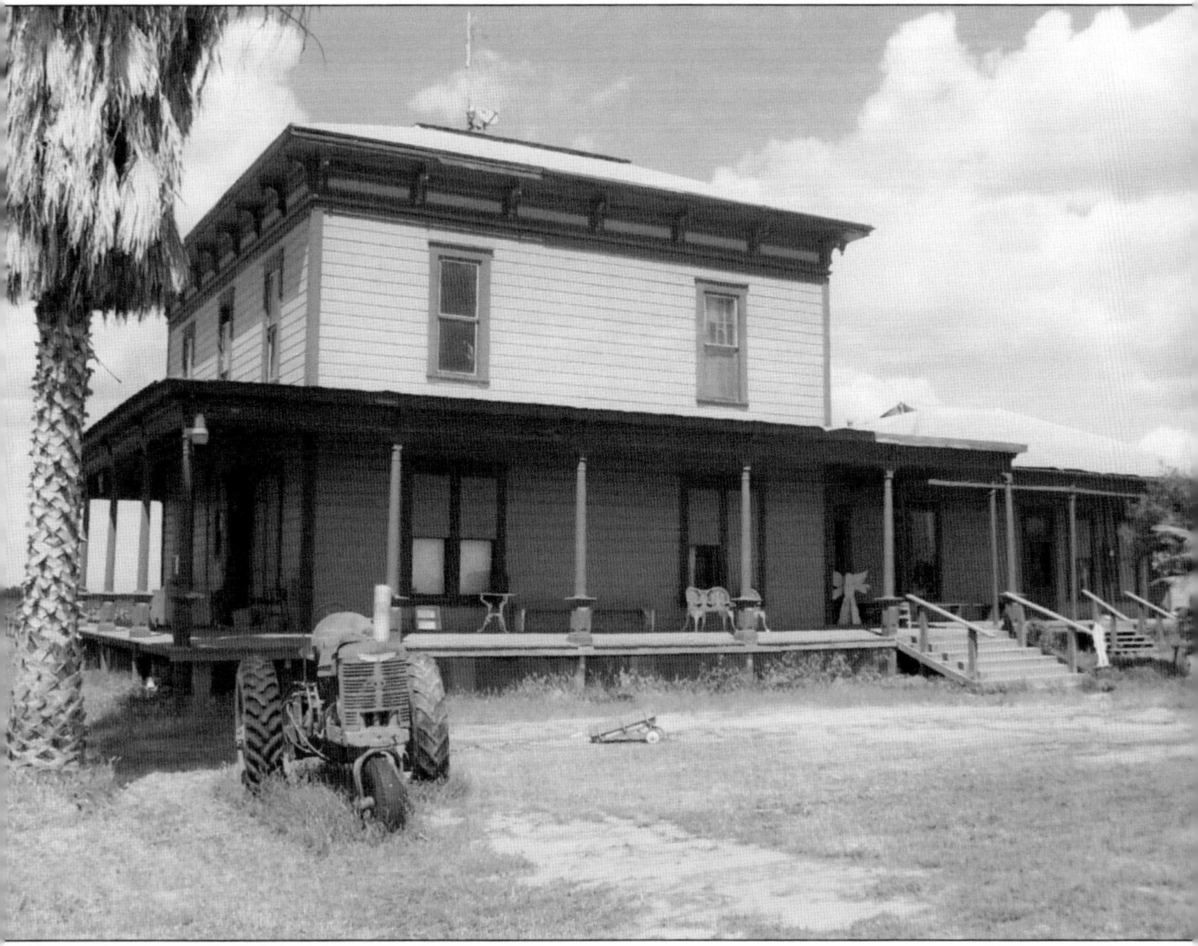

The J.B. Zumwalt house, owned by the Renaud family, is pictured in 2013 without its second-floor porches. The main 1884 building was 36 by 40 feet and two stories high, with a hip roof—all sides slope downward toward the walls and deck. It had eight large rooms with lofty ceilings—four upstairs and four downstairs. The connecting hallways are broad and the stairs had a very gradual and easy rise. At the time of construction, it was surrounded by double porches to protect it from the direct rays of the sun. Behind the main building, the kitchen measured 20 by 40 feet and included a pantry and bathroom. The cost of the porches was $2,000. (Author's collection.)

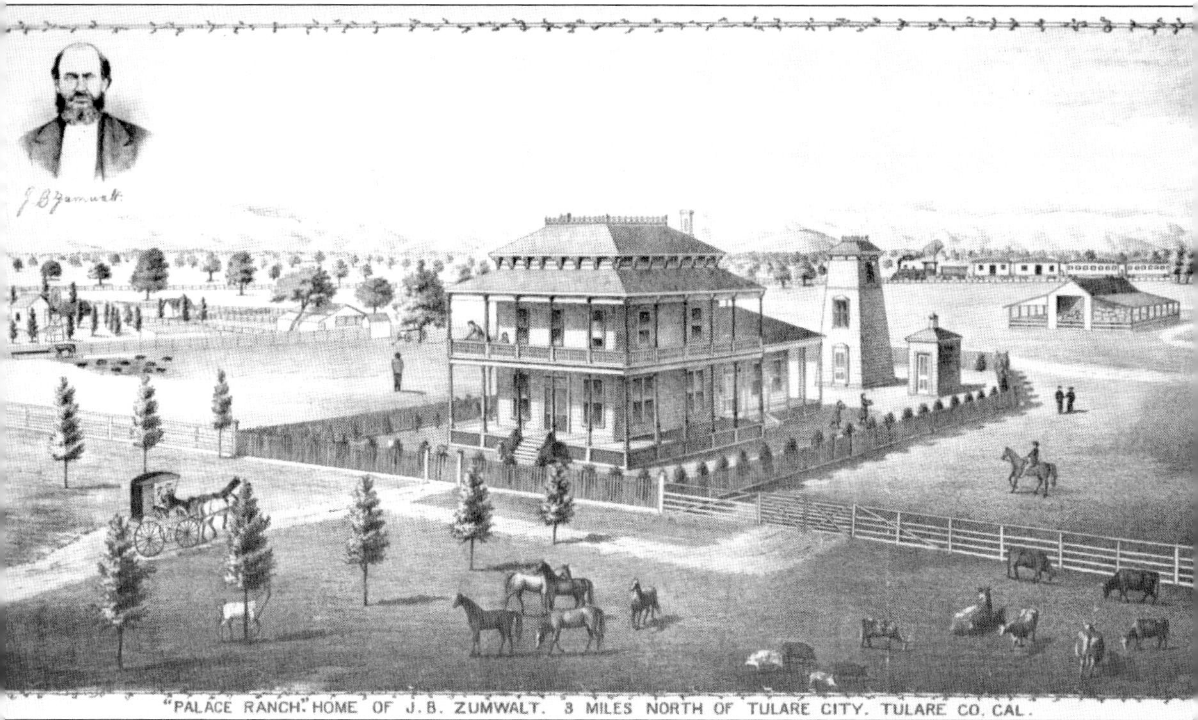

The Palace Ranch house of J.B. Zumwalt is pictured—along with a small inset of Zumwalt himself. In 1891, when Zumwalt died, his widow continued to live in the home while Emerie Renaud (1856–1941) leased the acreage from the family and in 1895 moved his family into the massive house. In 1903, Renaud purchased the Zumwalt Ranch. The family still owns the home. (Author's collection.)

Six

People

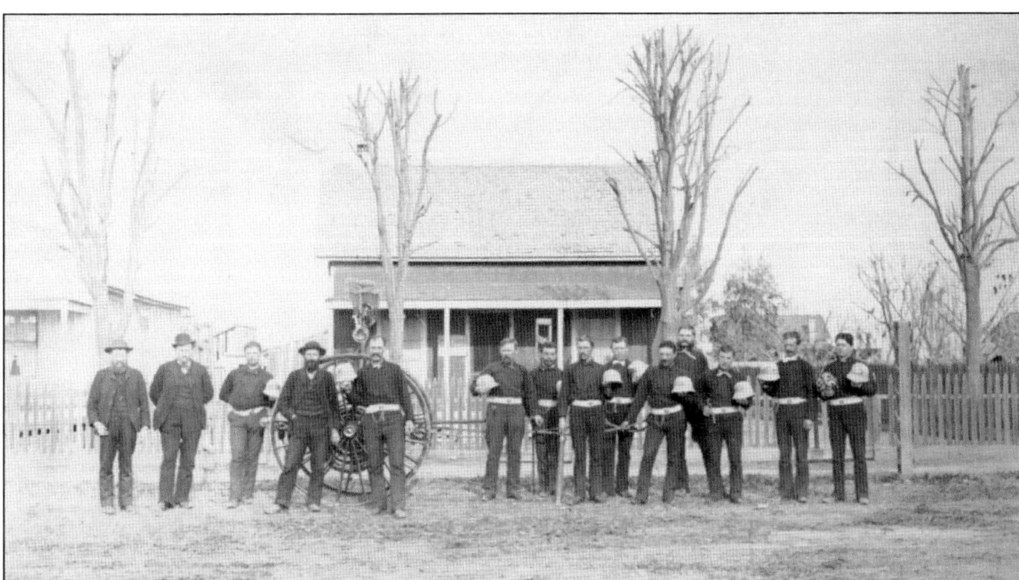

After winning the valley championship hose-cart race, the Tulare Fire Department team poses in front of the Dodson house on March 17, 1896, in the 100 block of South K Street. (Tulare County Library.)

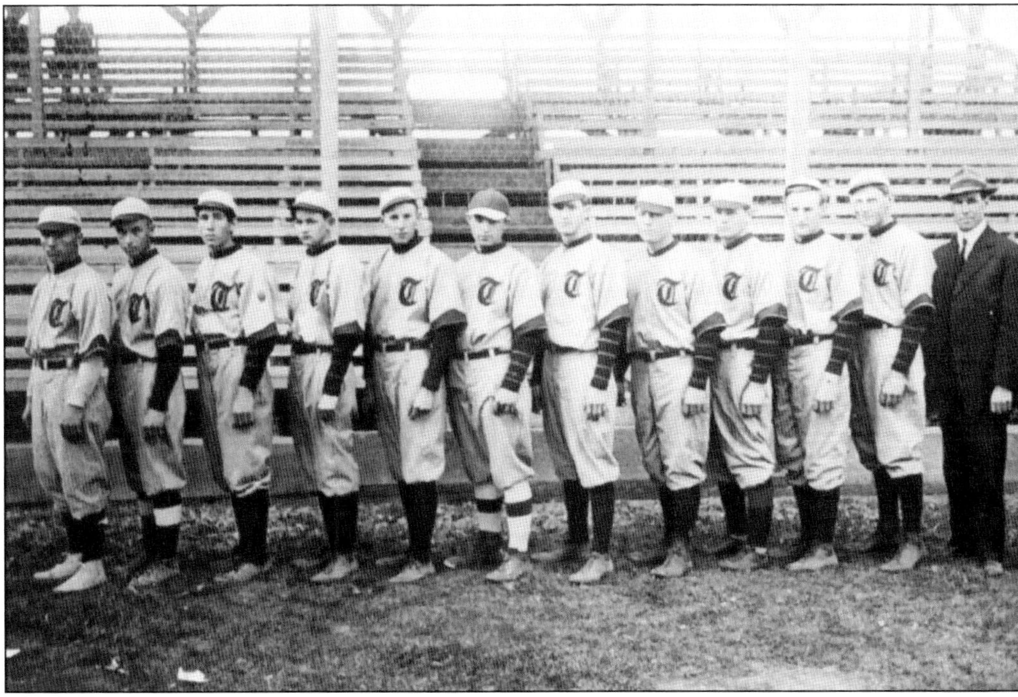

The Tulare baseball team is pictured in front of the grandstand about 1910. From left to right are Wood, Dunlap (who died in 1974), Smith, Foster, Ellis (who died in 1956), Pell (who died in 1913), Specklemere, Dye, Beford, Harris, Hopkins, and Professor Walton. (Author's collection.)

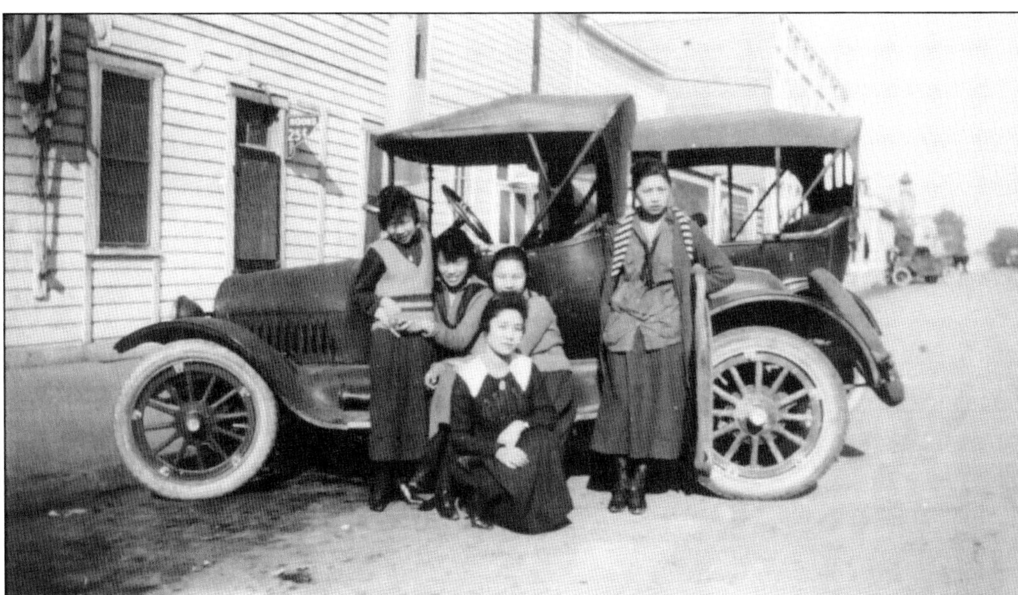

The Ling family poses in front of an automobile in Tulare's old Chinese section on the west side of the 200 block of South K Street, with Daisy Joe Fung in the center front in front of Shanghai Café. (Tulare County Library.)

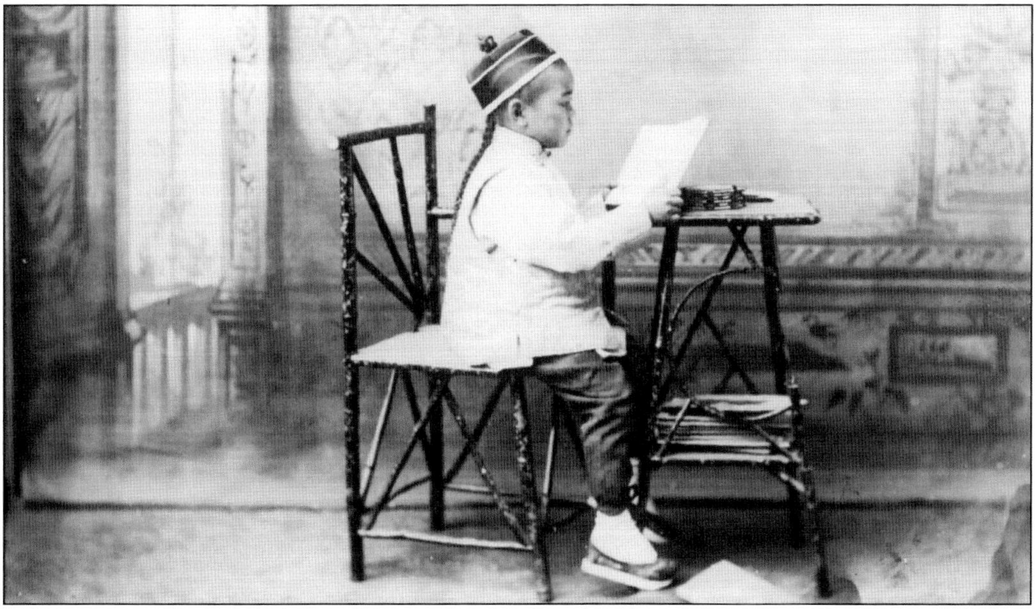

This unidentified Chinese boy is reading a book while his portrait is being taken at Doran Studios in Tulare in the early 1900s. Tulare once had a thriving Chinese community until a group of extremists gathered the entire local Chinese population, loaded them into a railroad car, and shipped them off. (Author's collection.)

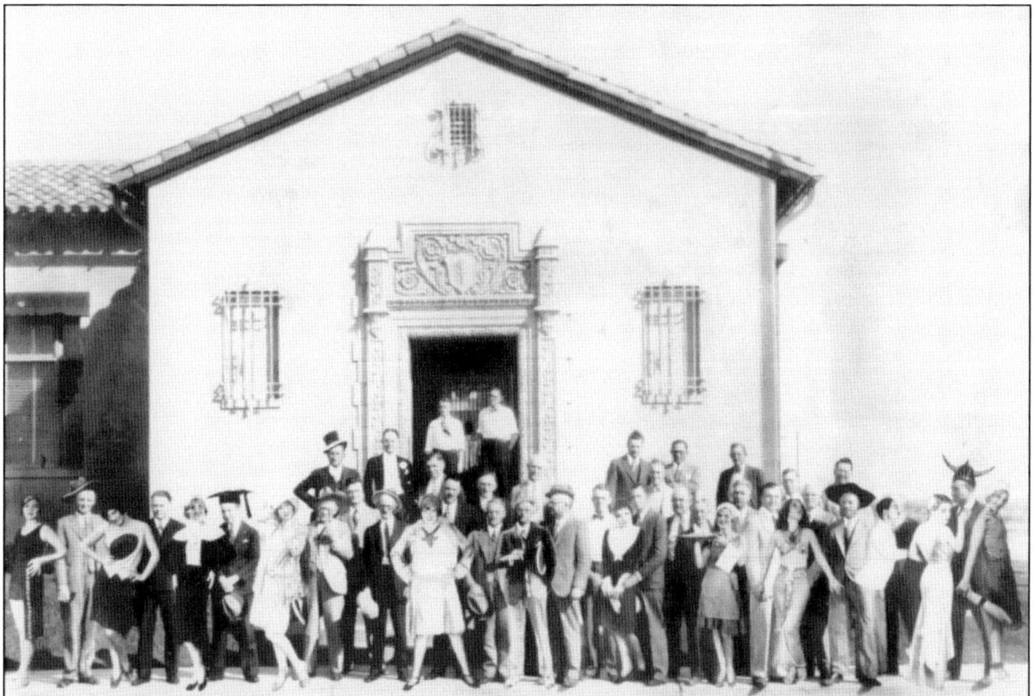

Members of the Tulare Rotary Club with fake paper cutouts are guests at the local chamber of commerce office in the 1930s. This photograph was taken on the south end of the building at K Street and what would become Martin Luther King Jr. Avenue. (Tulare County Library.)

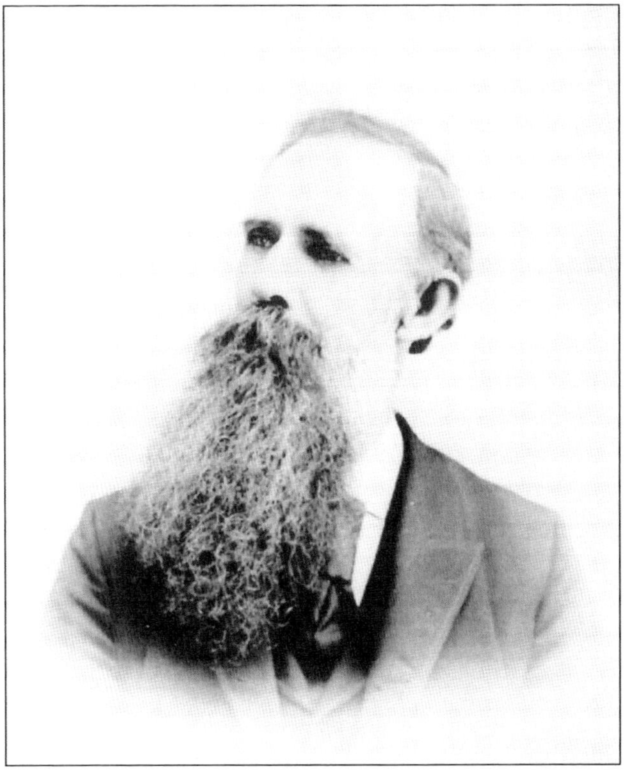

Daniel K. Zumwalt started the first creamery in Tulare County near the current site of the Liberty School. He came to Tulare County in 1869 and set up a farm dedicated to dairying and the raising of shorthorn cattle between Tulare and Visalia. In 1890, Zumwalt was instrumental in getting Congress to protect and set up General Grant National Park (forerunner to Kings Canyon National Park). (Author's collection.)

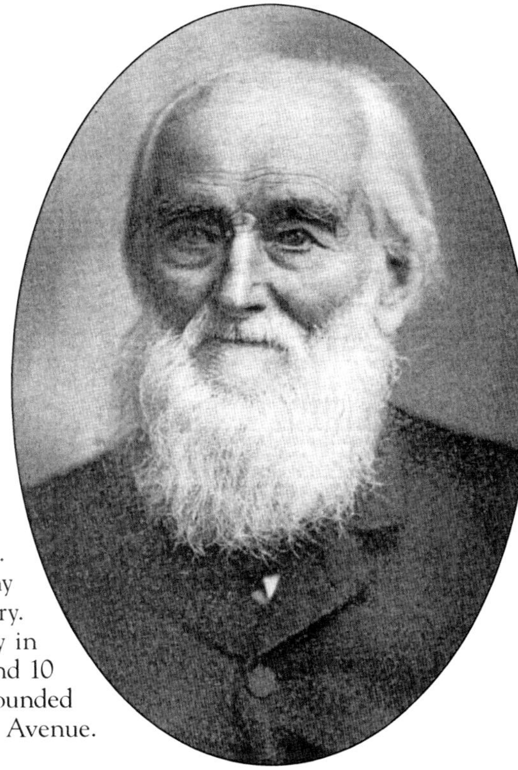

William F. Cartmill is pictured in his later years. He is the father of Wooster Cartmill, whom many consider to be the father of Tulare's dairy industry. The elder Cartmill arrived in Tulare County in 1861 and soon bought a quarter section of land 10 miles southwest of Visalia. When Tulare was founded in 1872, he built a home at 304 West Tulare Avenue. (Author's collection.)

Ezra Lathrop arrived in Tulare in 1873. Shortly after, he began to farm his land—and soon bought other acreage—until he began his lumber business in 1882. He sold the lumber business in 1884 to Puget Sound Lumber Company. He later was appointed agent for the San Joaquin Lumber Company In 1885, he assisted in the organization of the Bank of Tulare, the oldest in town. He was president until his death on November 17, 1908. (Author's collection.)

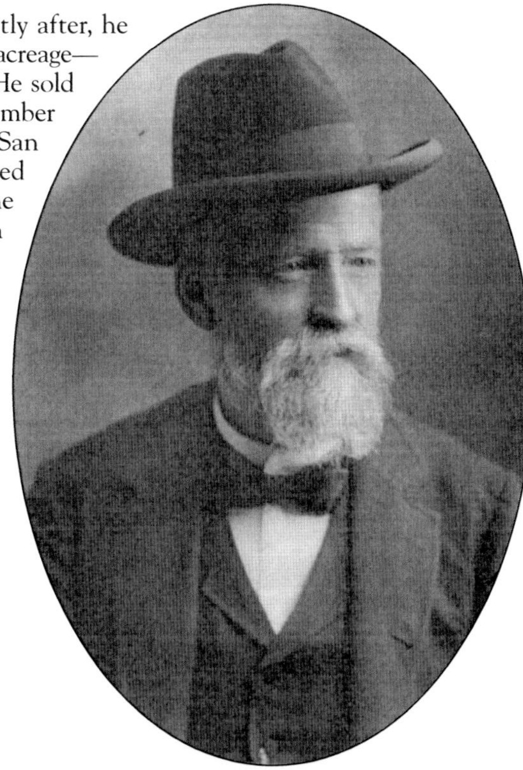

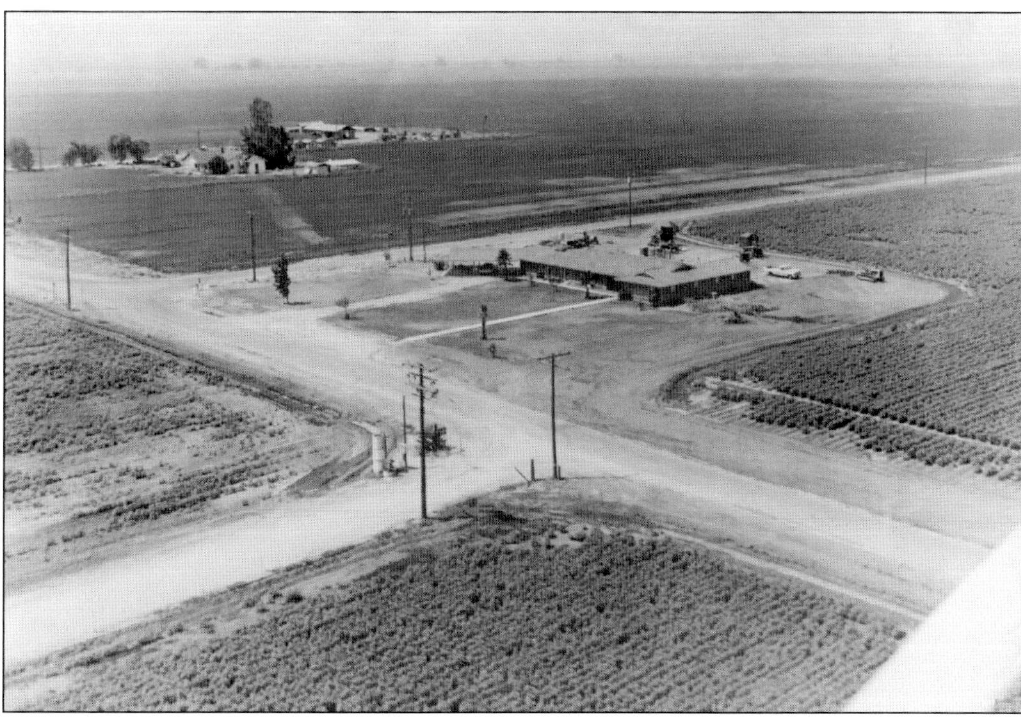

This image shows what was once the Torrez family home, long since sold to a local diary. (Richard Torrez and the Tulare Athletic Club)

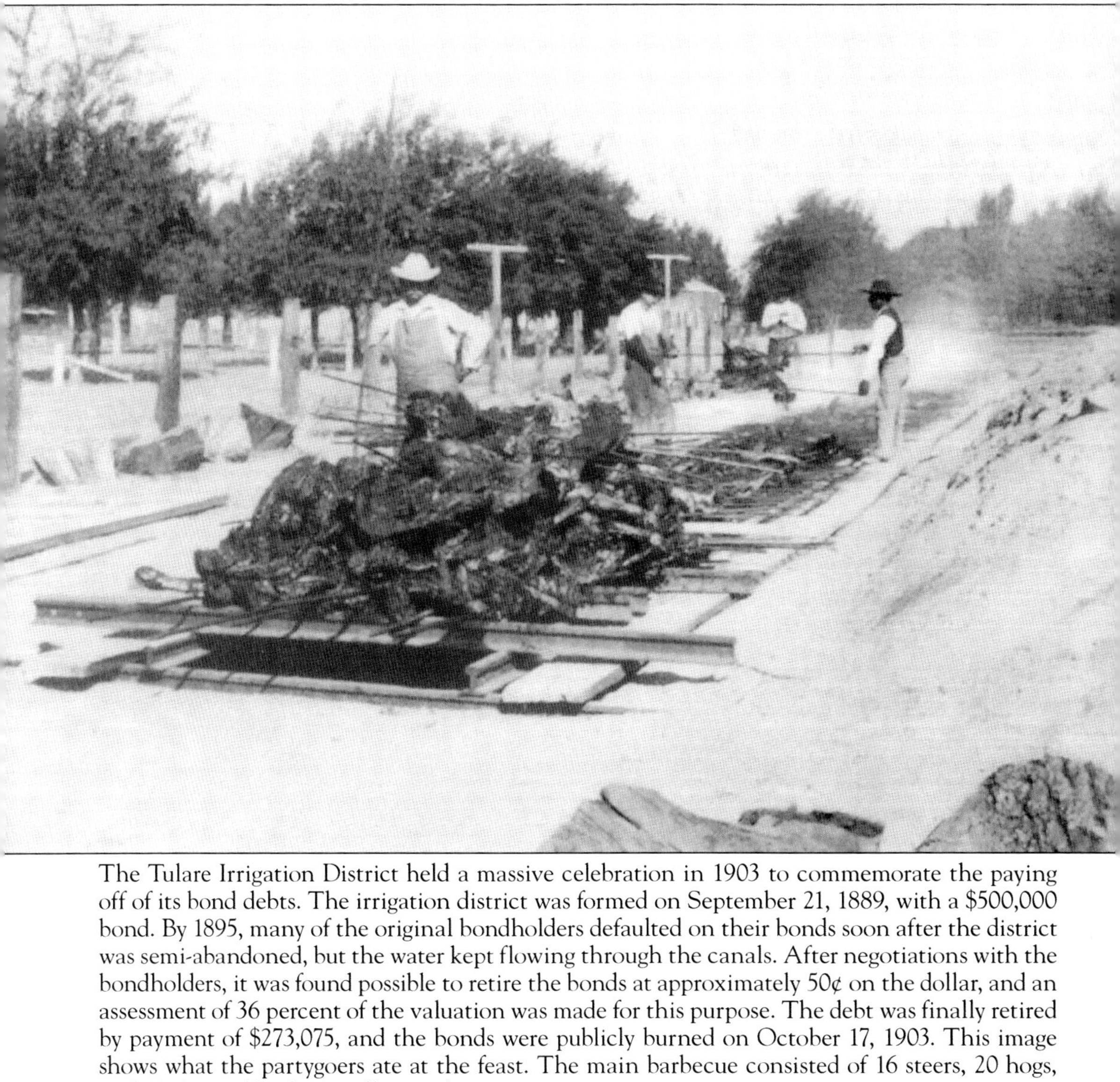

The Tulare Irrigation District held a massive celebration in 1903 to commemorate the paying off of its bond debts. The irrigation district was formed on September 21, 1889, with a $500,000 bond. By 1895, many of the original bondholders defaulted on their bonds soon after the district was semi-abandoned, but the water kept flowing through the canals. After negotiations with the bondholders, it was found possible to retire the bonds at approximately 50¢ on the dollar, and an assessment of 36 percent of the valuation was made for this purpose. The debt was finally retired by payment of $273,075, and the bonds were publicly burned on October 17, 1903. This image shows what the partygoers ate at the feast. The main barbecue consisted of 16 steers, 20 hogs, and 20 sheep. (Author's collection.)

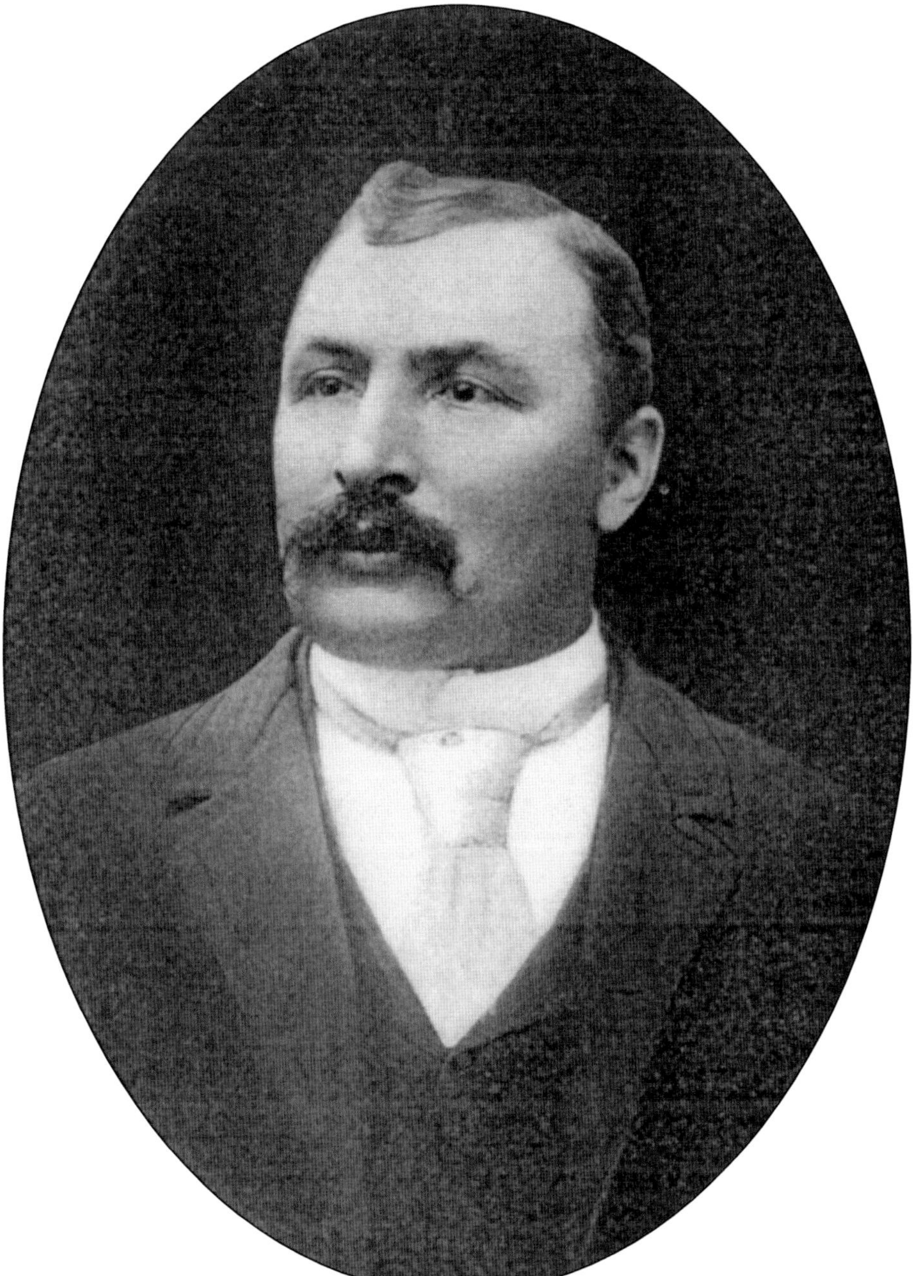

Joseph LaMarche was born in Montreal, Canada, and came to Tulare County in 1883. He was prominent in organizing the Dairymen's Cooperative Creamery Company and was elected one of its directors three months after it began business. In 1906, he was a director in the Cooperative Creamery Company of Tulare. LaMarche was also one of the organizers of the Rochdale Company and was a stockholder in the Tulare Canning Company and the Tulare Milling Company. He was also a director of the Fair Association of Tulare County, which constructed a racetrack and held fairs for two years, and he was the owner of the track. In 1908, LaMarche was elected president of the Bank of Tulare. (Author's collection.)

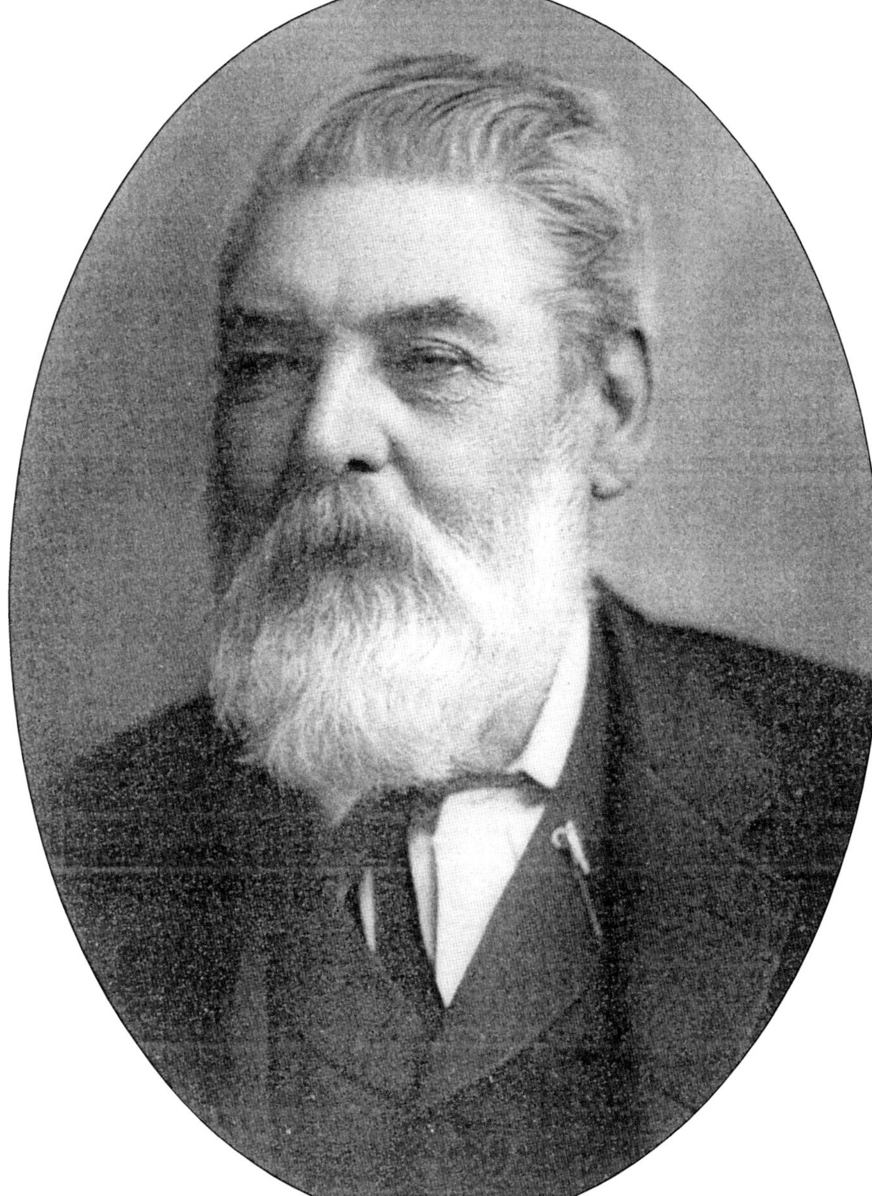

Josiah Otis Lovejoy was born in Duxbury, Massachusetts, on March 29, 1833. He lived in Boston until he went with his uncle to sea on a trading vessel bound for Honolulu in 1845. He sailed to California on his uncle's ship, *Roebuck*, which cast anchor at San Francisco on the Fourth of July, 1852, after a voyage of 150 days from Boston. In October, he started to mine in Mariposa, and in 1855, he bought a sawmill on Snow Creek. In May 1871, Lovejoy moved to Tulare County and established his home in July. In December 1871, his family joined him. When Lovejoy arrived in town, the roof was just being placed on the railroad depot. For 16 years, he served as justice of the peace and public notary, and acquired many dairy and fruit farms. Emma Lovejoy, his wife, died in San Francisco on July 17, 1917, at the age of 88. Of their 13 children, only Mrs. Jessie Garrison remained in Tulare. (Author's collection.)

On the far right is Manuel Torrez running track at Tulare Union High School in the 1940s; the other runners are unidentified. Manuel's son Richard Torrez is currently a board member of the Tulare Regional Medical Center and the director of the Tulare Athletic Club. (Richard Torrez and the Tulare Athletic Club.)

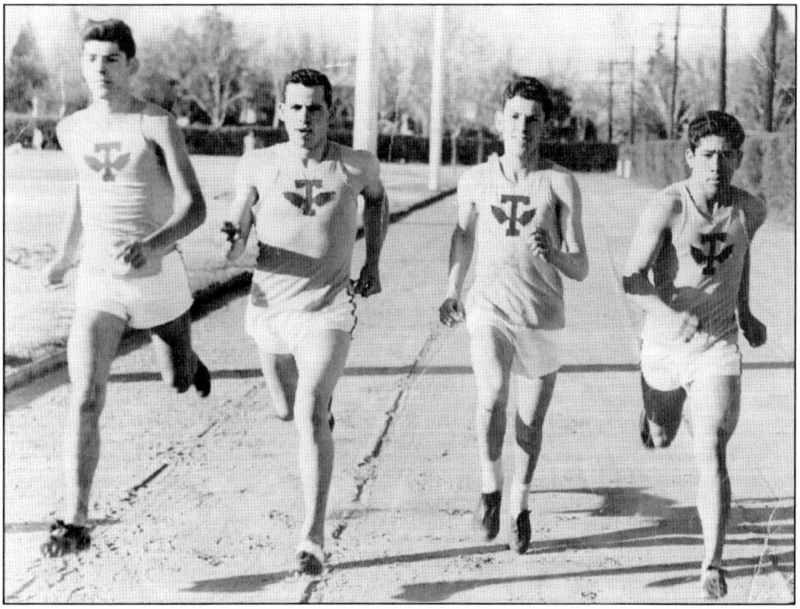

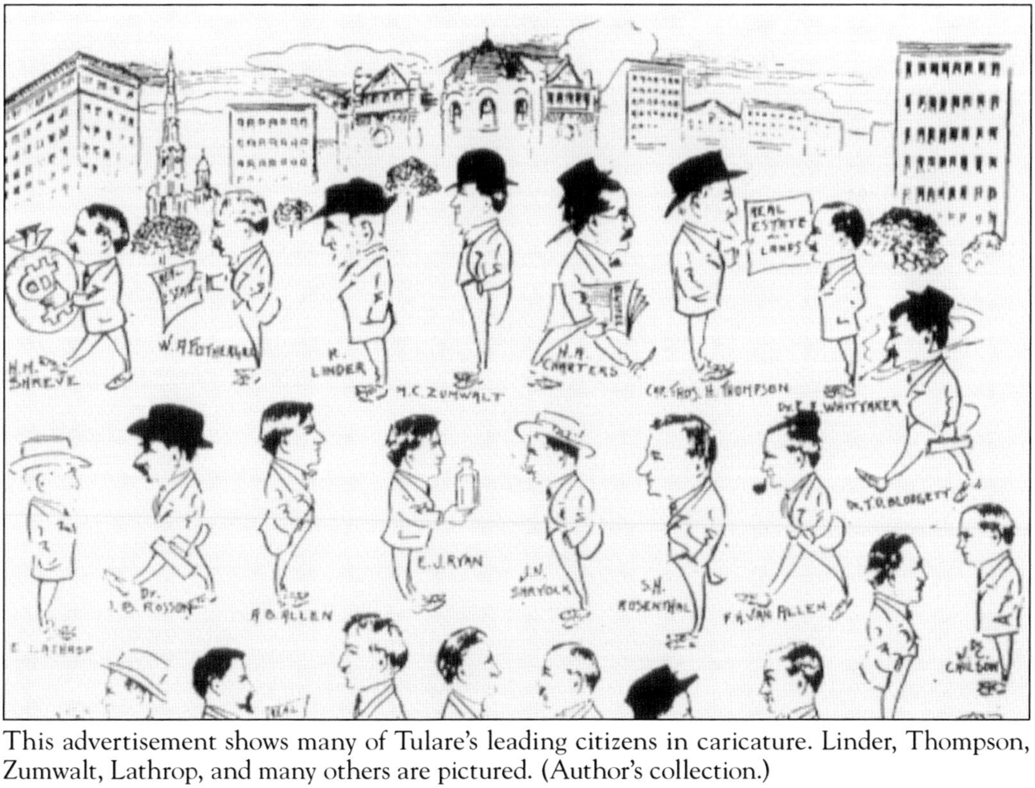

This advertisement shows many of Tulare's leading citizens in caricature. Linder, Thompson, Zumwalt, Lathrop, and many others are pictured. (Author's collection.)

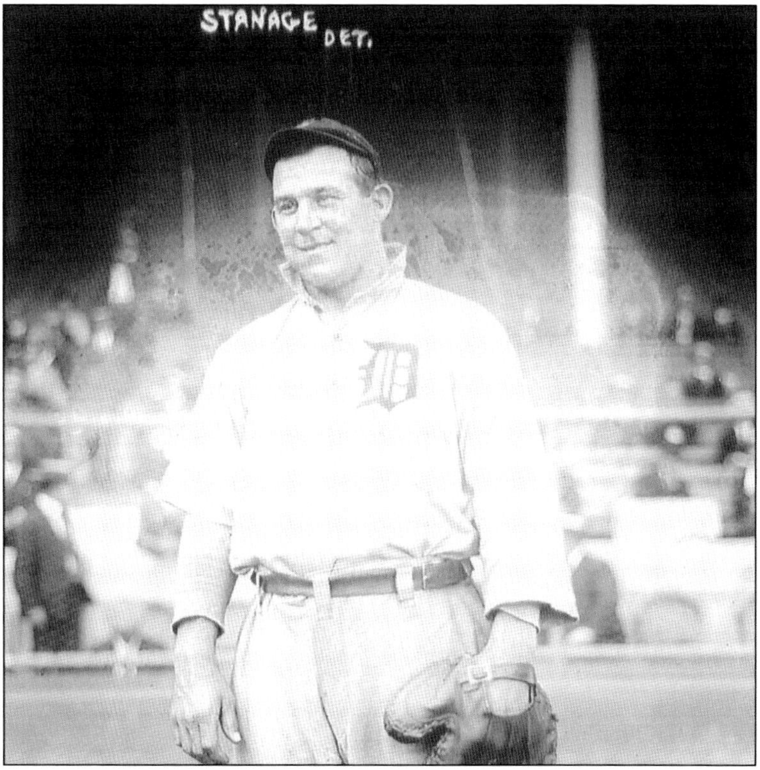

Oscar Stanage played for the Detroit Tigers and in Los Angeles and Sacramento of the Pacific Coast League. In 1920, newly appointed player-manager Ty Cobb released Stanage, making room for Johnny Bassler as the Tigers catcher. Cobb hired Stanage as a coach in 1925, and he coached with the Pittsburgh Pirates from 1927 to 1931. He died in Detroit in 1964 at 81 and is buried in that city's Evergreen Cemetery. (Library of Congress.)

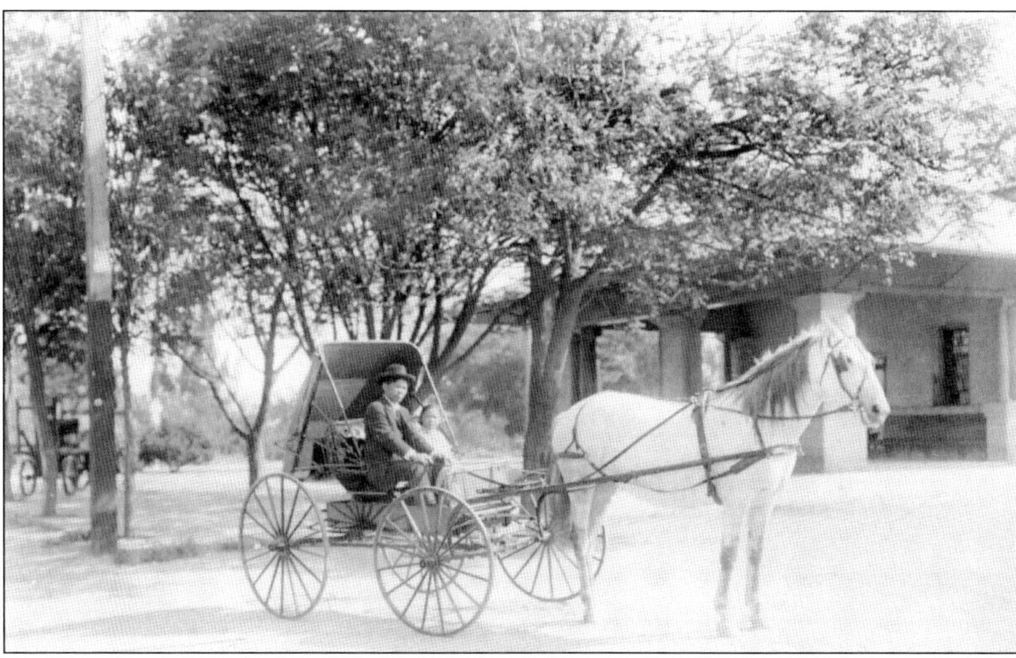

Ling Joe and his daughter Nunn Reve, 7, are seen in a horse-drawn carriage in front of the Santa Fe Railway depot in Tulare in 1908. The Santa Fe depot was located on the north side of tracks just east of K Street, north of San Joaquin Avenue. One of its later uses was as a clubhouse for a model railroad club. (Tulare County Library.)

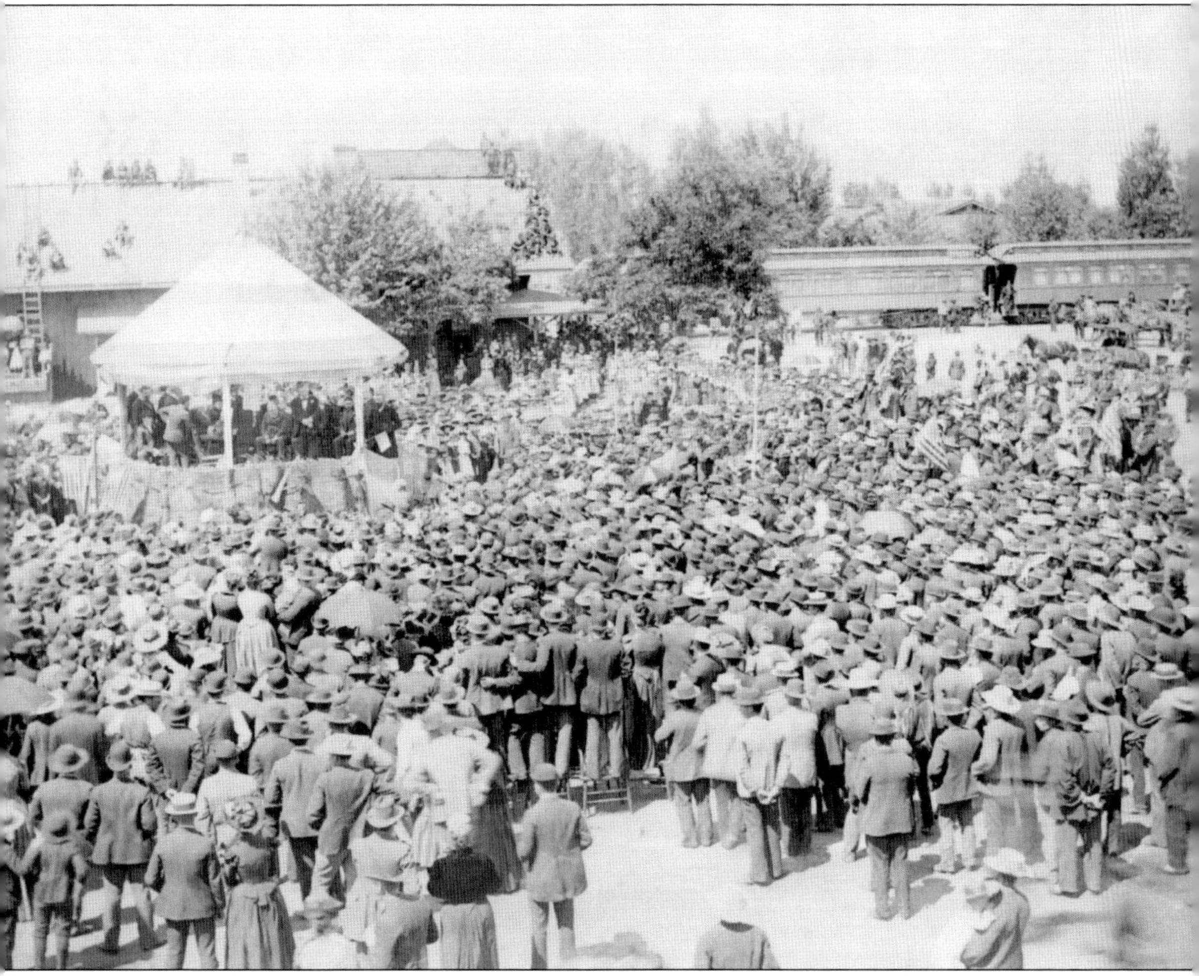

Benjamin Harrison made a campaign stop in Tulare on April 25, 1888. The speech was given on a section of a fallen giant sequoia that Capt. Thomas H. Thompson, president of the committee for the entertainment, brought to town. The stump had a diameter of 29 feet. Harrison arrived at 10:00 a.m., and after being introduced by future governor Henry Markham, he delivered his short speech in front of 6,000 people. Harrison began, "My Friends—This seems to be a very happy and smiling audience and I am sure that the gladness which is in your hearts and in your faces does not depend at all upon the presence of this little company of strangers who tarry with you for a moment" and ended his speech, "God bless them [children], every one; keep them in the lives they are to live and from all that evil, fill their little hearts with sunshine and their mature lives with grace and usefulness." (Annie R. Mitchell History Room, Tulare County Library.)

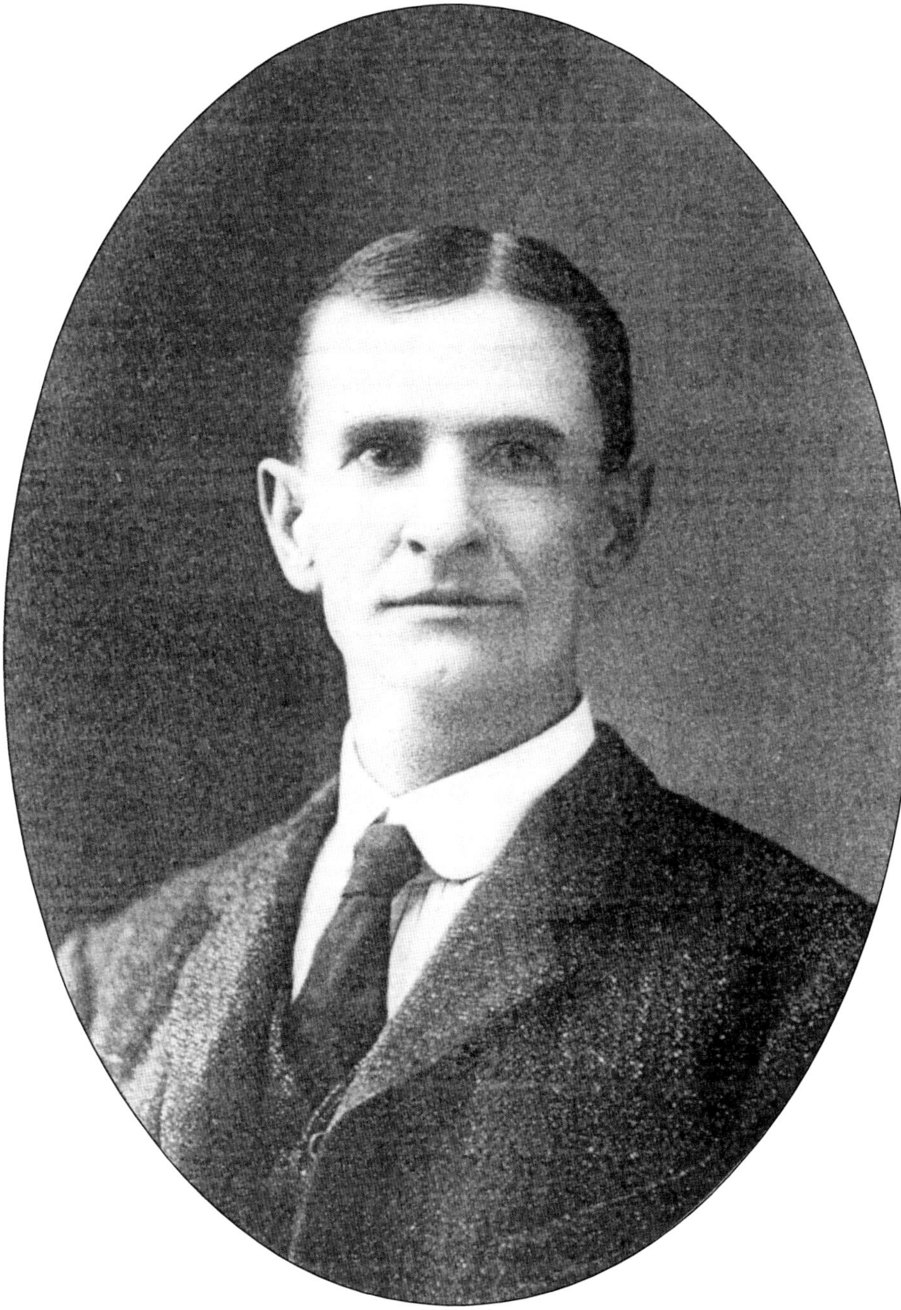

Tulare postmaster William P. Radcliff, shown here in 1913, was very popular. Radcliff came to Tulare in 1882 and become a brakeman on the Southern Pacific Railroad. A year later, he was made a conductor on the route between Tulare and Huron. In 1888, he left the railroad for a position with Braly & Blythe, a real estate agency. Radcliff resigned in 1892 to become cashier for the Tulare County Bank and the Tulare Savings Bank. In August 1896, he became assistant cashier of the Bank of Tulare. In 1901, he contracted typhoid fever and upon regaining his health he resumed his duties at the Bank of Tulare. In April 1902, Pres. Theodore Roosevelt appointed him postmaster of Tulare. (Author's collection.)

Seven

AGRICULTURE

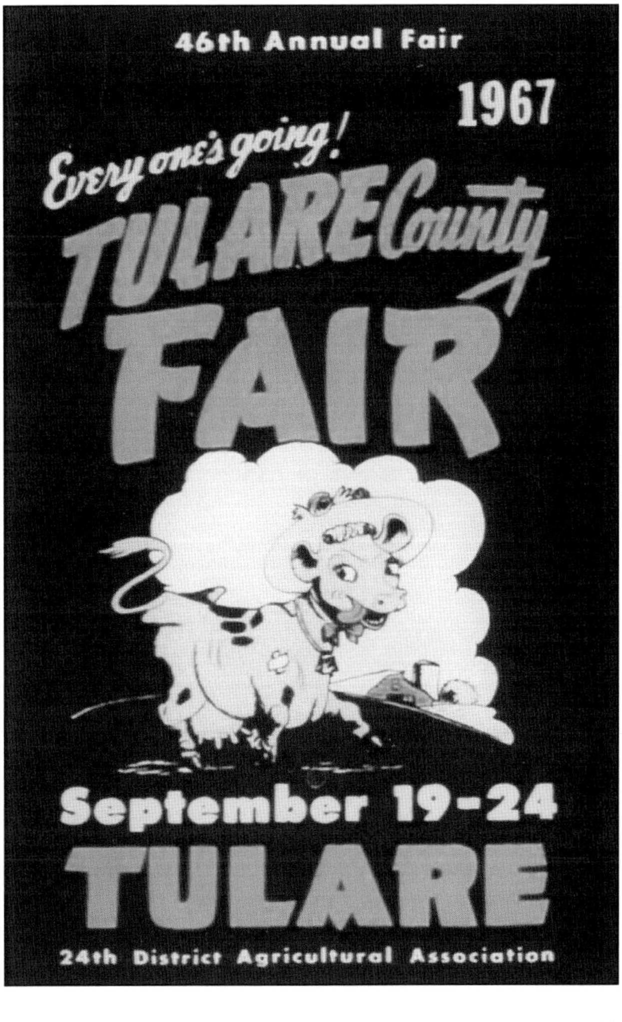

This 1967 poster is for the 46th annual Tulare County Fair. The original county fair began in Tulare and was known as the Citrus Fair. In the early days, the fair was held at the City Park (later Zumwalt Park) and used the pavilion at the park for its covered areas. (Author's collection.)

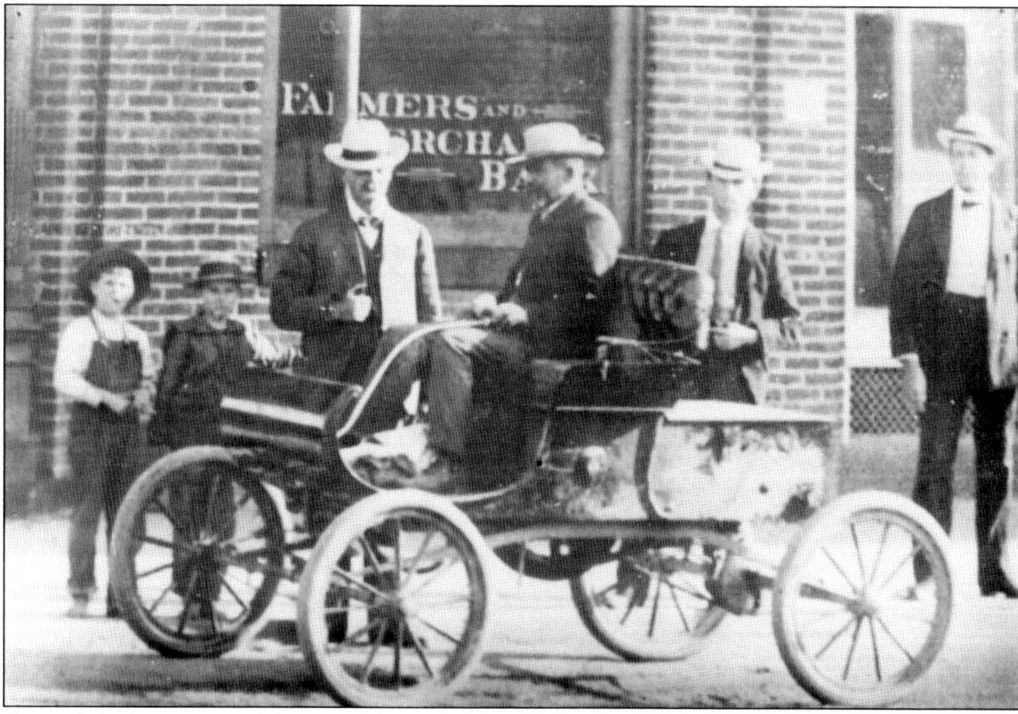

One of the first automobiles in Tulare was owned by John Goble, pictured here in front of the Farmers and Merchants Bank at K Street and Kern Avenue. The driver is Linford A. Moore, with Goble standing to the left. (Tulare County Library.)

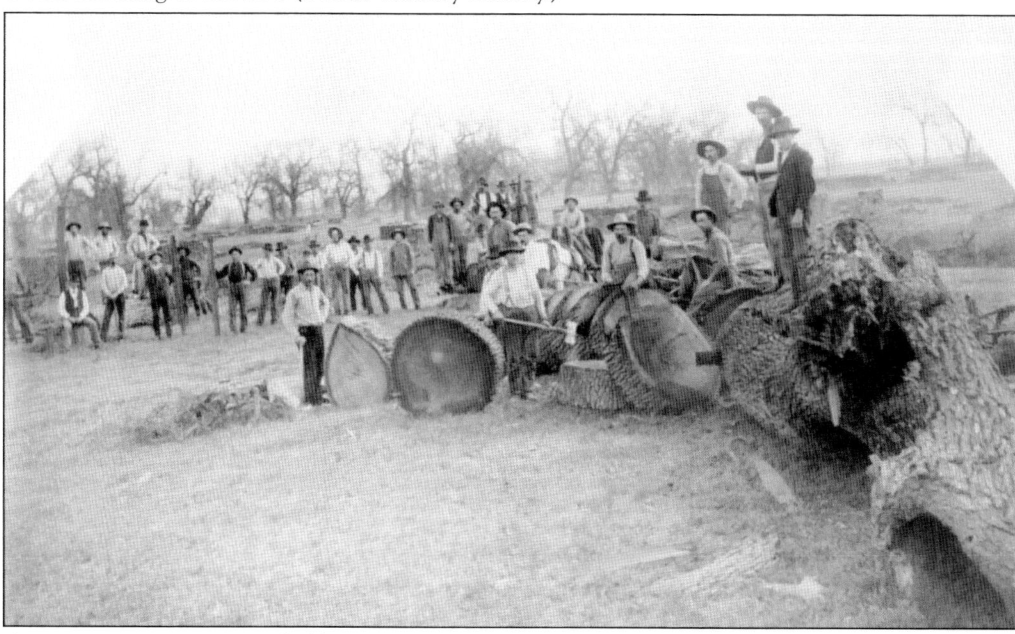

A tree-cutting contest was held at Centennial Grove, which encompassed a large section of Tulare and the surrounding area in the late 1800s. The early pioneers who wanted to farm sections that were flat cleared the area of the oak woodland. The area pictured here is near J Street and Prosperity Avenue. (Tulare County Library.)

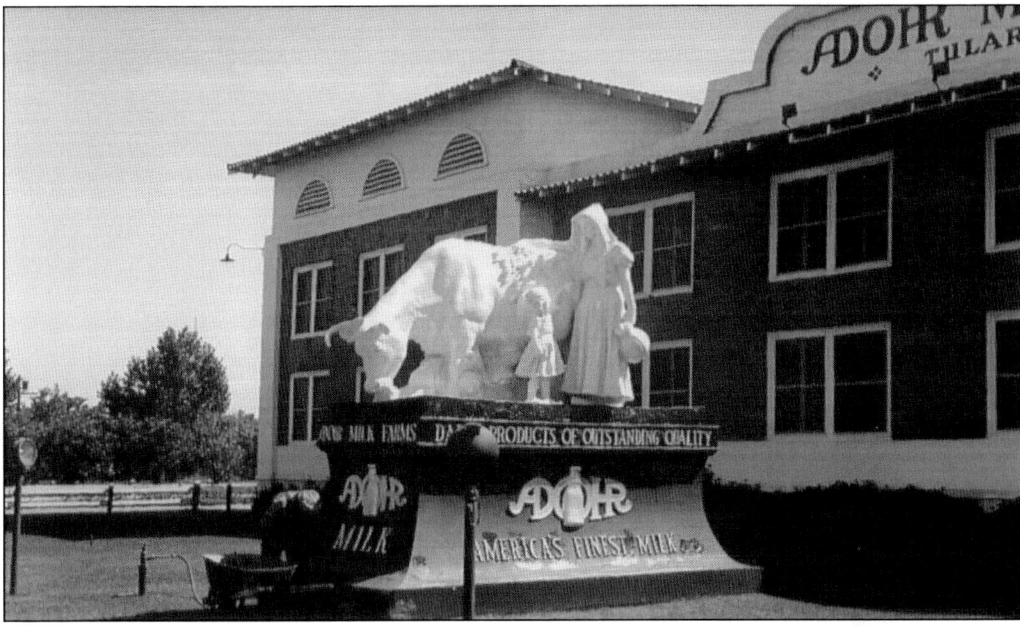

The *Adohr Milkmaid* is shown in this 1939 photograph in its original condition with the Adohr processing plant in the background. The statue is located on North J Street just past Cross Street on the right side a few blocks south of Pleasant Street. The dairy—"Rhoda" spelled backward—was named for the wife of Merritt Anderson, the company's founder. (Library of Congress.)

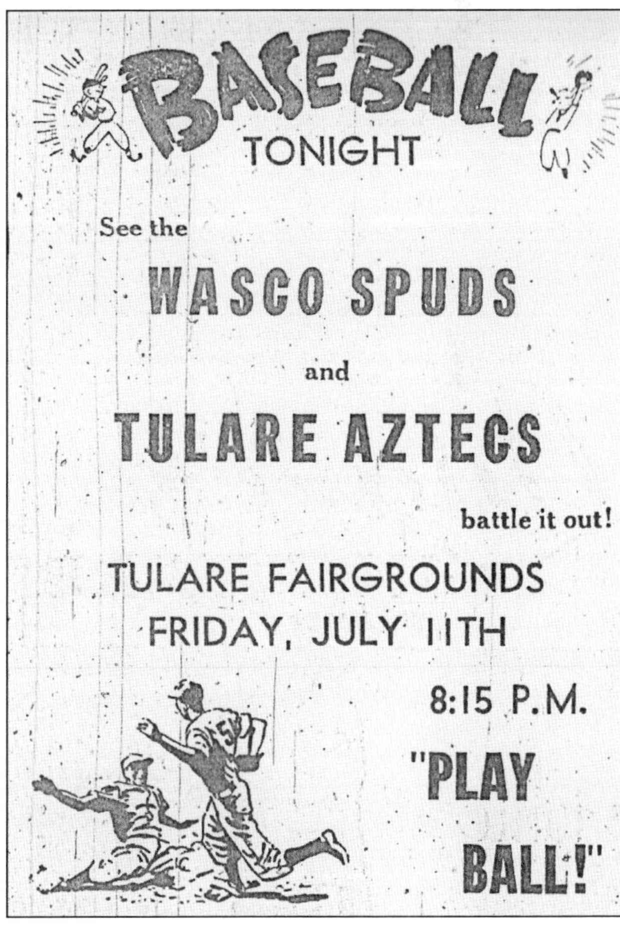

This advertisement is for a baseball game between the Tulare Aztecs and the Wasco Spuds in 1952. The manager of the Aztecs was Pilar Cuellar, who died in 2012. Cuellar was a very well-known baseball man in Tulare. (Author's collection.)

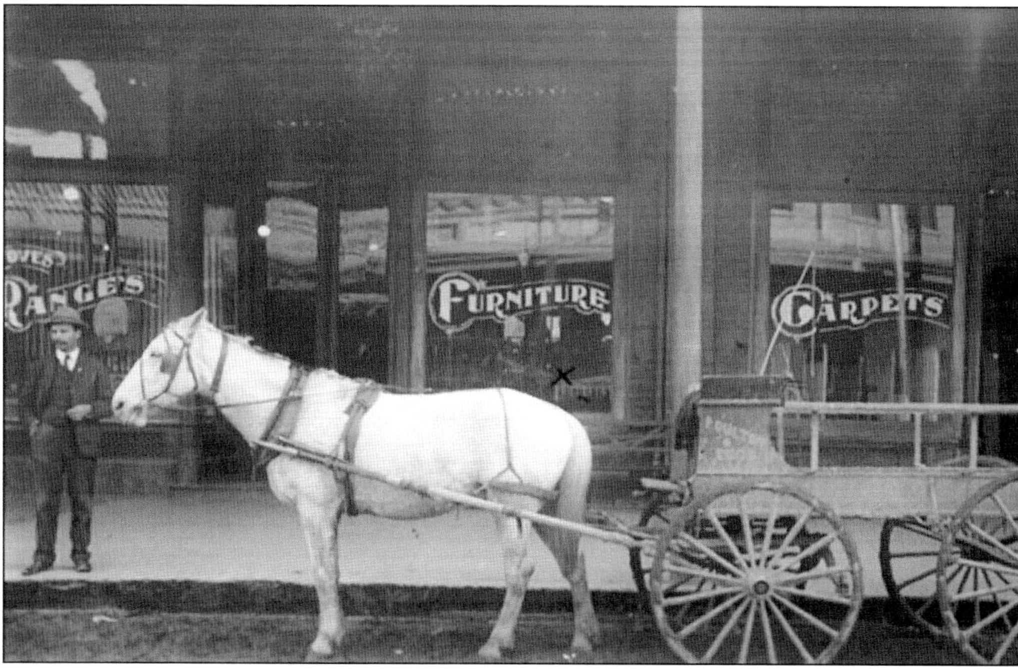

A wagon is pictured in front of store that sells stoves, carpets, and furniture. Note that the wheels on the wagon are covered with mud. (Tulare County Library.)

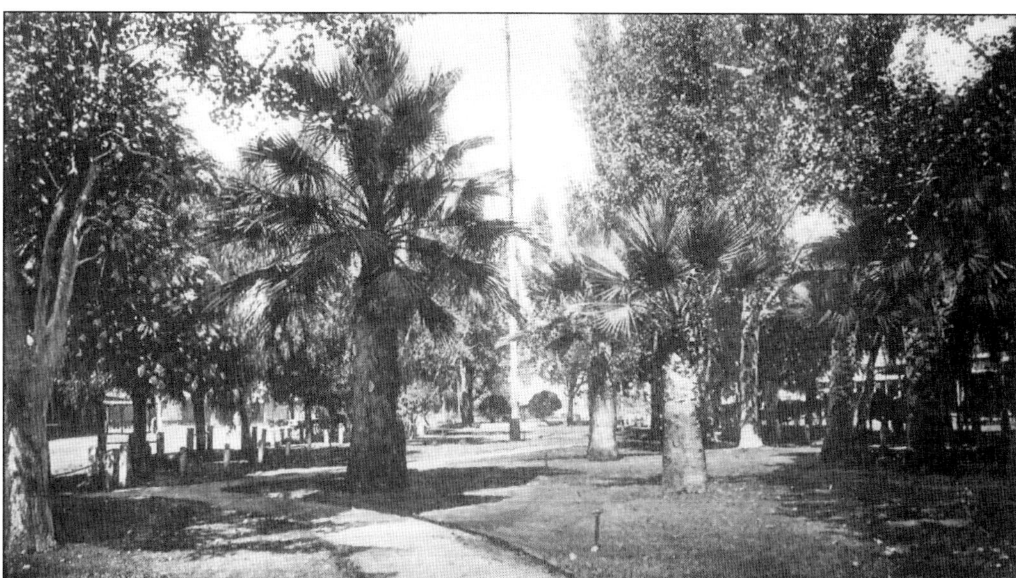

This is the view looking north in the south portion of Front Street Park. On the right is the business section, and on the left, the Southern Pacific depot is barely visible. One of the landmarks is a flagpole in the center of the park. Today, a Walgreens store is at this location. (Author's collection.)

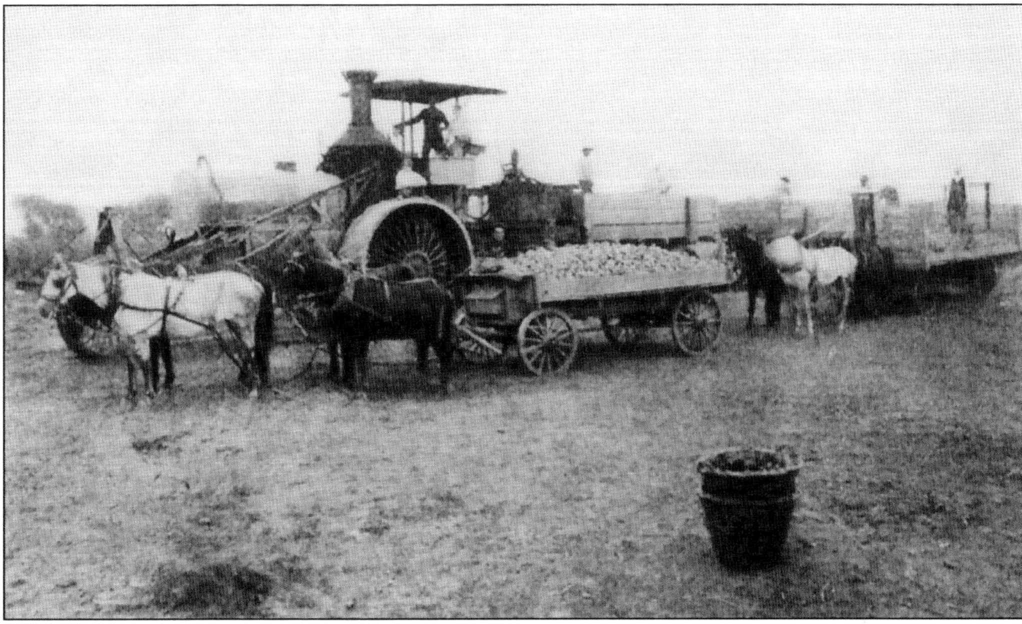

Early Tulare was primarily a railroad town, with machine shops, workshops, and a roundhouse. That ended in 1891, when the Southern Pacific relocated its roundhouse and machine shops to Bakersfield. The town turned to an agricultural-based economy. Besides farms for dairy, grapes, and other produce, beets were being hauled to Tulare and turned into sugar at the factory. (Author's collection.)

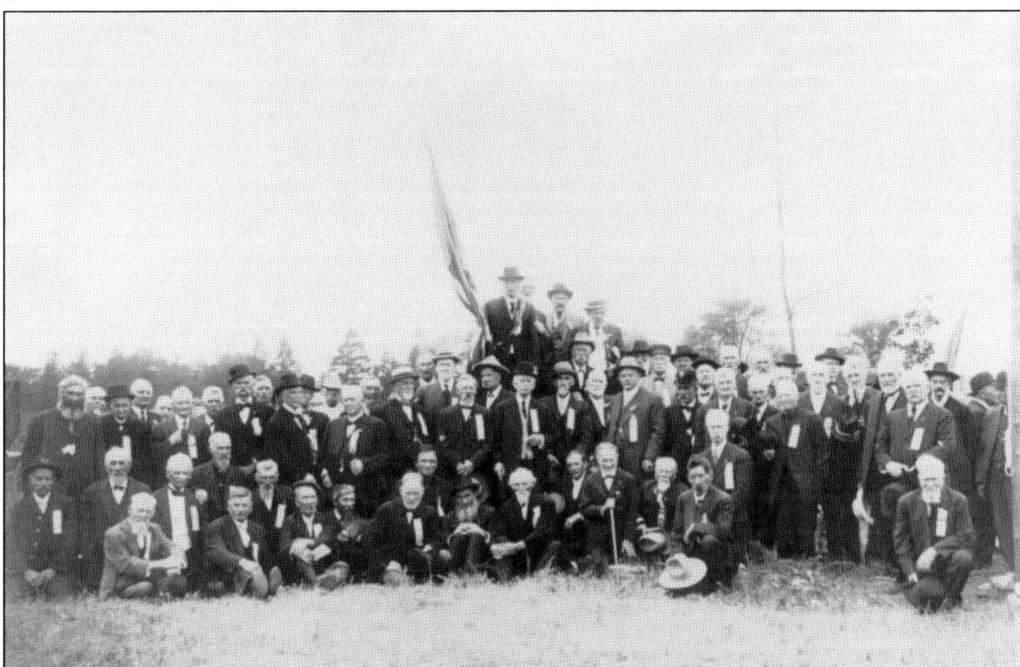

A group gathering of the California Chapter of the Grand Army of the Republic at City Park (Zumwalt Park) is held in 1892. Capt. Thomas H. Thompson was its commander until it disbanded. The GAR was an association of Union Civil War veterans. (Tulare County Library.)

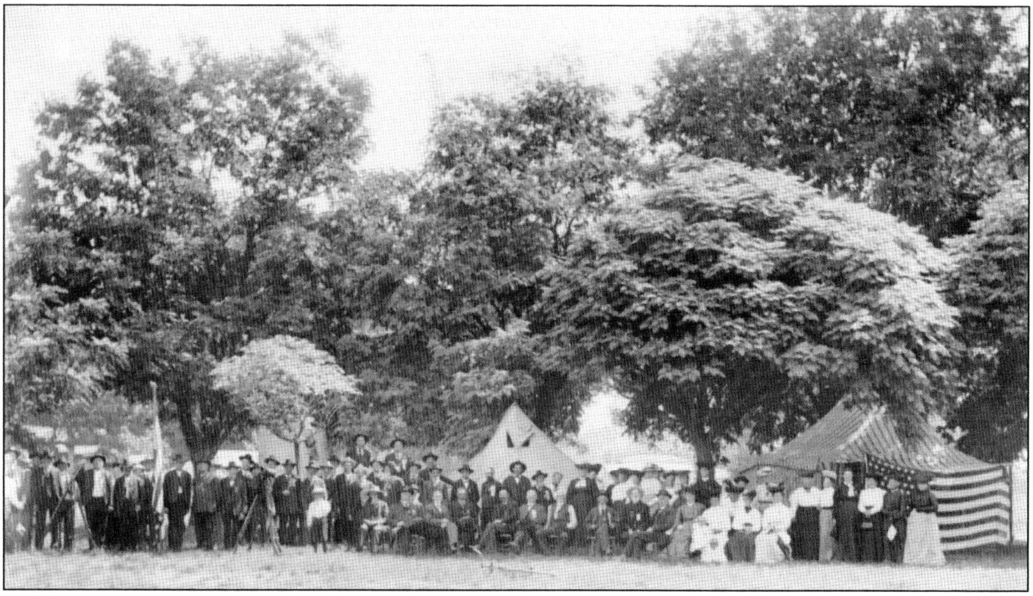

A Grand Army of the Republic encampment at City Park, now Zumwalt Park, is pictured in 1892. Note the large tree at the park and the bicycle that is in front of the group. (Tulare County Library.)

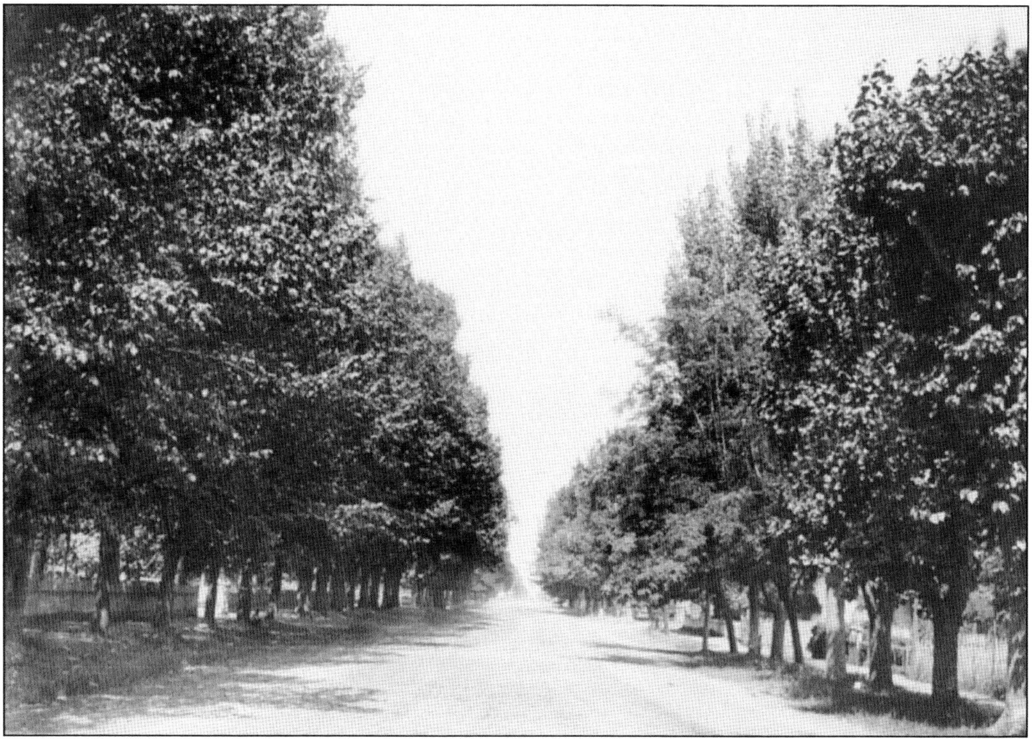

This is a view looking west to West Street along an unknown street in Tulare, possibly Tulare Avenue. On the left, someone sits under a tree. Most of these trees have been cut down or replaced with other trees, and Tulare Avenue no longer has the shady appearance it once had. (Author's collection.)

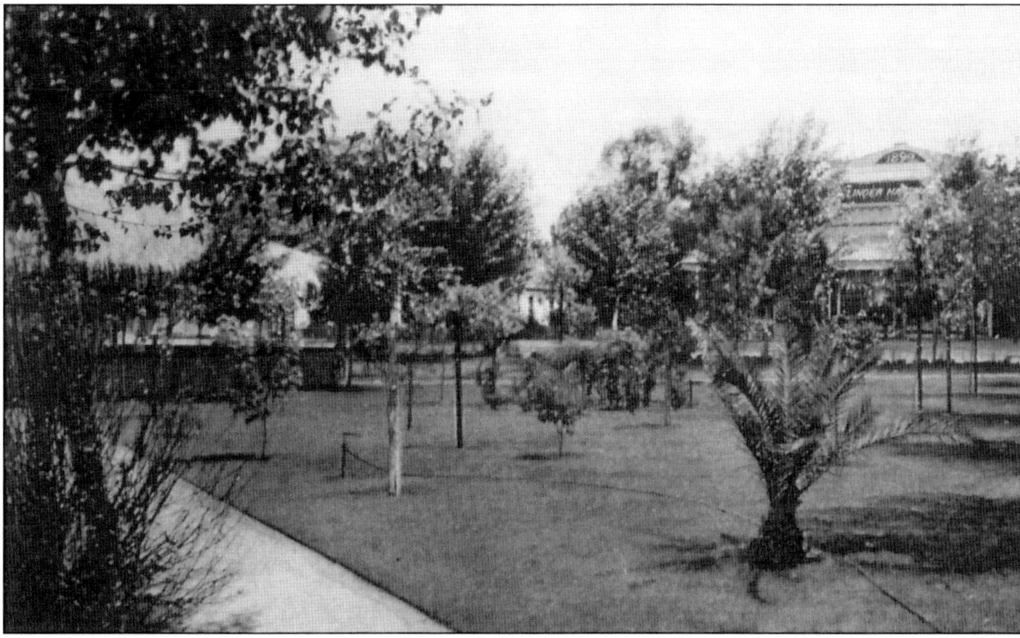

This is Linder Park with Linder Hardware in the background in the early 1900s before the First National Bank of Tulare was built on the corner site at Kern Avenue and K Street. (Author's collection.)

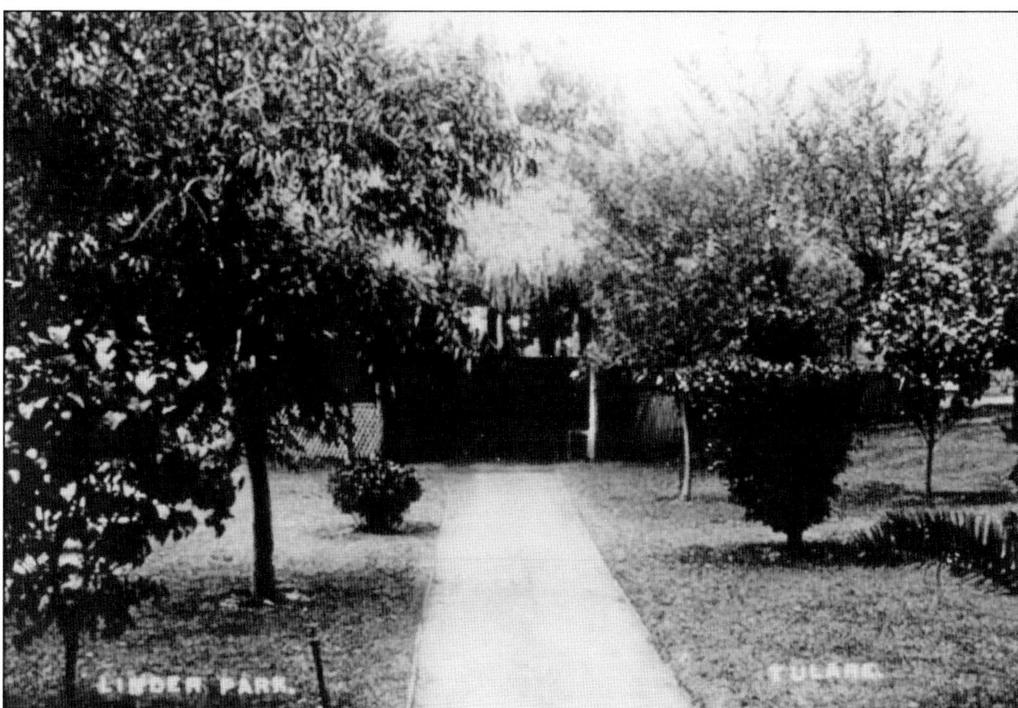

Linder Park is pictured with its thatched roof hut in the center and the old city hall and fire station to the right. To access the hut in the center of the park, the Linders had four paths constructed—one from each side. (Author's collection.)

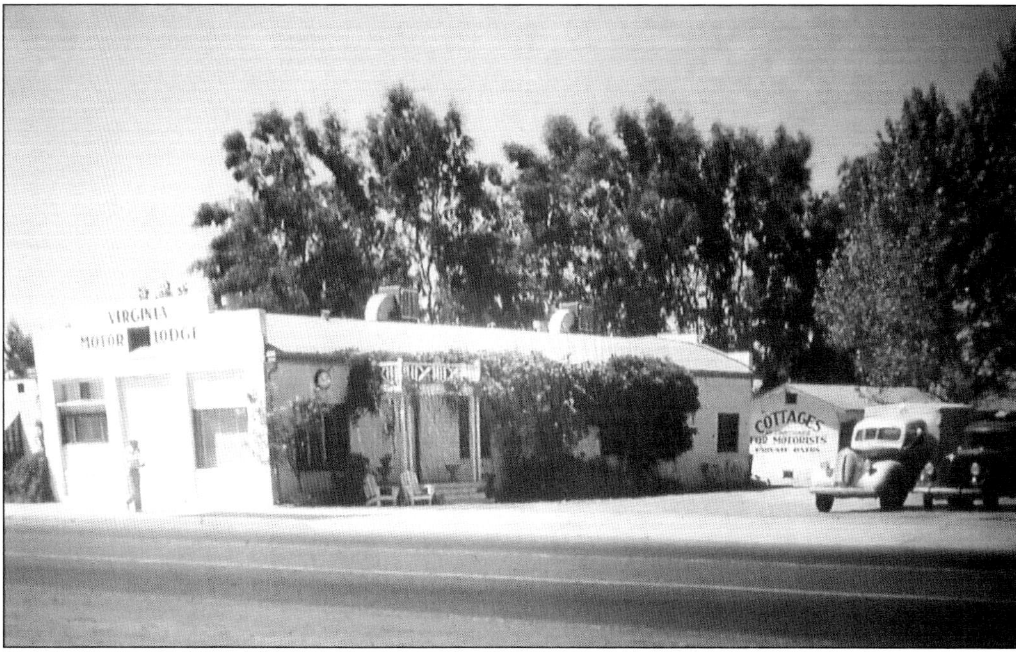

The Virginia Motor Lodge is shown with its cottages on South K Street as they appeared in the 1940s. (Author's collection.)

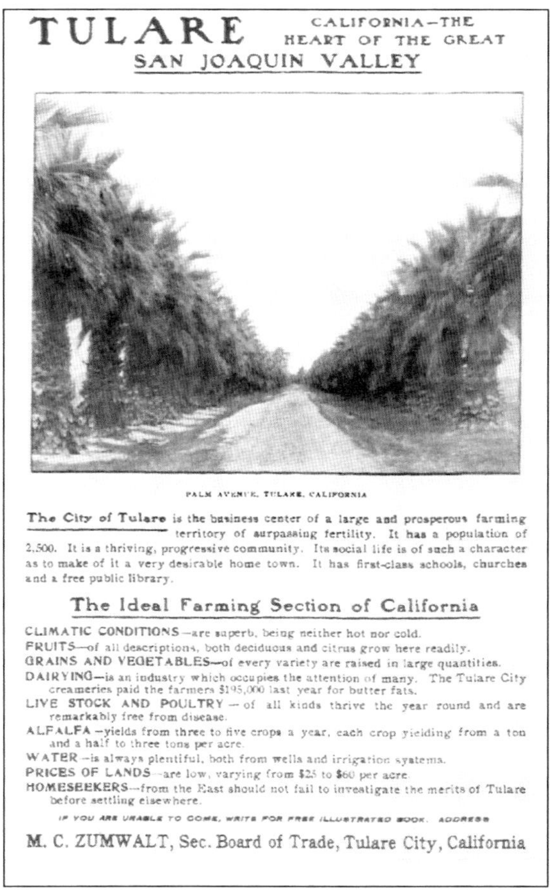

This advertisement for Tulare land shows Palm Drive and indicates Marcus C. Zumwalt, son of James B. Zumwalt, as the contact person. The palms led to the main house on the Paige and Morton Ranch in the early 1900s. The advertisement lists the price of land at $25 to $60 per acre. (Author's collection.)

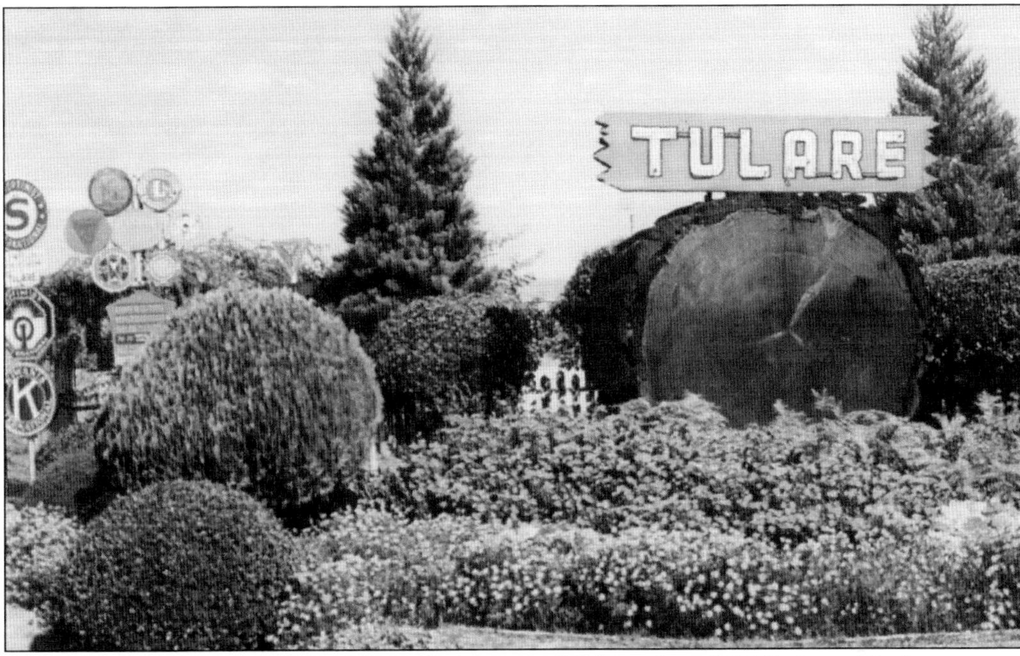

This is an old sign located on the northern edge of Tulare along US Highway 99. At one time, there were two signs with tree stumps to greet visitors into and out of Tulare—one at each end of town. (Author's collection.)

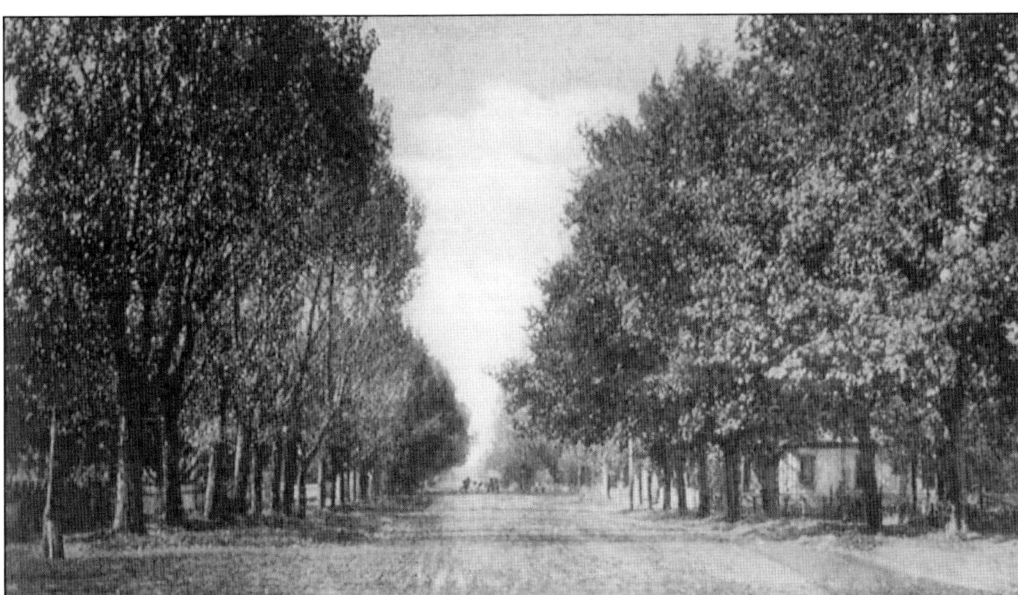

Pictured here are street views of Tulare Avenue. Trees were mature but have been since been removed or replaced. At right is a house, probably at the corner of I Street and Tulare Avenue. (Author's collection.)

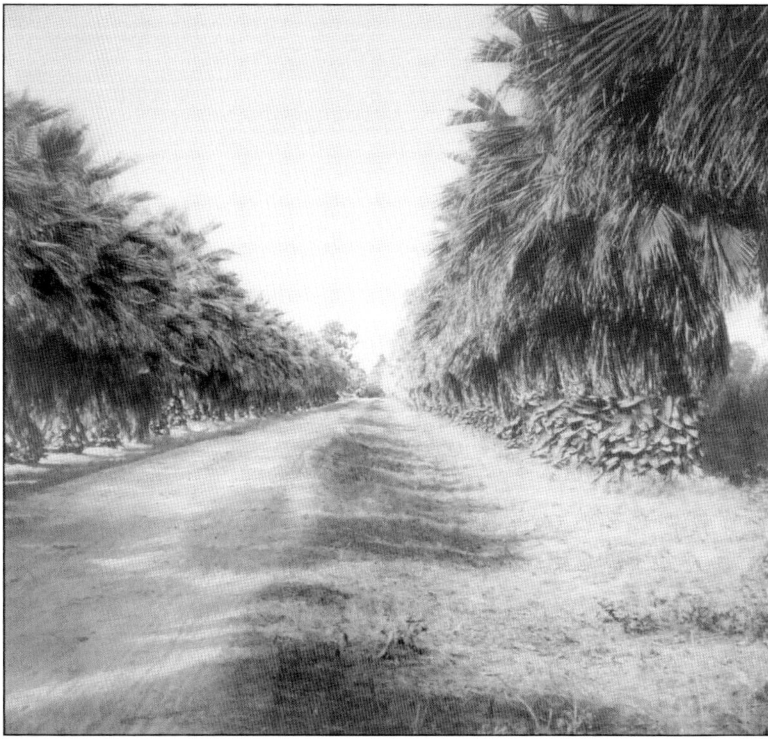

This image shows Palm Drive when the palms were not as tall as they are today. (Author's collection.)

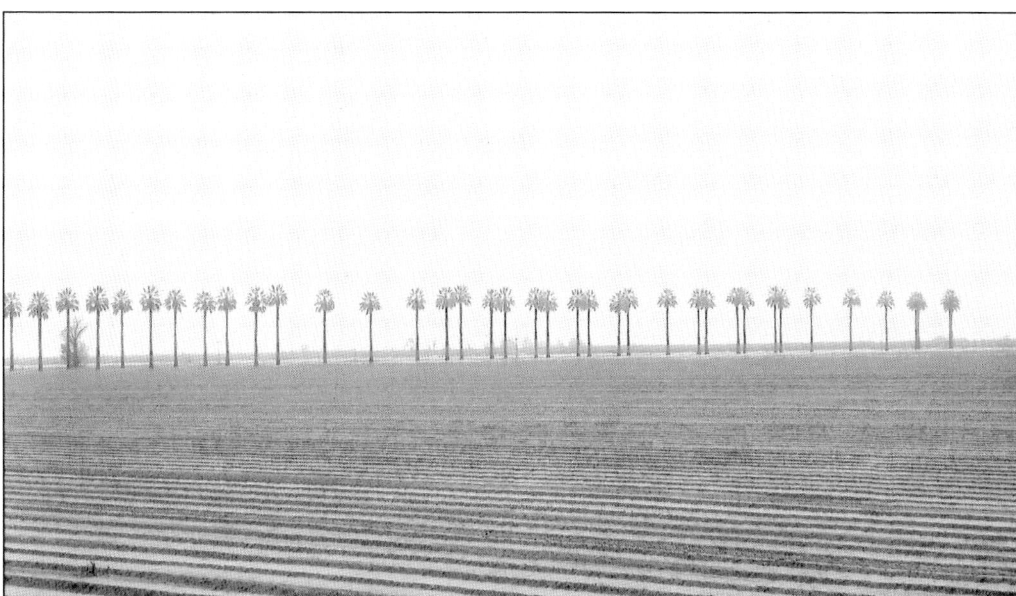

This is Palm Drive as it appears today. The only difference is that the Paige and Morton Ranch has been replaced by many small farms. (Author's collection.)

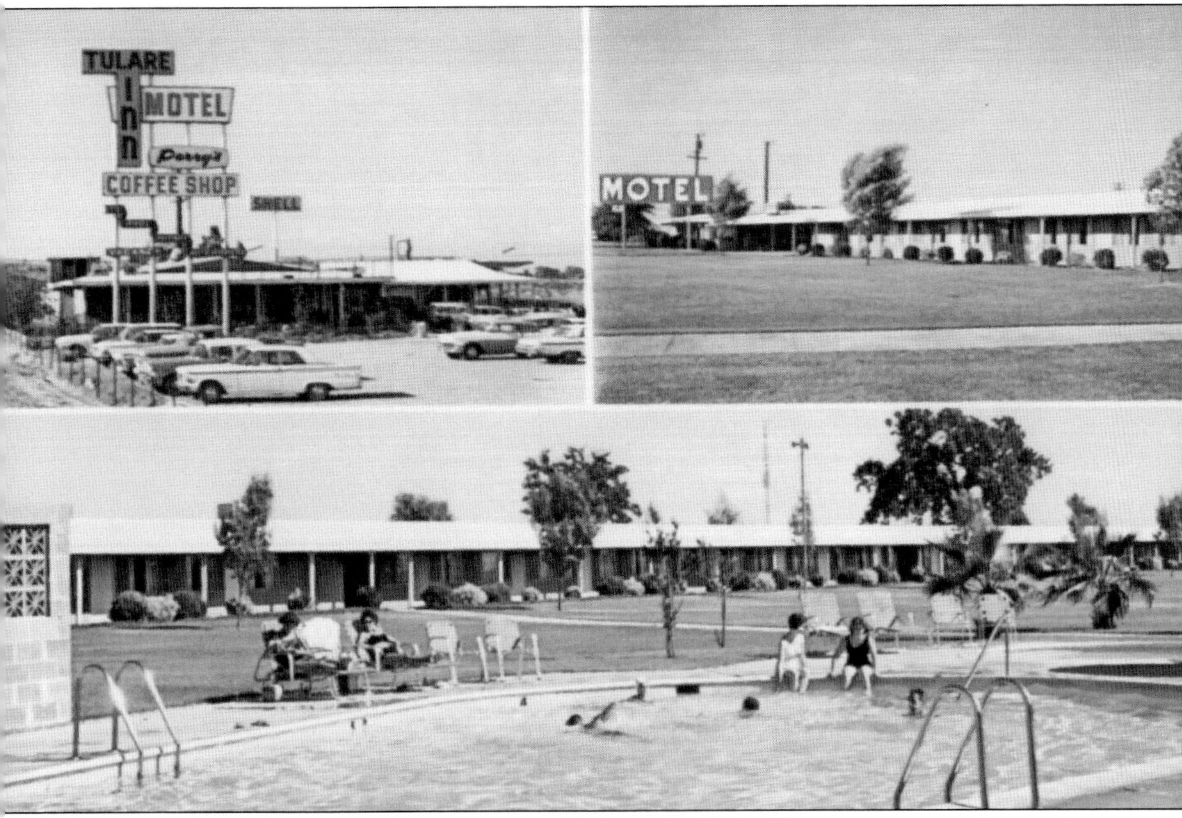

This is the Tulare Inn with Perry's restaurant in the early 1950s. The swimming pool is on the right off US Highway 99 and Paige Avenue. (Author's collection.)

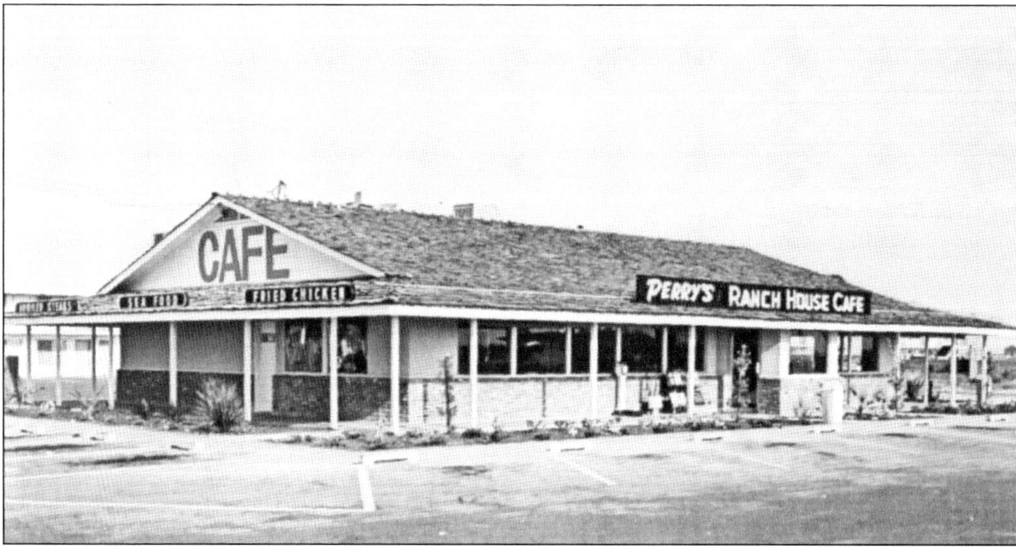

This is a side view of Perry's Ranch House Café, the original location of the Perry's restaurant chain. When US Highway 99 was completed in the early 1950s, Perry decided to build Perry's Sky Ranch Café at its intersection with Avenue 200. (Author's collection.)

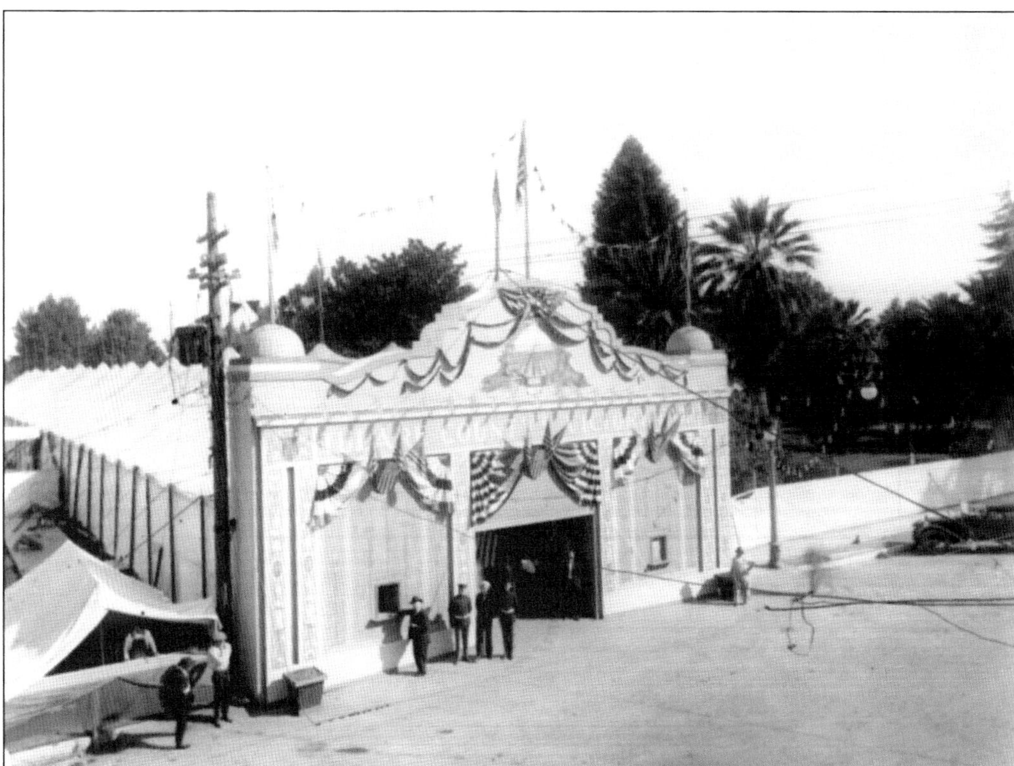

This photograph shows the pavilion of a tent show presented in Tulare in 1905. The event was the Tulare County Victory Fair. The location is probably the City Park, now called Zumwalt Park. (Tulare County Library.)

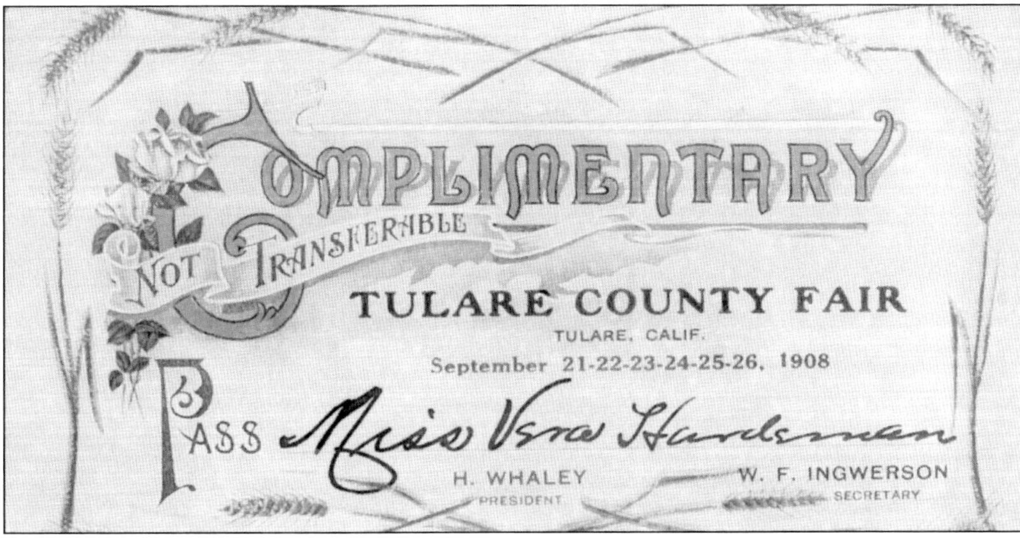

This is a Tulare County Fair pass from 1908. The president of the fair board was H. Whaley, and the secretary was W.F. Ingwerson. The county fair ran from September 21 until September 26 in 1908. (Tulare County Library.)

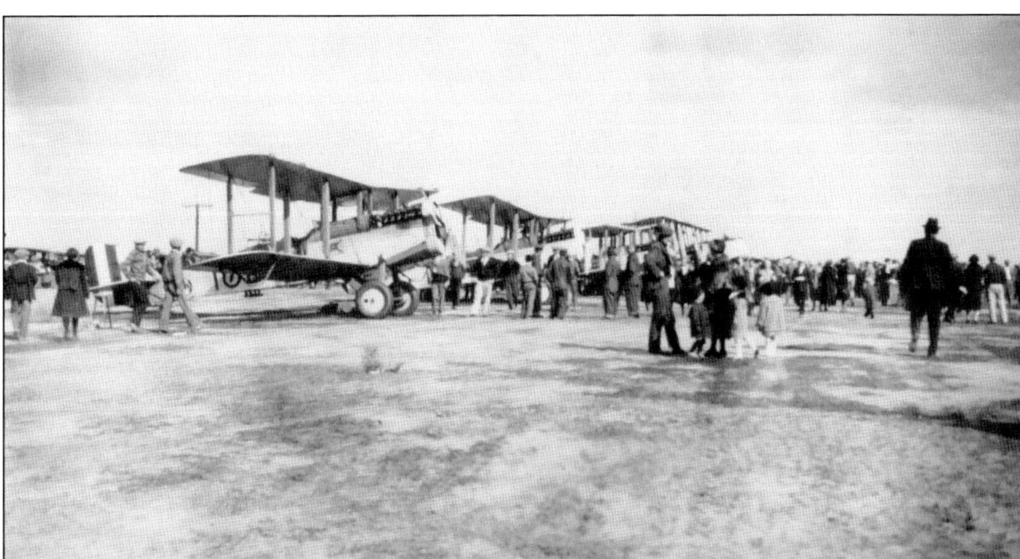

This is the Tulare airfield with planes on display for an air show about 1925. (Tulare County Library.)

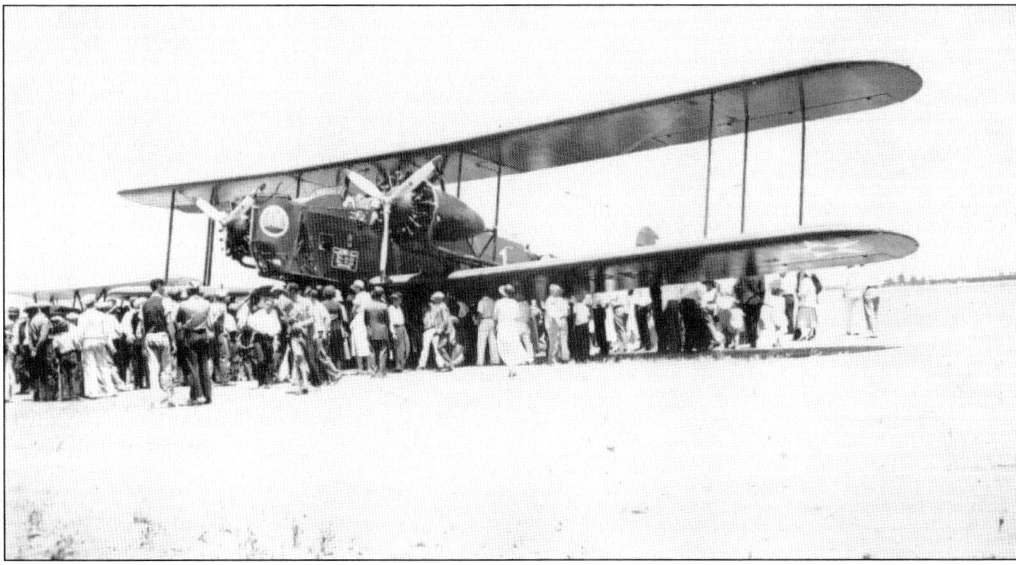

This airplane is on display about 1925 and was demonstrated at an air show in Tulare. (Tulare County Library.)

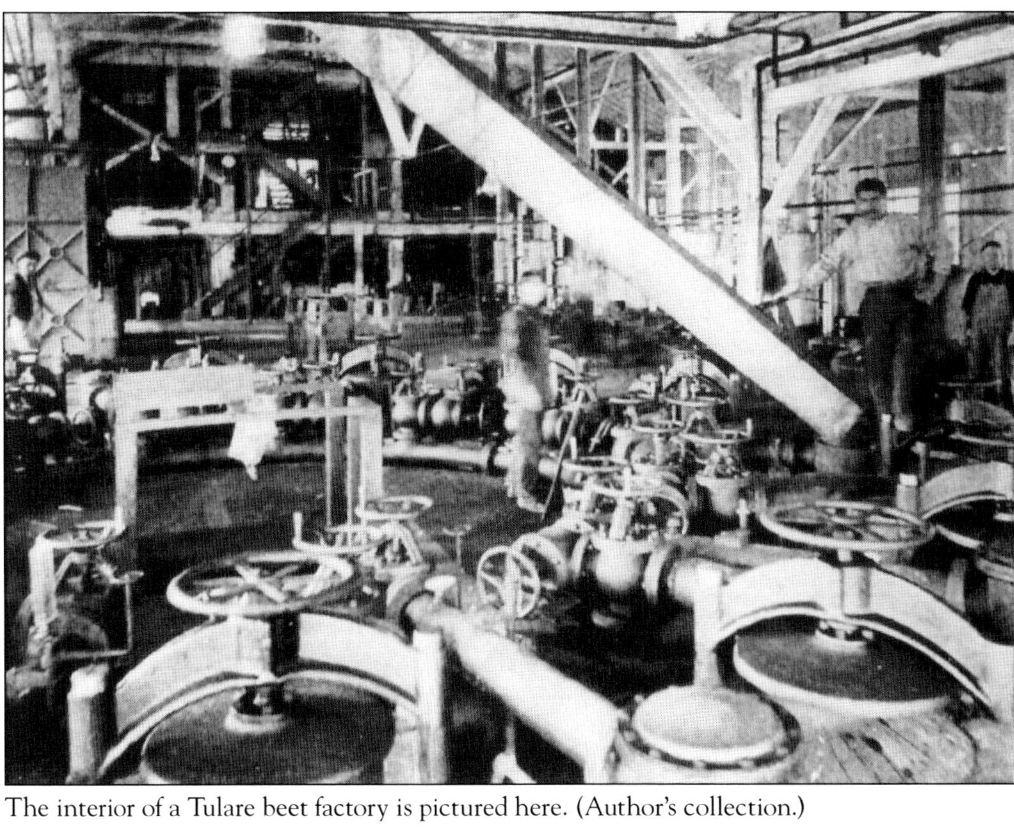

The interior of a Tulare beet factory is pictured here. (Author's collection.)

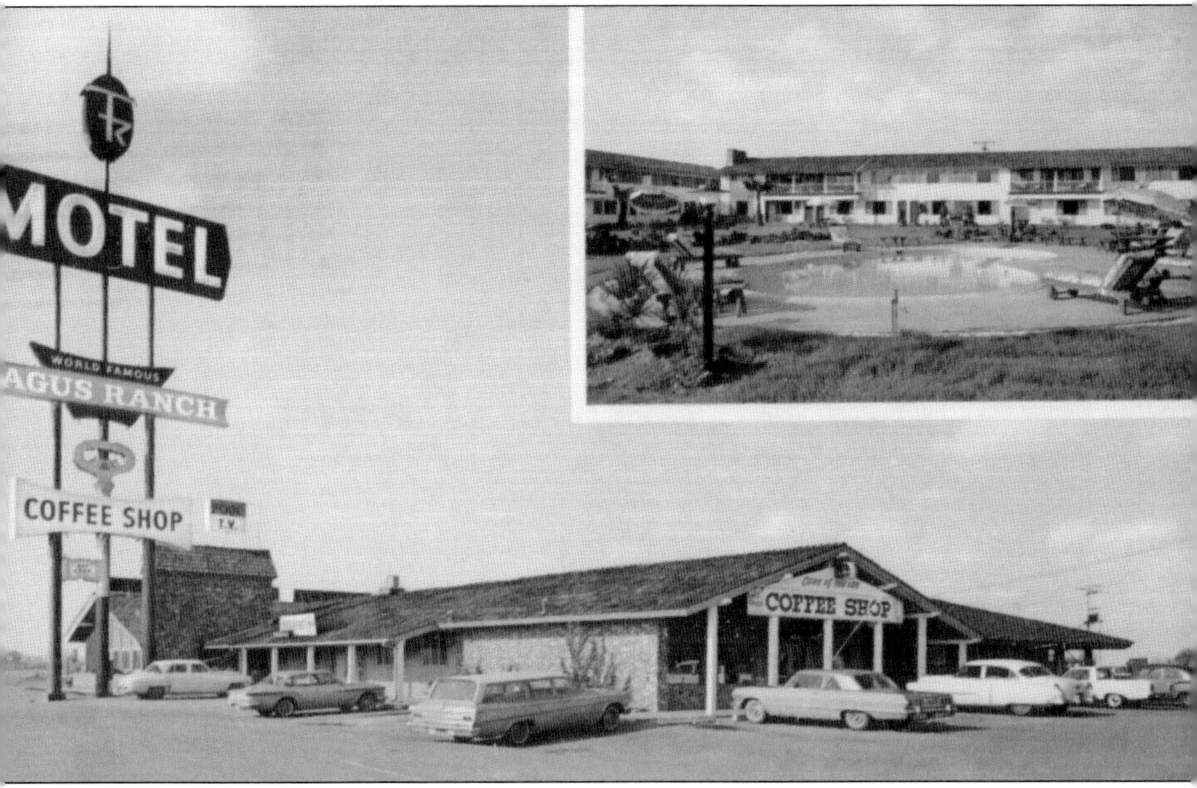

Tagus Ranch and Motel is pictured just north of Tulare as it looked at its peak, in the 1950s–1960s era. Now abandoned, it has become an eyesore and a haven for graffiti artists and vandals. (Author's collection.)

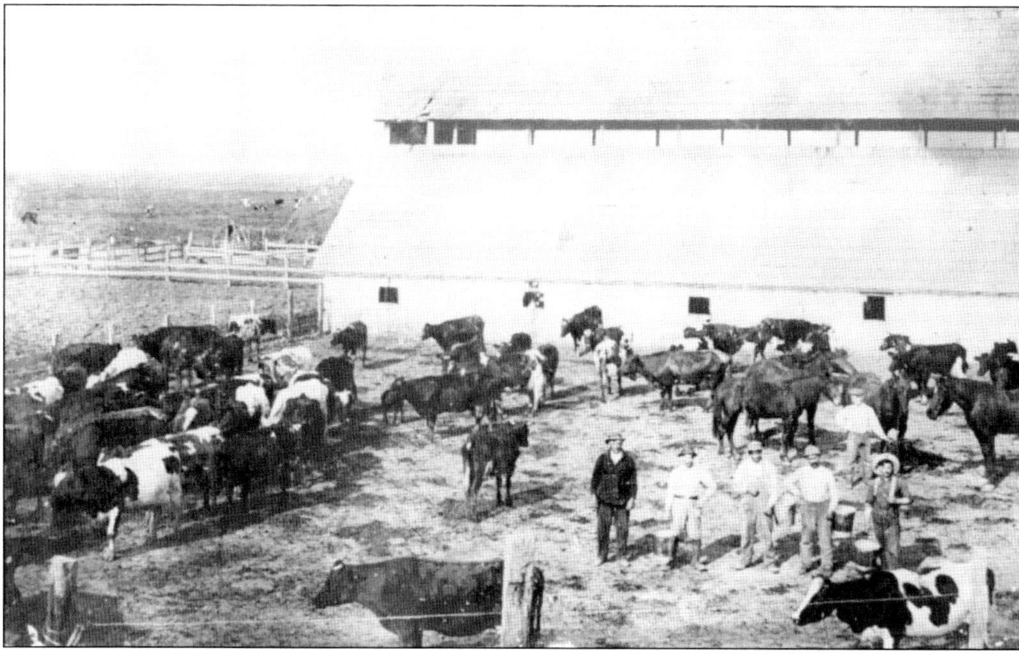
A group of dairymen poses among a mixed herd of cows, horses, and mules in 1905 at the Newman dairy ranch in Tulare. (Tulare County Library.)

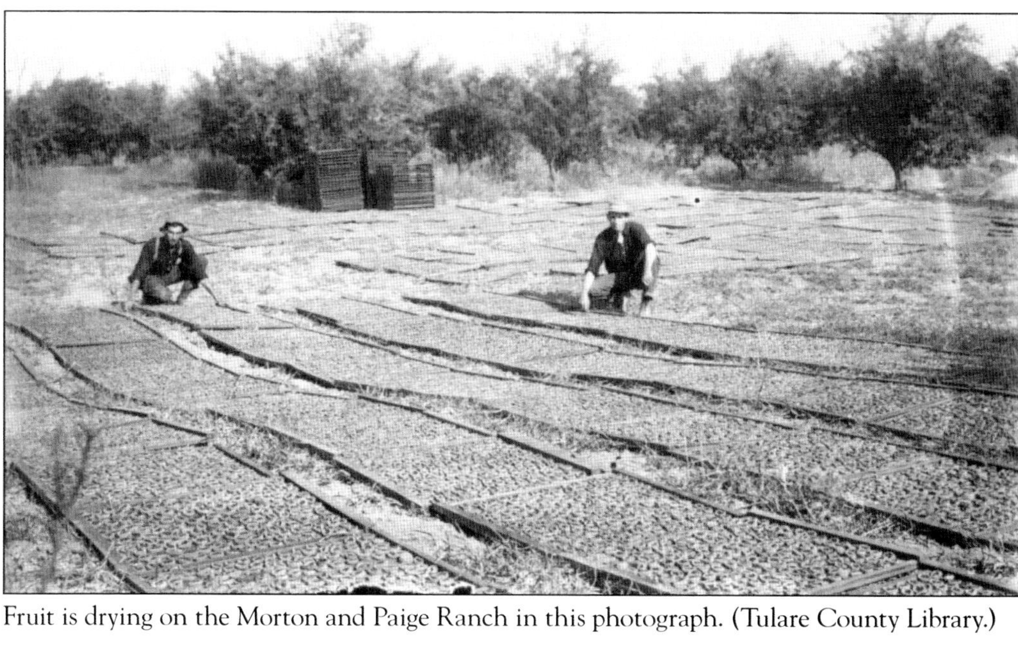
Fruit is drying on the Morton and Paige Ranch in this photograph. (Tulare County Library.)

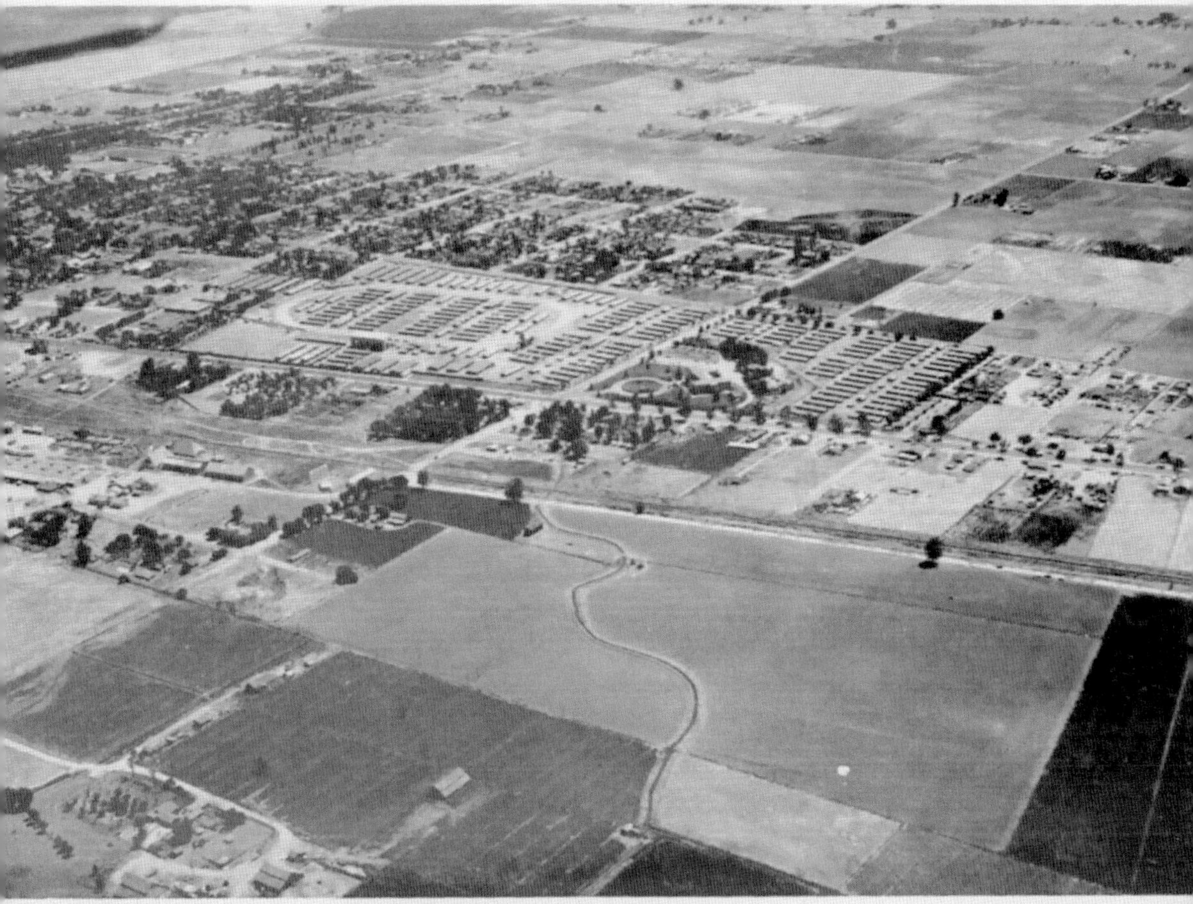

FIGURE 16-n—TULARE ASSEMBLY CENTER

This is an aerial view of the Tulare Assembly Center in 1942. The center occupied the entire fairgrounds complex and even spilled over across the street onto the Tulare County General Hospital property. This photograph shows where Bardsley Avenue divides the center into northern and southern sections. (Author's collection.)

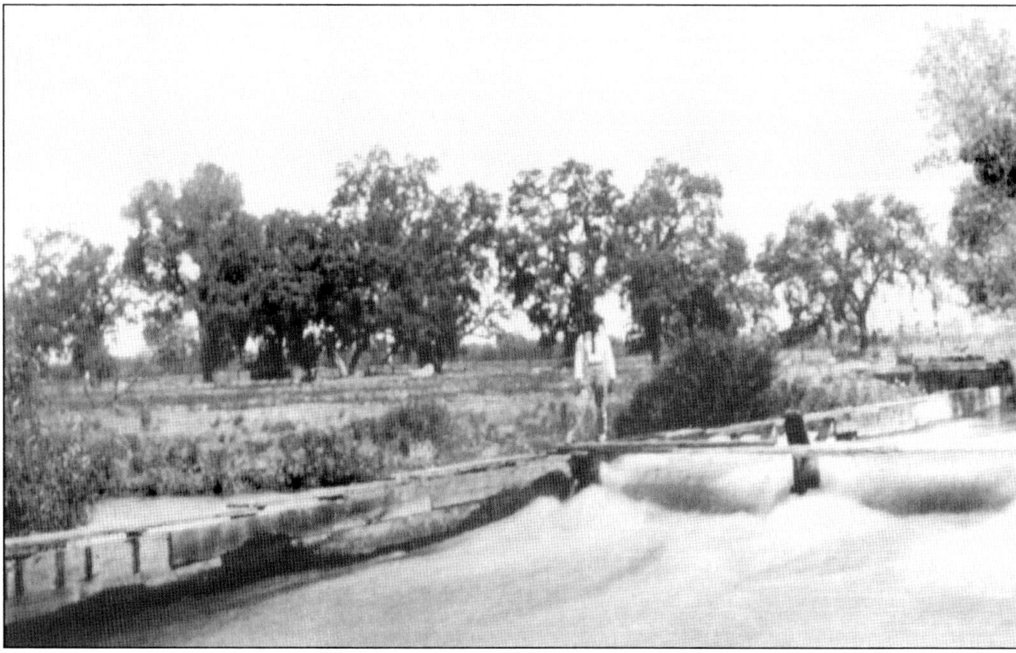

The Tulare Irrigation District main canal is shown in the early 1900s. Here, an unidentified man stands on the gate of the main canal. Interestingly, the irrigation district had a canal running through Tulare in the early days, with people having to use a small bridge to cross to the other side. (Author's collection.)

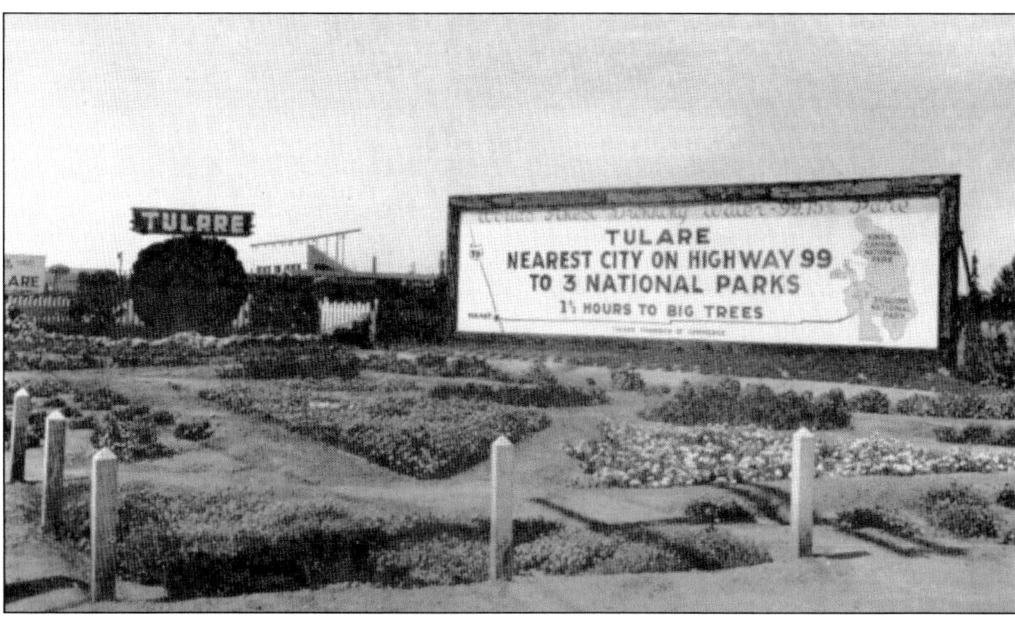

Tulare had two large signs along Highway 99 to greet travelers as they entered town. This one was located at the corner of K Street and Bardsley Avenue. In the background, the county fair grandstand is visible. The large sign stating that Tulare has pure clean water and is the nearest city to the national parks is gone now. (Author's collection.)

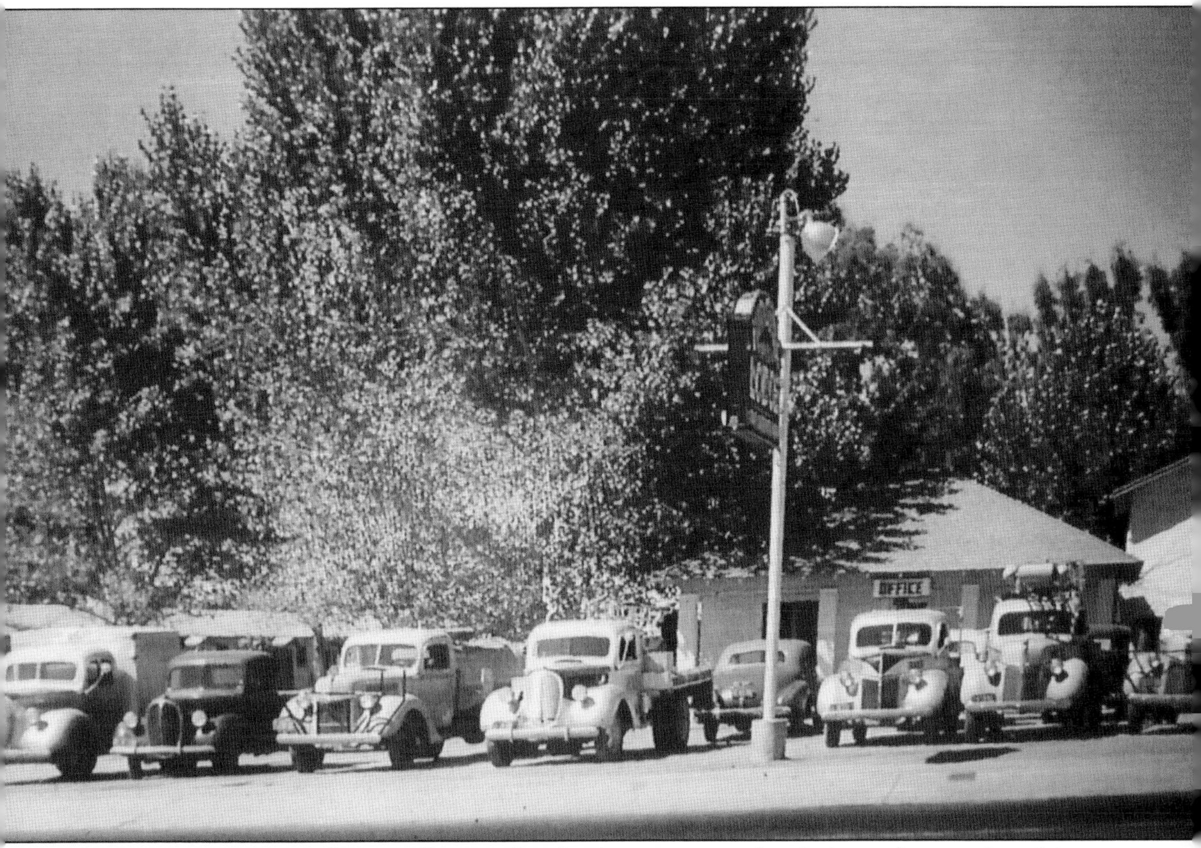

The Virginia Motor Lodge is still around today but is not used as lodging for travelers. Most occupants are long-term residents or low-income people who have taken up residence at the lodge. Adjacent to the lodge was a Texaco service station, which is still there but has been closed for many decades. In the 1940s, it was very active, as evident by the traffic and congregation of Texaco trucks parked in front. (Author's collection.)

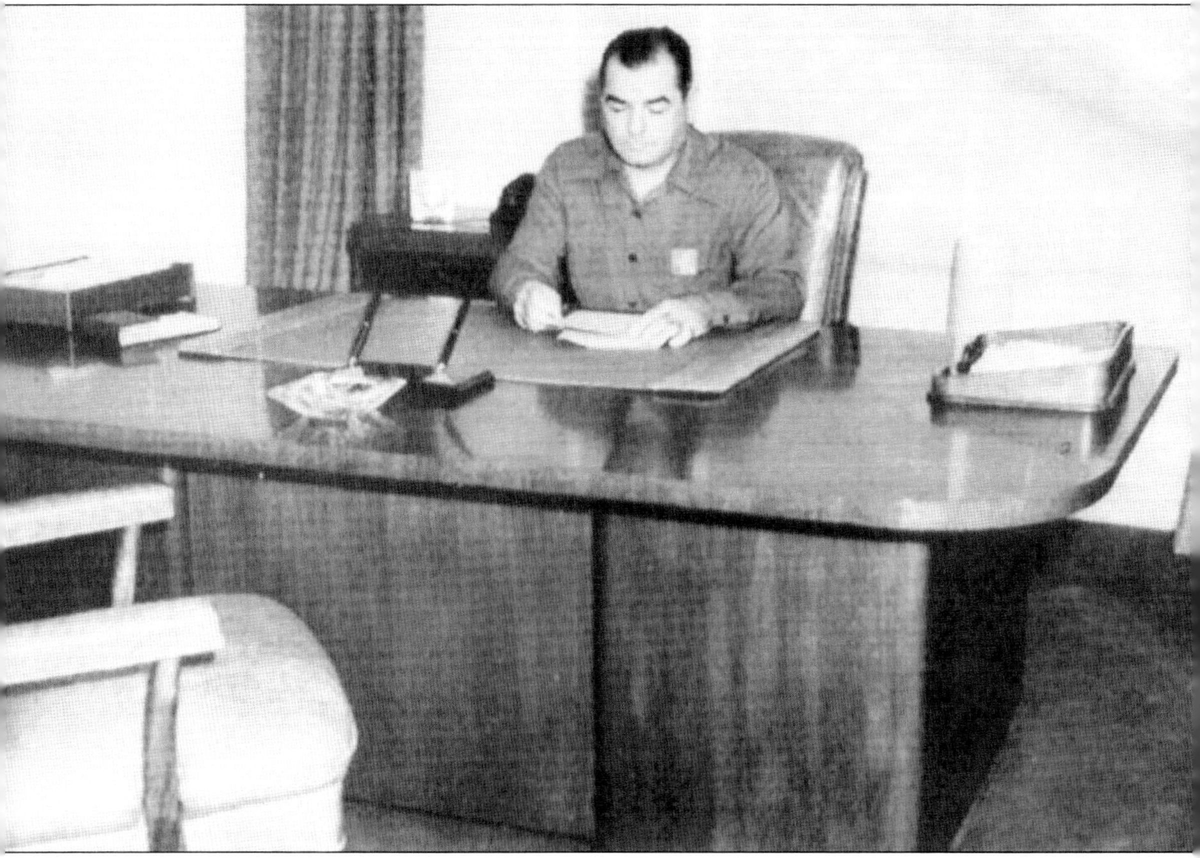

Rankin Field was established by Tex Rankin (shown here at work in 1943) in 1940 when he signed a contract with the War Department to open a school to train US Army Air Corps flight cadets. The Rankin Aeronautical Academy Inc. was established and began basic (level 1) pilot training in February 1941 at Mefford Field, located about six miles west of Rankin Field, still under construction at that time. Classes were moved to Rankin Field in May 1941. During its operation, over 10,000 pilots were trained. (Author's collection.)

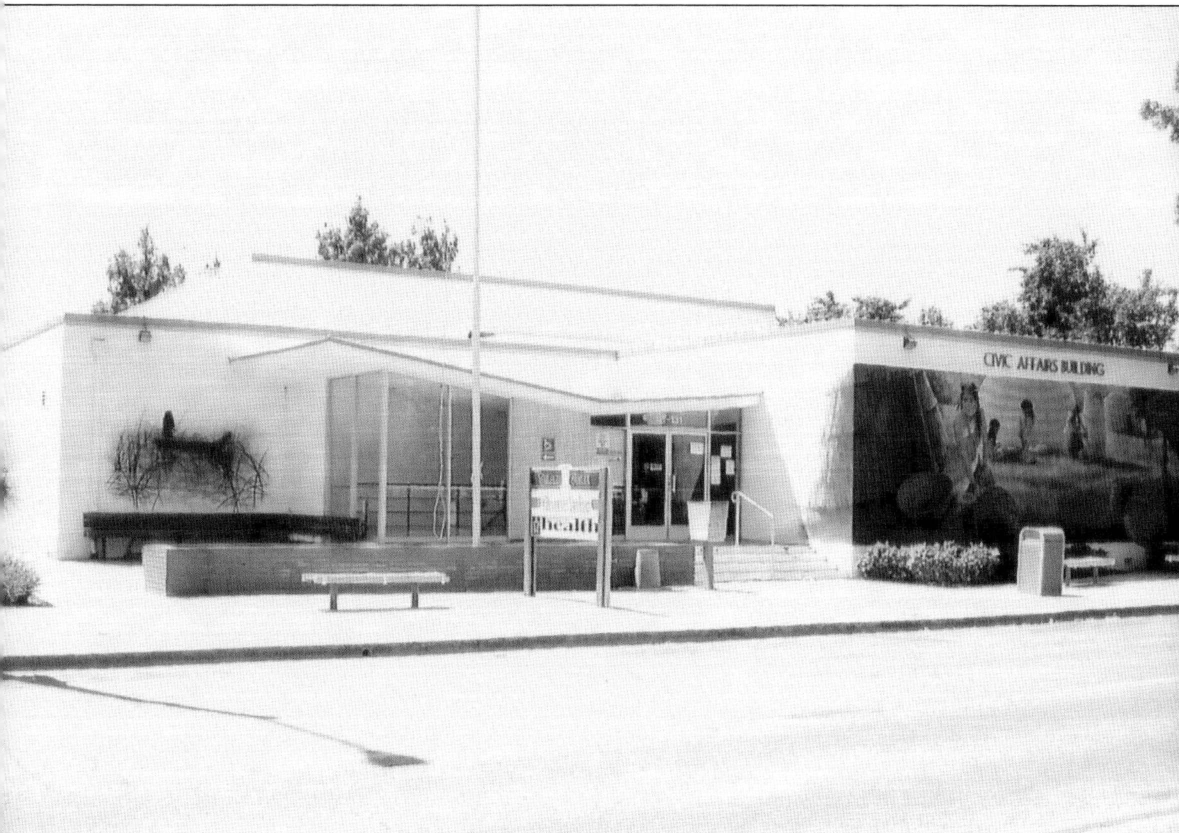

The onetime Tulare Veterans Memorial building is pictured in its early years before the new Veterans Memorial building was constructed in the 1950s near Tulare Avenue and Laspina Street. This building has undergone some changes to the front entrance, but the basic design is still the same. For a long time, this venerable structure was home to city council meetings and other city affairs. (Author's collection.)

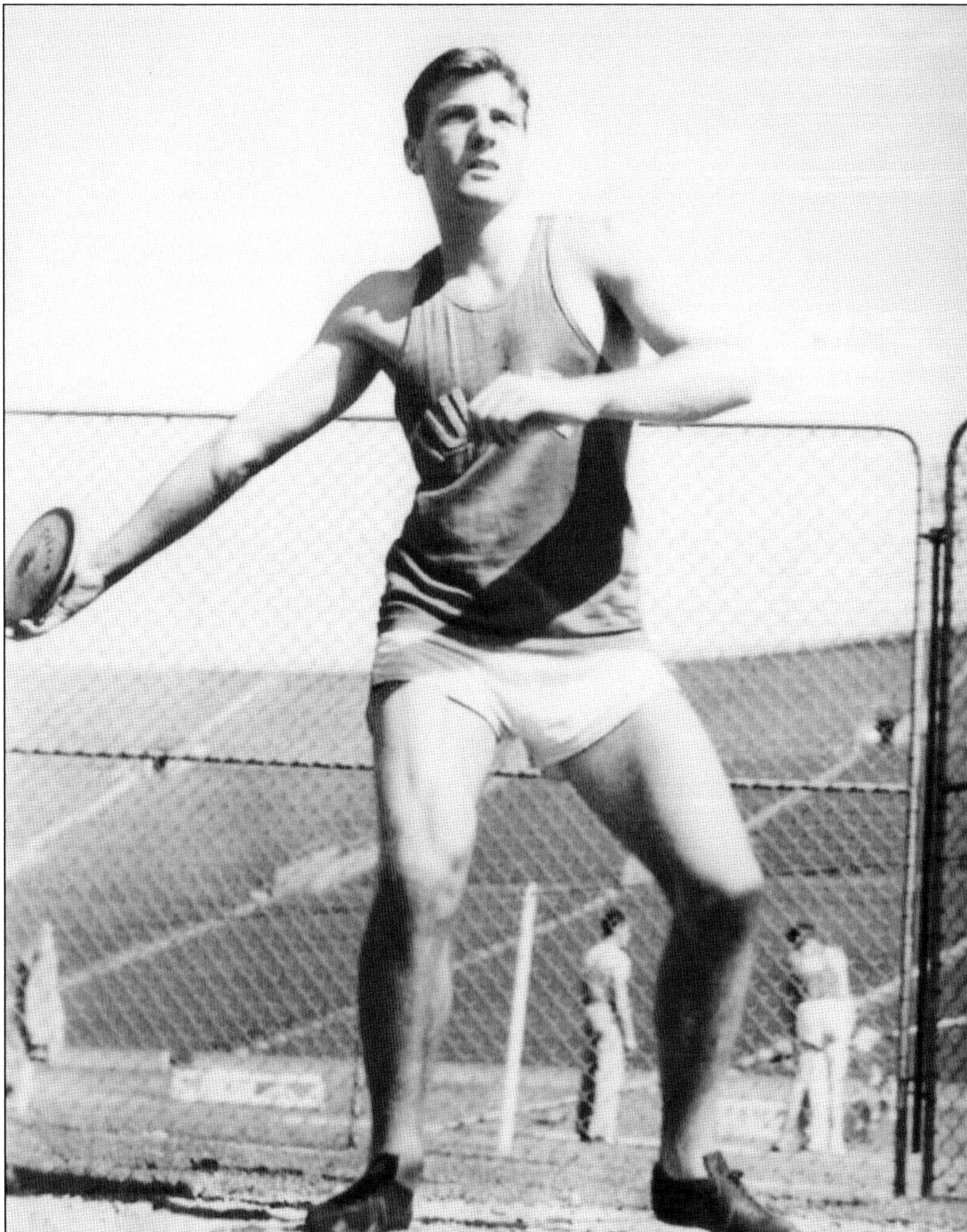

In this wire photograph, Tularean and future Olympian and US congressman Bob Mathias is shown throwing a discus. Mathias is wearing his Tulare track uniform with large lettering across the top. (Author's collection.)

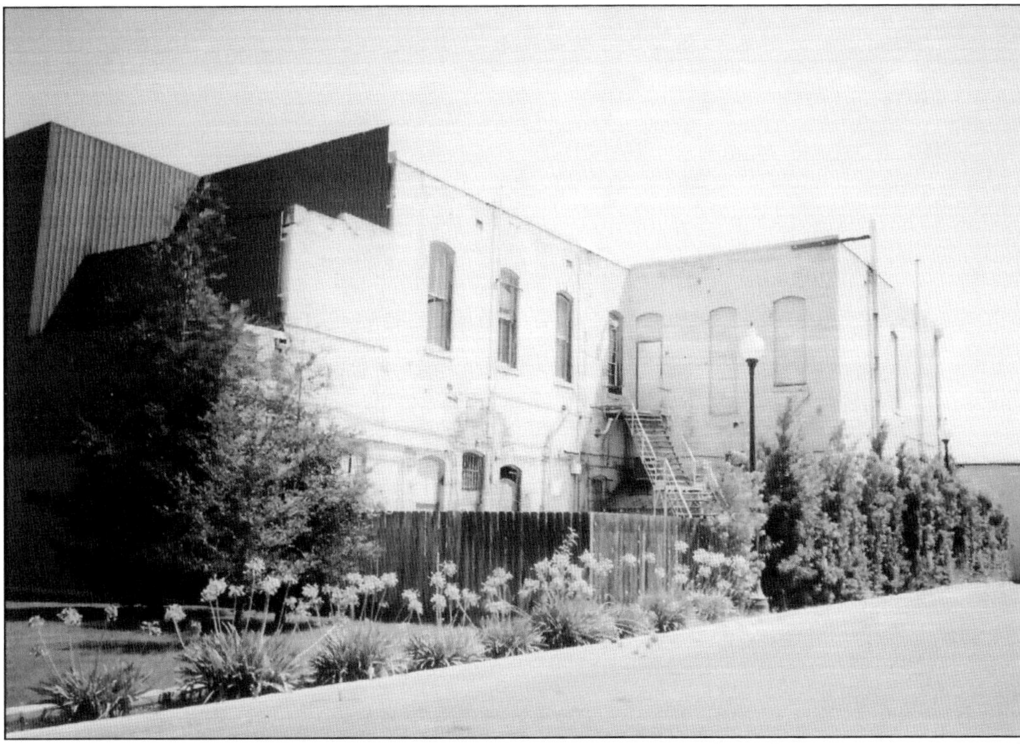

This is the former Elks building at the corner of Kern Avenue and south K Street in 2001, with green space to the left. The green space is now the site of a food court with outdoor tables. Its name is China Alley, harking back to old Tulare. (Author's collection.)

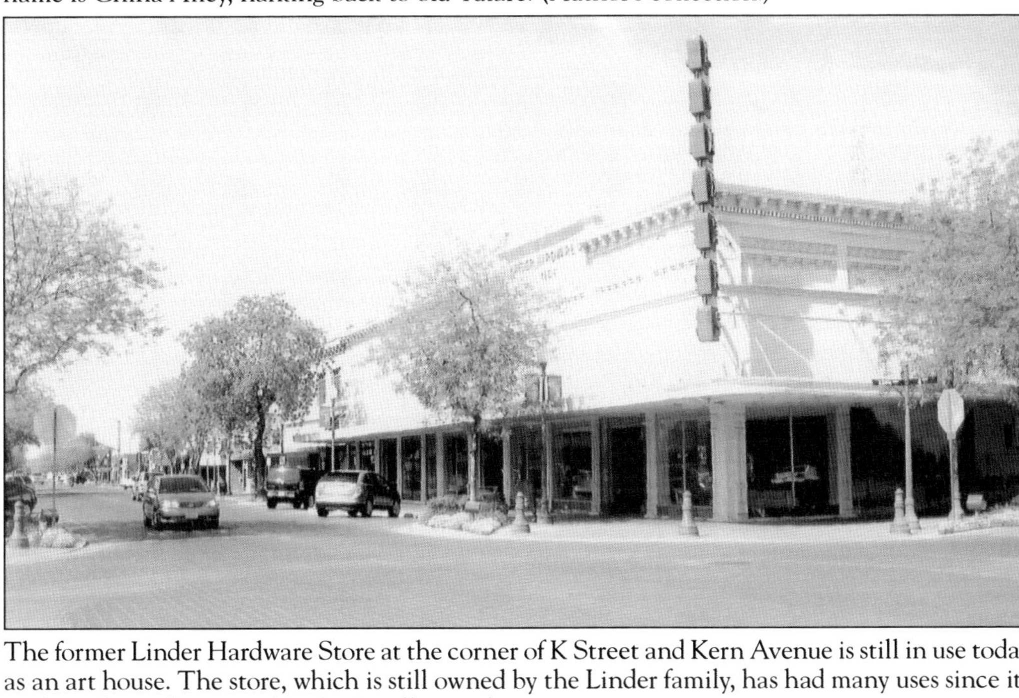

The former Linder Hardware Store at the corner of K Street and Kern Avenue is still in use today as an art house. The store, which is still owned by the Linder family, has had many uses since its peak in the early 1900s. (Author's collection.)

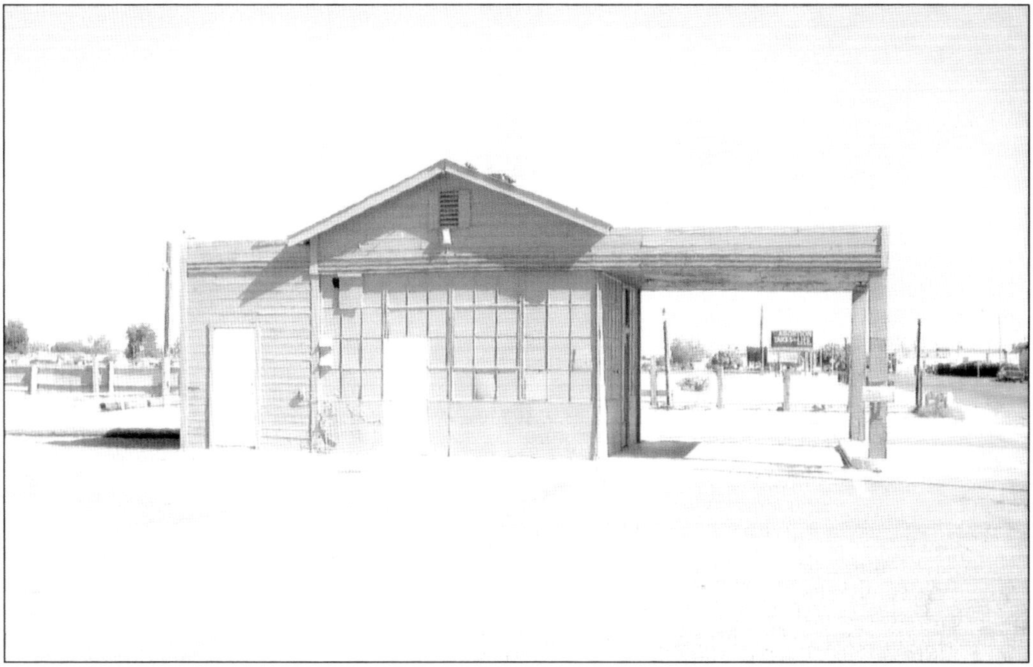

This is the former Texaco gas station on K Street, across from the Tulare County Fairground. (Author's collection.)

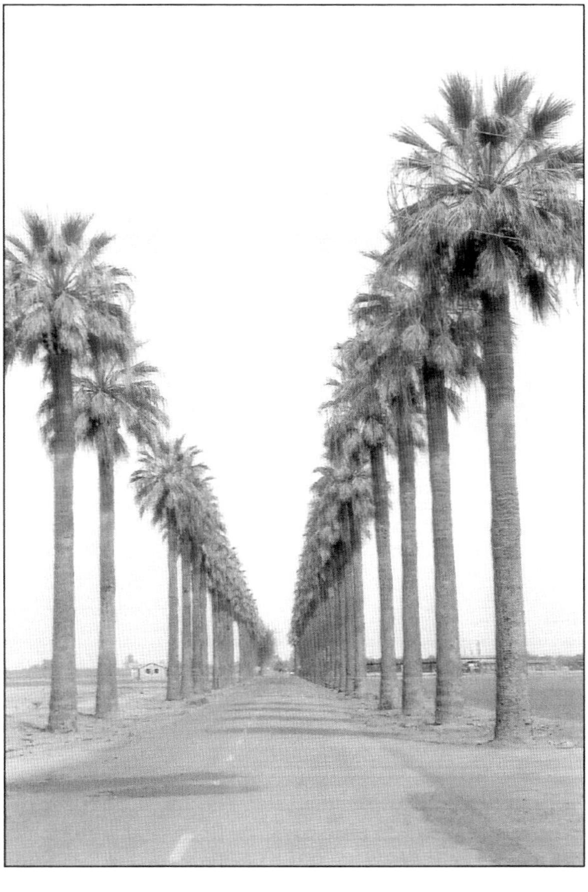

Palm Drive is seen here from Tulare Avenue. Palm Drive is also known as Road 76 and used to lead to the Paige and Morton Ranch. All that remains are the many palm trees. (Author's collection.)

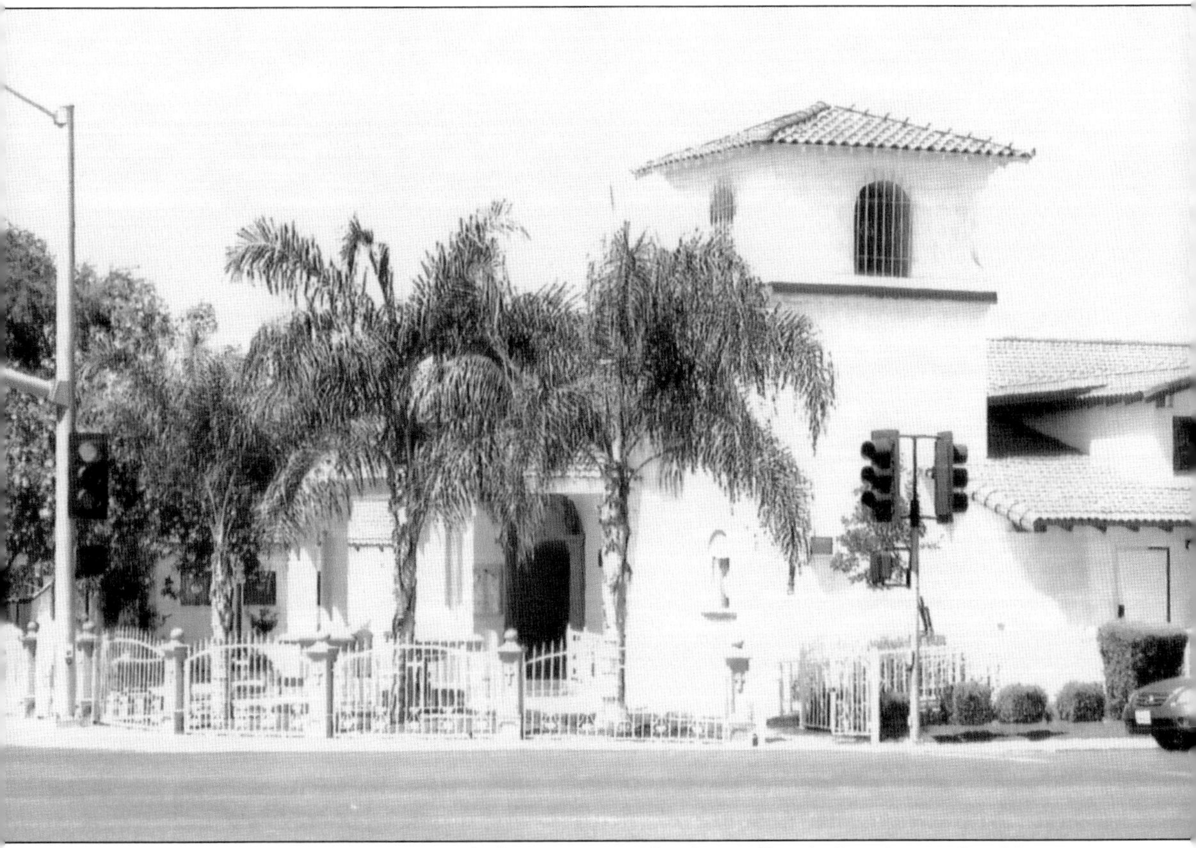

Since the 1880s, Tulare has had Catholic services. The first official church was St. Aloysius, in the 1800s. Since 1967, St. Rita has provided services for parishioners on the west side and southern parts of Tulare. St. Rita is located on the corner of Bardsley Avenue and O Street. (Author's collection.)

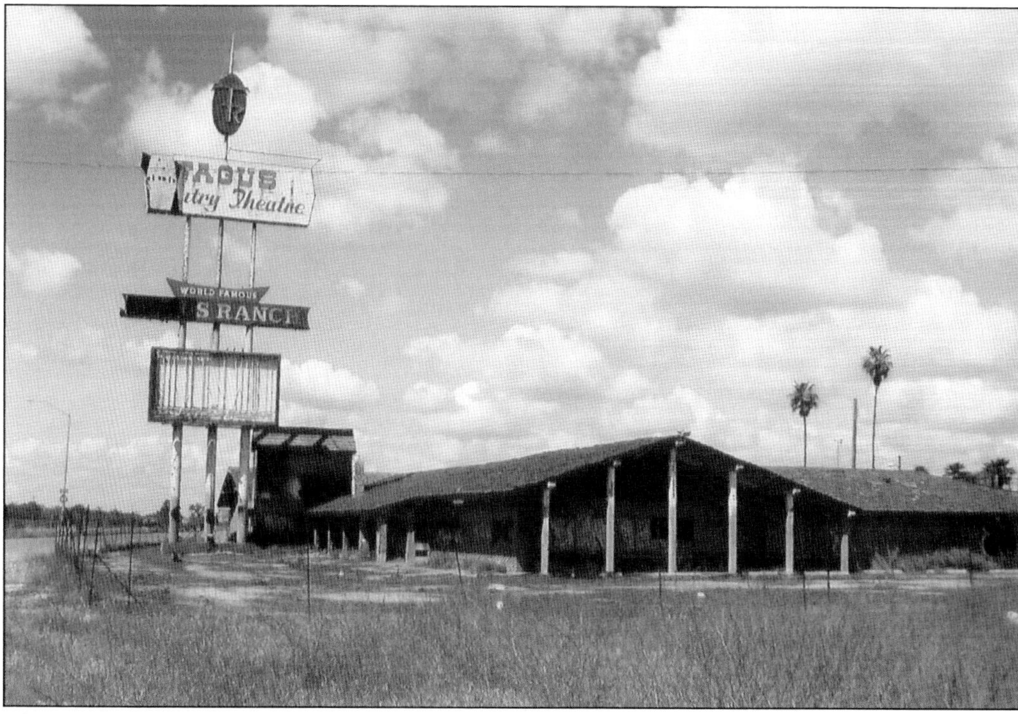

The Tagus Ranch has been abandoned for several years. It once boasted a store, motel, gas station, fruit stand, and restaurant. (Author's collection.)

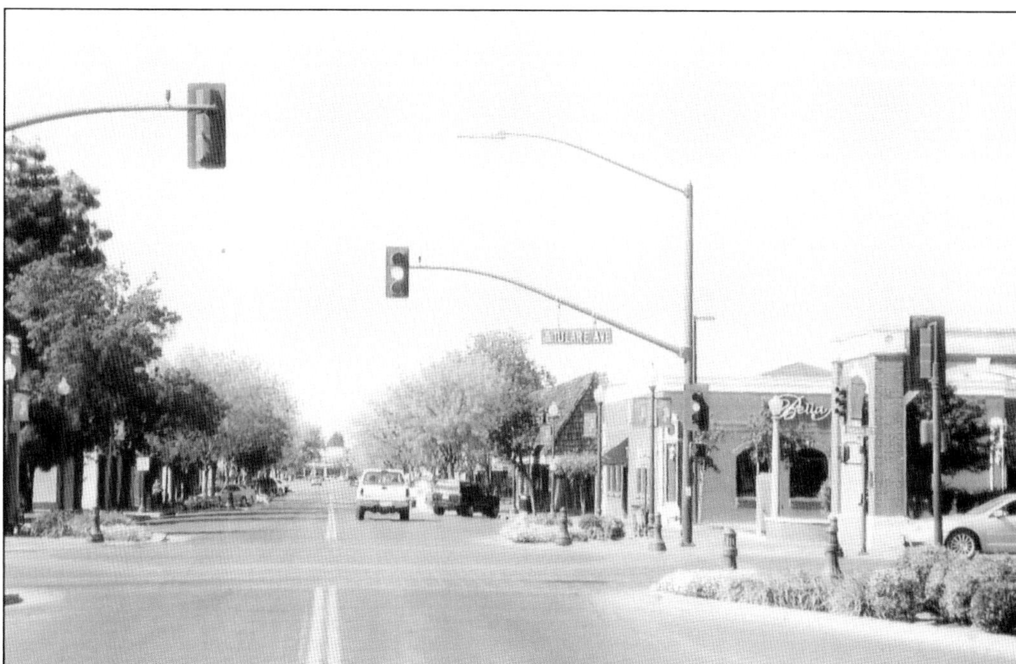

In this image, the Tulare Hotel stands at the corner of Tulare Avenue and K Street. A parking lot and two arches with a plaque as a reminder of this grand hotel have since replaced it at this site. (Author's collection.)

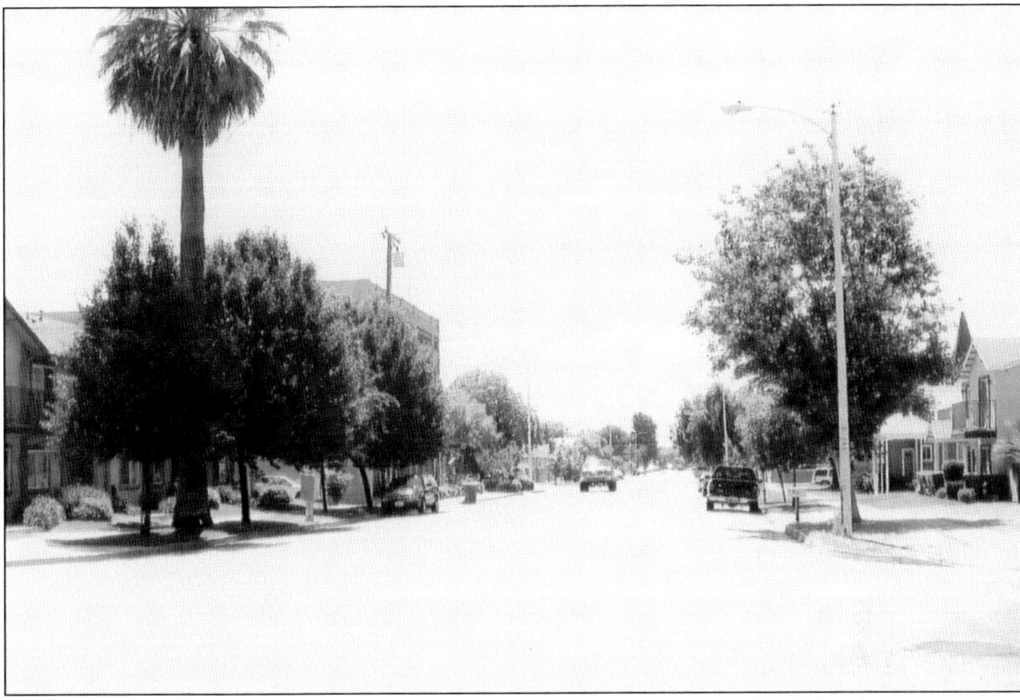

Present-day Tulare Avenue is pictured in this view looking west. To the left side, one can see a large two-story building, which is the Masonic Temple. (Author's collection.)

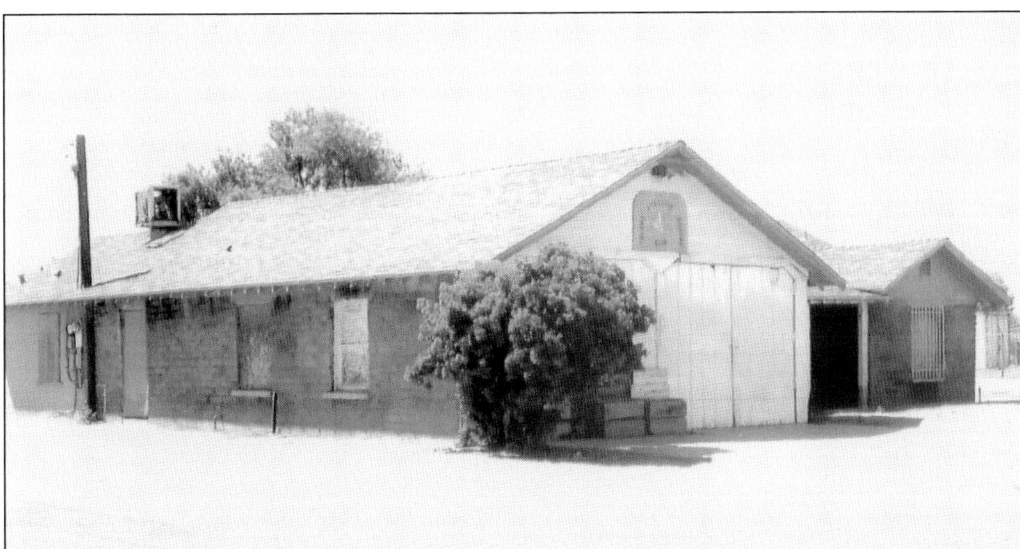

The Tulare Athletic Club is located at the corner of O Street and East O'Neal Avenue. The club was founded in 1945 by Manuel Torrez and is now under the leadership of his son, coach Richard Torrez. (Author's collection.)

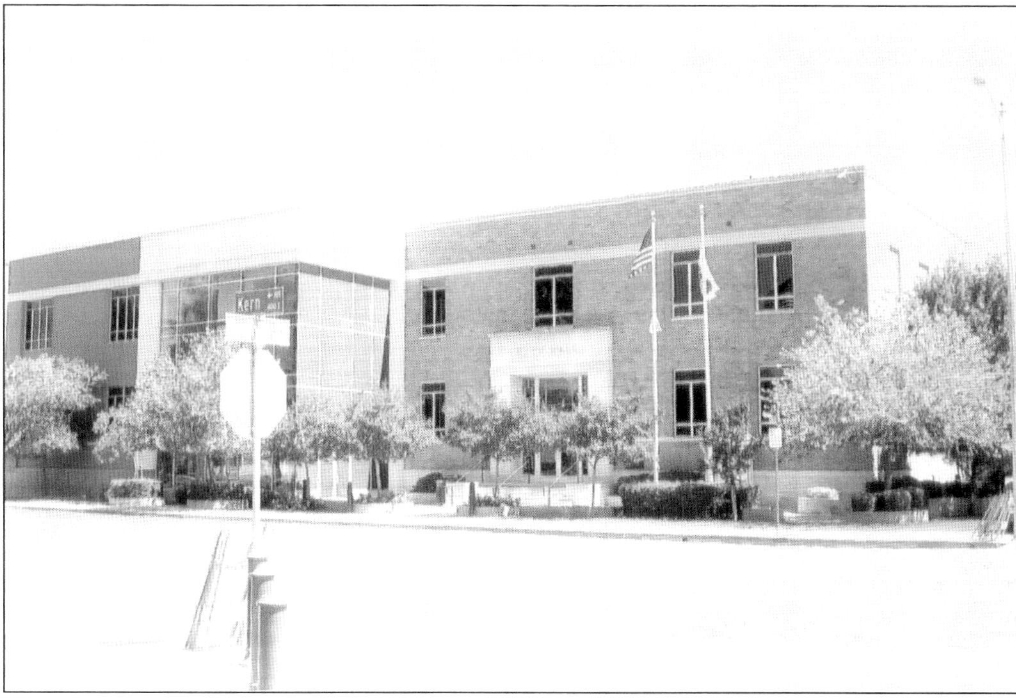

This is a present-day look at Tulare's city hall; an addition was completed in the 1990s. (Author's collection.)

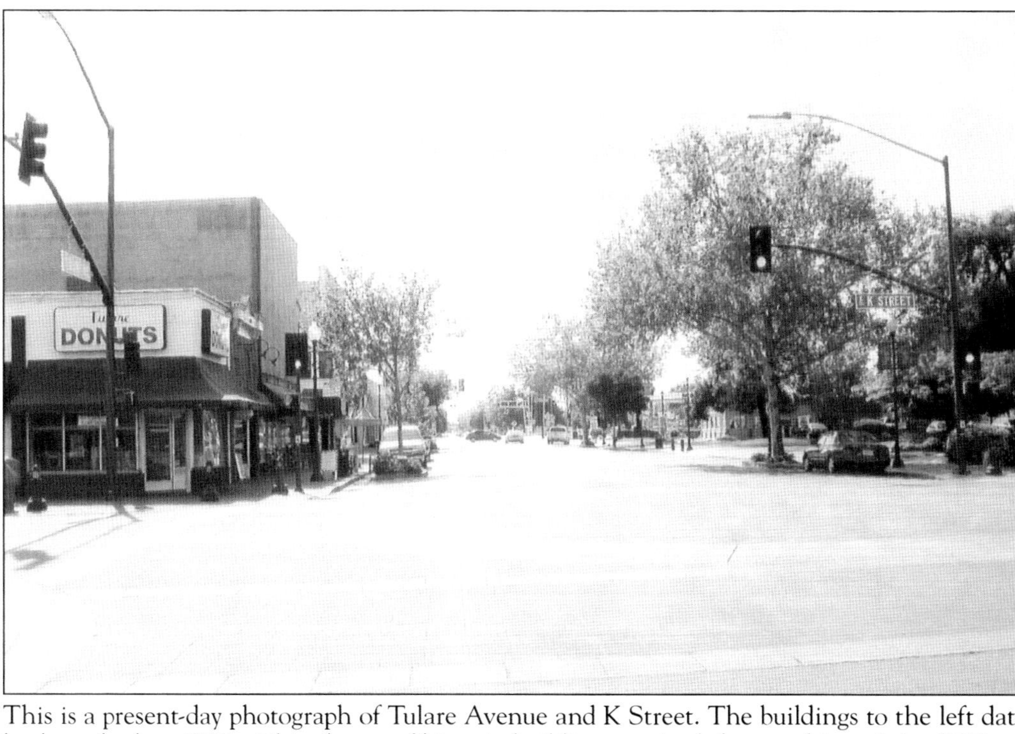

This is a present-day photograph of Tulare Avenue and K Street. The buildings to the left date back to the late 1800s. This cluster of historic building survived the wrecking of the 1950s to 1970s. (Author's collection.)

David W. Madden was one of Tulare's earliest pioneers and entrepreneurs. He ran the Pacific Hotel and also started the town's water system when he dug out two wells. For many years, he basically *was* the water system. In one of the Tulare fires, his tower collapsed because it caught on fire and thus left the city without any water to combat the growing blaze. (Tulare County Library.)

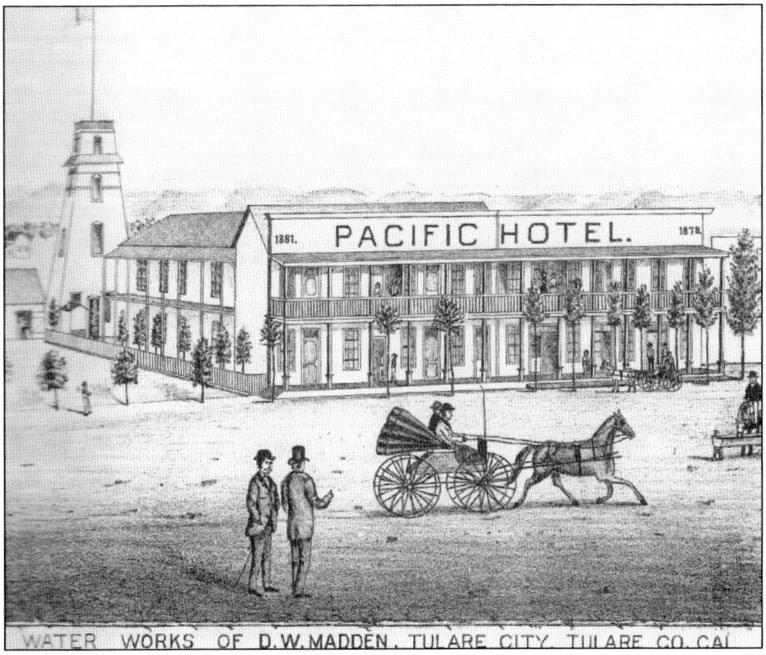

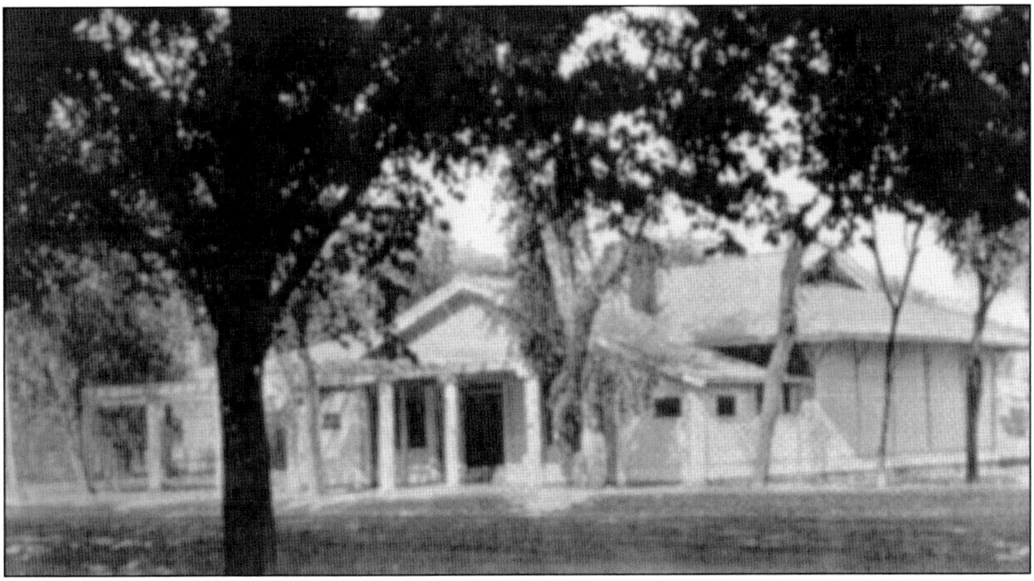

By 1914, the old library hall was converted into a Women's Club for the ladies of Tulare. Today, it is still known as the Women's Club and is the oldest building in Tulare. (Author's collection.)

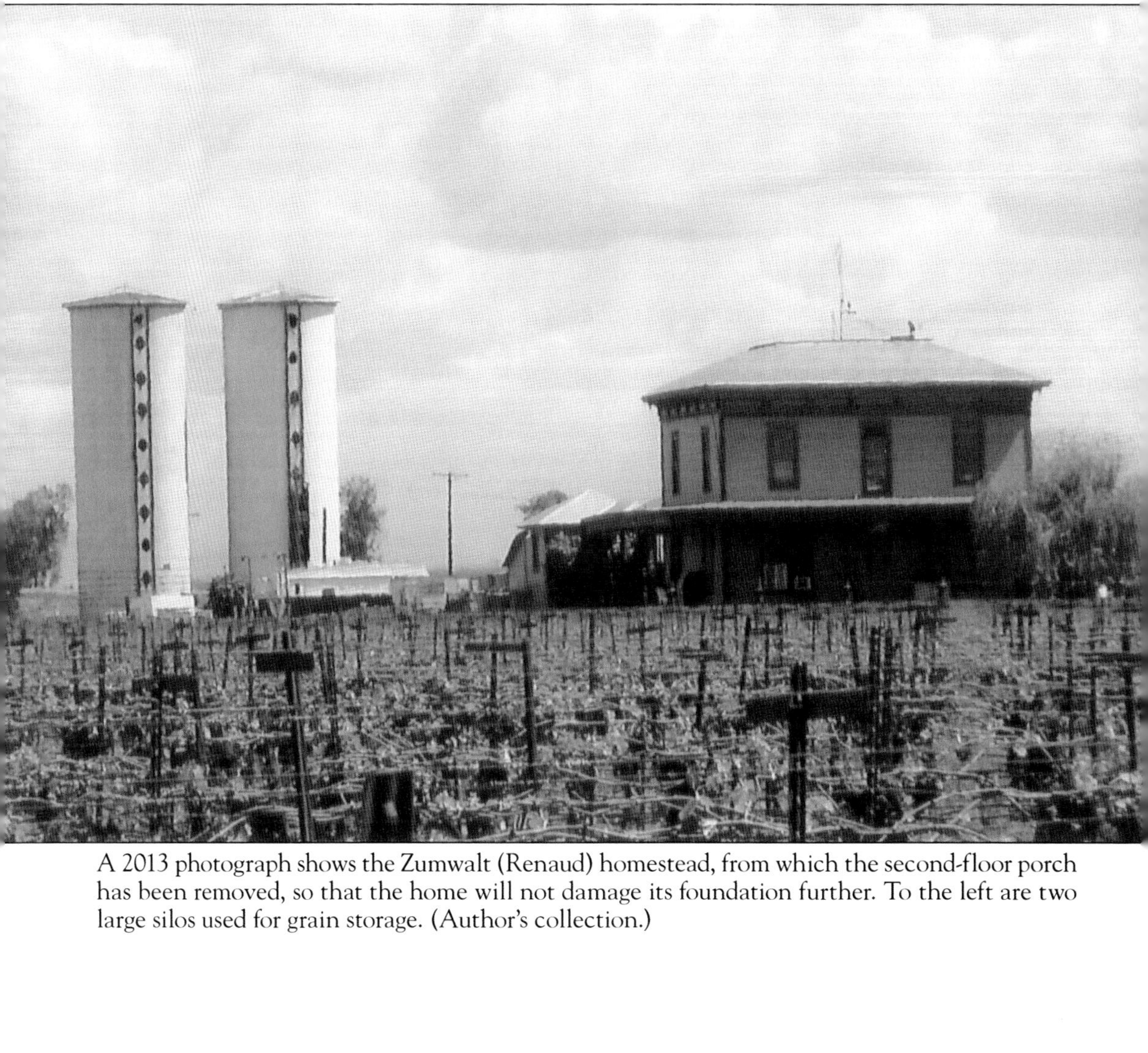

A 2013 photograph shows the Zumwalt (Renaud) homestead, from which the second-floor porch has been removed, so that the home will not damage its foundation further. To the left are two large silos used for grain storage. (Author's collection.)

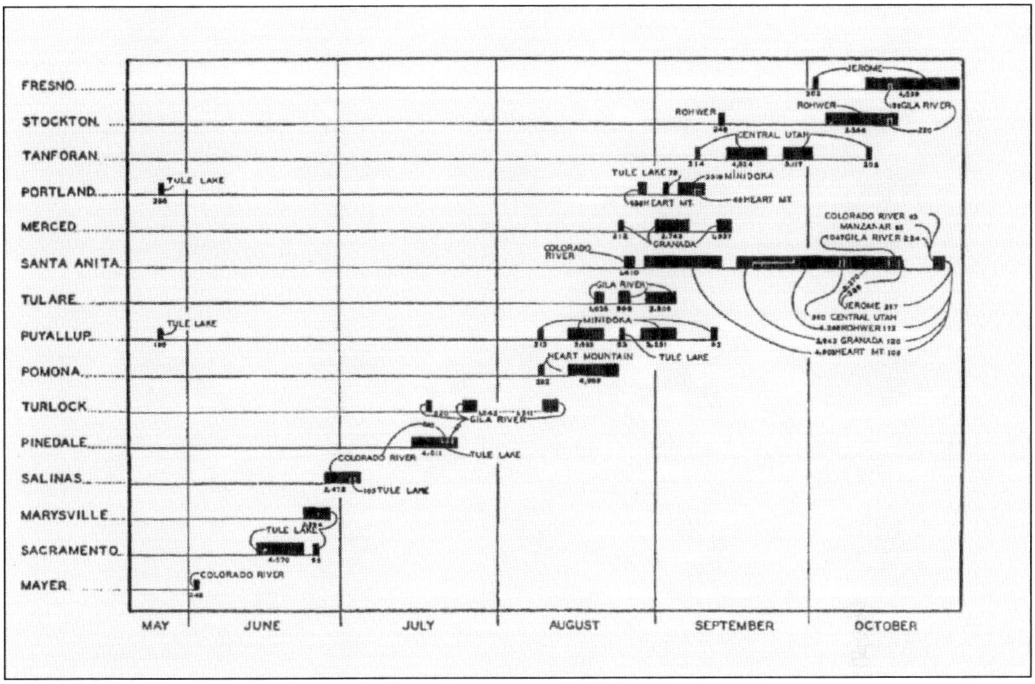

The table here lists all the assembly centers in California that held Japanese internees during World War II. The graph shows that the majority of the Tulare internees were sent to the Gila River area. Once the center was abandoned, the fairground reverted to local control again, but it was not until the late 1940s that the county fair was revived. (Author's collection.)

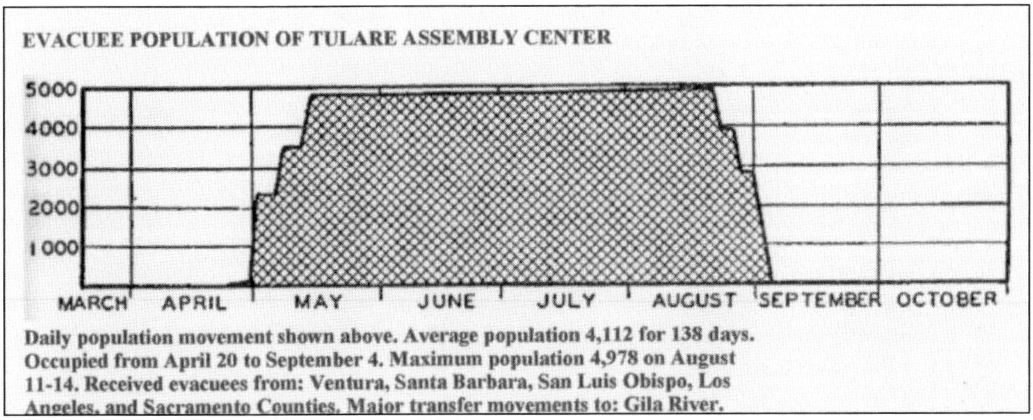

In this table, the population of the Tulare Assembly Center is shown during its operation in 1942. Starting on April 20, through September 4, 1942, it had a peak population of almost 5,000 Japanese Americans within its confines. The majority of these internees came from Ventura, Santa Barbara, San Luis Obispo, Los Angeles, and Sacramento Counties. Later, when the center was shut down, the majority were moved to the Gila River Center. (Author's collection.)

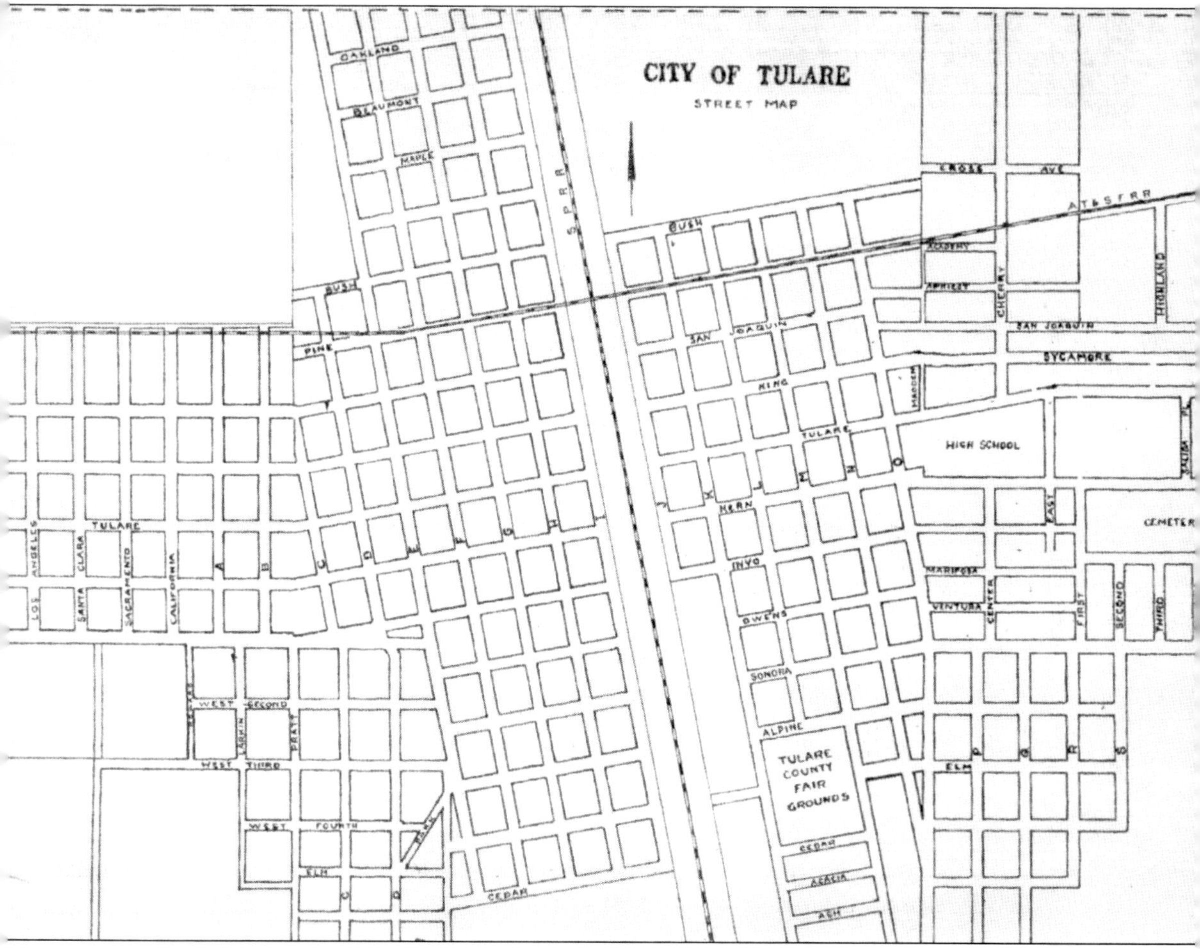

Tulare city limits have changed a lot since 1930. The eastern boundary was at one time Blackstone Street and the cemetery. Today, that boundary goes a few miles east of Mooney Boulevard. In 1930, the northern boundary was at about Bush Avenue, later renamed Cross Avenue. (Author's collection.)

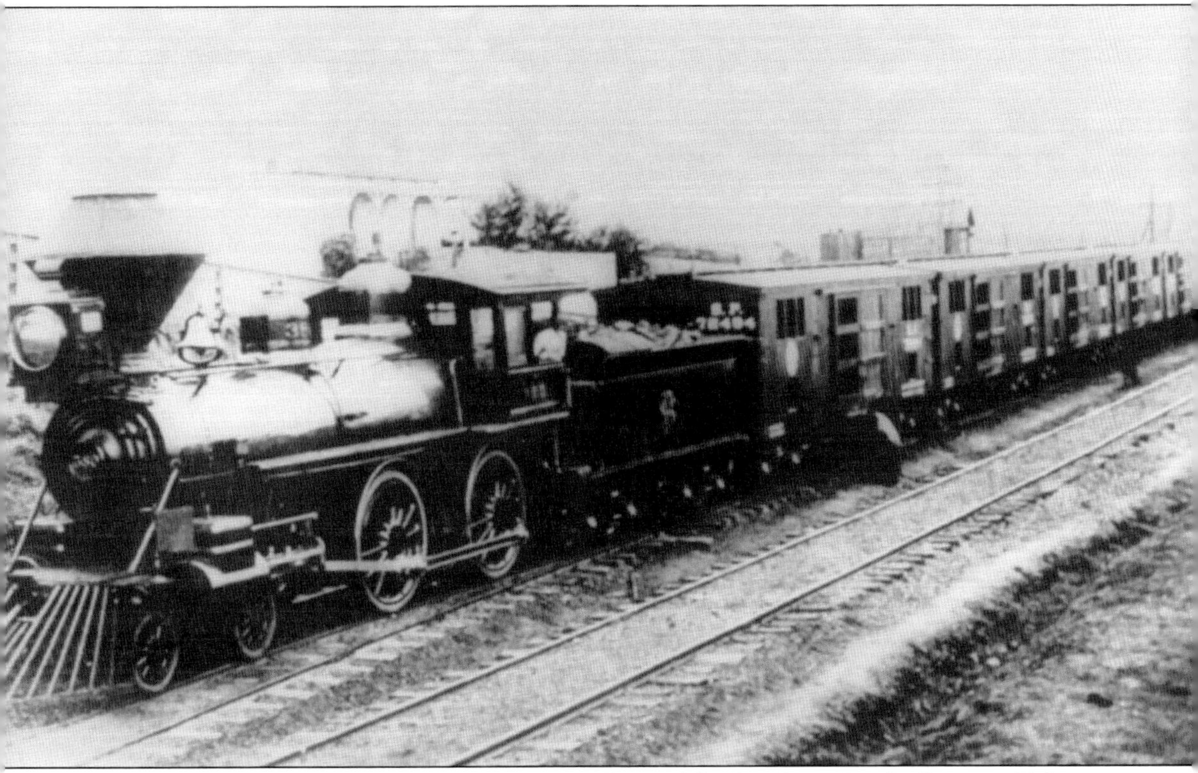

In 1889, a Southern Pacific freight train arrives in front of the Southern Pacific Depot in Tulare. (Tulare County Library.)

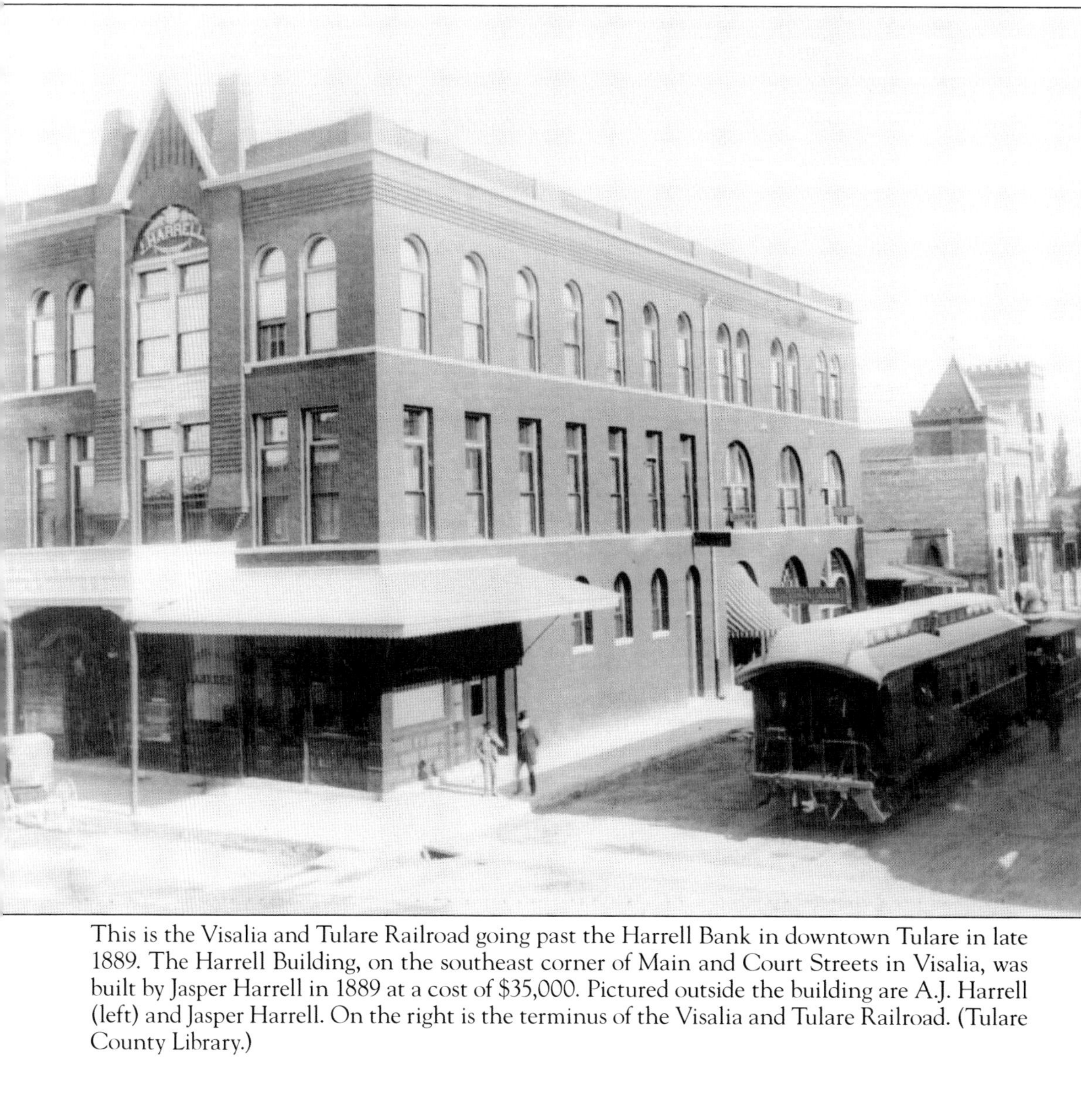

This is the Visalia and Tulare Railroad going past the Harrell Bank in downtown Tulare in late 1889. The Harrell Building, on the southeast corner of Main and Court Streets in Visalia, was built by Jasper Harrell in 1889 at a cost of $35,000. Pictured outside the building are A.J. Harrell (left) and Jasper Harrell. On the right is the terminus of the Visalia and Tulare Railroad. (Tulare County Library.)

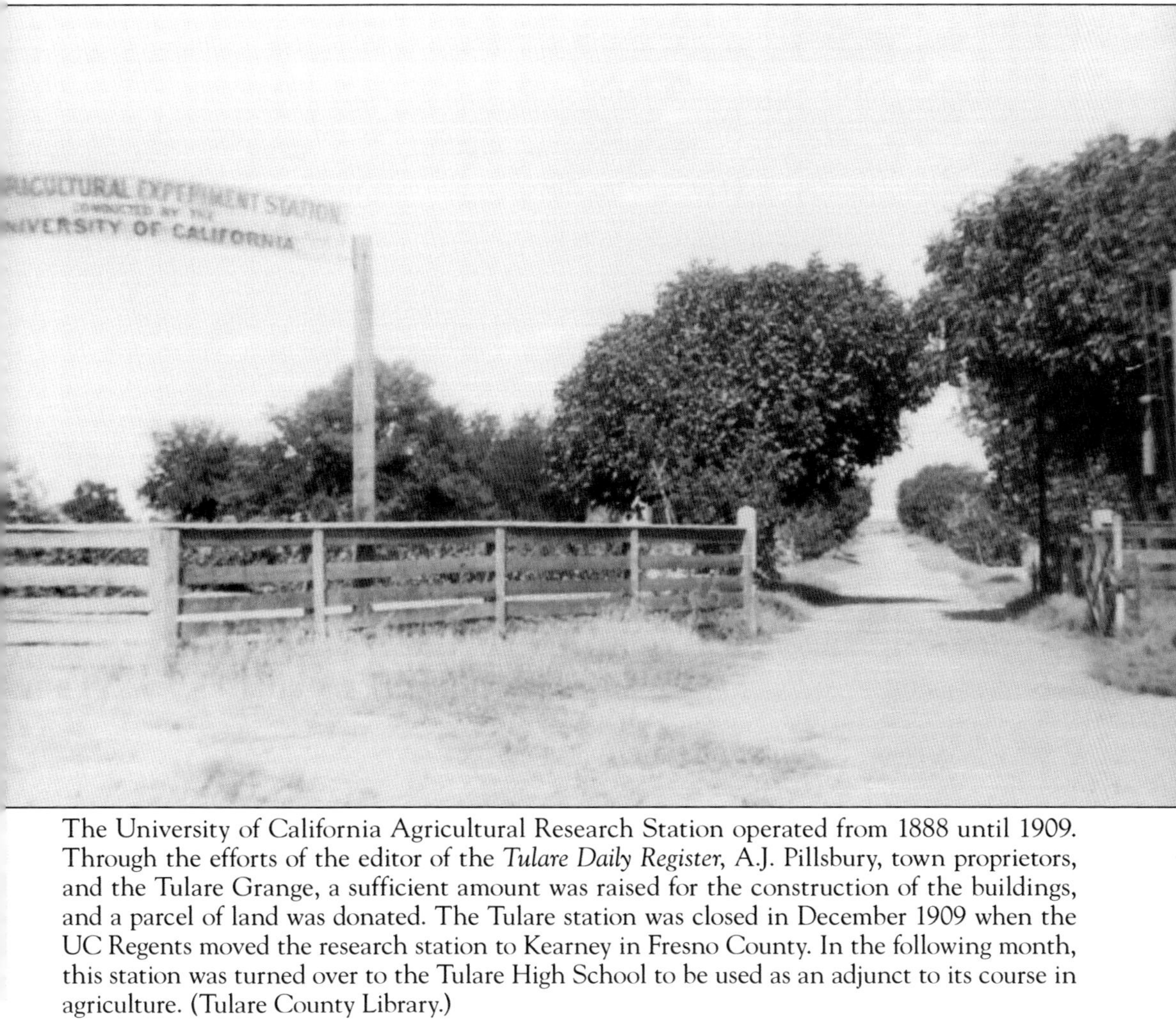

The University of California Agricultural Research Station operated from 1888 until 1909. Through the efforts of the editor of the *Tulare Daily Register*, A.J. Pillsbury, town proprietors, and the Tulare Grange, a sufficient amount was raised for the construction of the buildings, and a parcel of land was donated. The Tulare station was closed in December 1909 when the UC Regents moved the research station to Kearney in Fresno County. In the following month, this station was turned over to the Tulare High School to be used as an adjunct to its course in agriculture. (Tulare County Library.)